A Gr[eenville] Burial Ground

Human Remains and Mortuary Elements in British Columbia Coast Prehistory

Jerome S. Cybulski

with contributions by
Darlene Balkwill
Gregory S. Young
and
Patricia D. Sutherland

Archaeological Survey of Canada
Mercury Series Paper No. 146

Canadian Museum of Civilization

© Canadian Museum of Civilization 1992

Canadian Cataloguing in Publication Data

Cybulski, Jerome S., 1942–

A Greenville burial ground: human remains and mortuary elements in British Columbia Coast prehistory

(Mercury series, ISSN 0316-1854)
(Paper/Archaeological Survey of Canada, ISSN 0317-2244; no. 146)
Includes an abstract in French.
Includes bibliographical references.
ISBN 0-660-14008-X

1. Niska Indians — Mortuary customs.
2. Excavations (Archaeology) — British Columbia — Pacific Coast. 3. Indians of North America — British Columbia — Pacific Coast — Mortuary customs. 4. Pacific Coast (B.C.) — Antiquities.
I. Balkwill, Darlene. II. Young, Gregory S. III. Sutherland, Patricia D. IV. Canadian Museum of Civilization. V. Title. VI. Title: Human remains and mortuary elements in British Columbia Coast prehistory. VII. Series. VIII. Series: Paper (Archaeological Survey of Canada); no. 146.

E99.N734C97 1992   971.1'100497   C92-090931-0

Printed and bound in Canada

Published by
Canadian Museum of Civilization
100 Laurier Street
P.O. Box 3100, Station B
Hull, Quebec
J8X 4H2

Cover photo:
View of the Greenville village
Photo by Jerome S. Cybulski

Paper Coordinator: Richard E. Morlan

Production Coordinator: Lise Rochefort

Cover Design: Francine Boucher

Canadä

OBJECT OF THE MERCURY SERIES

The Mercury Series is designed to permit the rapid dissemination of information pertaining to the disciplines in which the Canadian Museum of Civilization is active. Considered an important reference by the scientific community, the Mercury Series comprises over three hundred specialized publications on Canada's history and prehistory.

Because of its specialized audience, the series consists largely of monographs published in the language of the author.

In the interest of making information available quickly, normal production procedures have been abbreviated. As a result, grammatical and typographical errors may occur. Your indulgence is requested.

Titles in the Mercury Series can be obtained by writing to:

Mail Order Services
Publishing Division
Canadian Museum of Civilization
100 Laurier Street
P.O. Box 3100, Station B
Hull, Quebec
J8X 4H2

BUT DE LA COLLECTION MERCURE

La collection Mercure vise à diffuser rapidement le résultat de travaux dans les disciplines qui relèvent des sphères d'activités du Musée canadien des civilisations. Considérée comme un apport important dans la communauté scientifique, la collection Mercure présente plus de trois cents publications spécialisées portant sur l'héritage canadien préhistorique et historique.

Comme la collection s'adresse à un public spécialisé celle-ci est constituée essentiellement de monographies publiées dans la langue des auteurs.

Pour assurer la prompte distribution des exemplaires imprimés, les étapes de l'édition ont été abrégées. En conséquence, certaines coquilles ou fautes de grammaire peuvent subsister : c'est pourquoi nous réclamons votre indulgence.

Vous pouvez vous procurer la liste des titres parus dans la collection Mercure en écrivant au :

Service des commandes postales
Division de l'édition
Musée canadien des civilisations
100, rue Laurier
C.P. 3100, succursale B
Hull (Québec)
J8X 4H2

Abstract

A midden excavation in the modern Nisga'a village of Greenville in west-central British Columbia yielded 36 human burial features, the skeletal remains of 57 individuals, 231 cultural artifacts, and 19, 389 pieces of non-human bone. Two burial components were identified, one in a shell layer dated A.D. 566 to 1010, the other in an overlying soil layer dated A.D. 1180 to 1290 in calibrated radiocarbon years. Dissimilar age and sex distributions suggest structural differences in the contributing populations, though a single lineage or social class could have been involved.

There was no evidence for habitation in terms of non-mortuary site features, but the faunal debris reflected an expected local ecological orientation in favour of anadromous fish resources, probably including food for the dead. All intact or partly intact human skeletons were flexed, most in square burial boxes or outlines. Sixteen were accompanied by concentrations of elderberry seeds, identifying a secondary use of food-storage boxes as coffins, a Tsimshian origin myth set in the Nass River valley, or "rich food" for the dead. Most of the adult females likely wore labrets, indicated by tooth-abrasion facets, possibly a sign of status attained through family wealth. One or two people were buried with dog crania, and canid bones other than skulls were underrepresented in the faunal assemblage as a whole, possibly also an indication that wealthy people were buried at the site.

Greenville accounts for eight per cent of all currently known prehistoric British Columbia coast burials starting at 5,500 years ago and seventy per cent of those assignable to the Late Developmental Stage, the last 1,300 years of Indian history before European contact. It may represent one of the last examples of midden burial as a significant cultural practice, replaced throughout the coast, possibly by A.D. 1300, by the historically known practices of above-ground corpse disposal. Infants, well represented at historic mortuary sites, may have been relegated to special burial areas in the prehistoric period. An unbalanced sex ratio in favour of males in many north-coast sites may identify female slaving practices related to warfare during the Middle and, possibly, Late Developmental Stages. Cranial morphology suggests the people who buried their dead at Greenville were biologically related to those of Prince Rupert Harbour, possibly denoting a common Tsimshian ancestry to 3,000 years ago. However, these two groups and Blue Jackets Creek on the Queen Charlotte Islands do not present images of a common north-coast, human biological complex in British Columbia for 4,000 or 5,000 years.

Résumé

Les fouilles d'un dépotoir du village nisga'a actuel de Greenville, situé au centre de la côte de la Colombie-Britannique, ont permis d'exhumer 36 éléments de sépultures humaines, les ossements de 57 personnes, 231 artefacts et 19 389 morceaux d'os d'animaux. Deux sépultures ont été identifiées : l'une située dans une couche de coquillages datant de 566 à 1010 apr. J.-C. et l'autre, recouvrant la première, que la datation au carbone 14 a fait remonter entre 1180 et 1290 apr. J.-C. La disparité entre l'âge et le sexe des populations mises au jour semble indiquer des différences structurelles, bien qu'il ait pu s'agir d'une seule lignée ou classe sociale.

On n'a retrouvé aucune trace d'habitation sur le site non mortuaire, mais les restes d'animaux témoignent de l'abondante consommation de poissons anadromes, dont une partie était peut-être destinée aux morts.

Tous les squelettes humains, en partie ou complètement intacts, ont été trouvés recroquevillés, la plupart à l'intérieur de tombes ou de périmètres carrés. Des quantités de graines de baies de sureau ont été trouvées près de seize squelettes, ce qui indiquerait que des boîtes d'entreposage de denrées auraient pu servir aussi comme cercueils. D'autre part, la présence de graines de baies de sureau pourrait ou refléter un mythe venant des Tsimshians de la vallée de la rivière Nass, ou encore représenter la «nourriture de choix» du mort.

L'usure des dents indique que la plupart des femmes adultes portaient, vraisemblablement, des labrets – signe, peut-être, du statut social lié à la richesse de la famille. Une ou deux personnes ont été enterrées avec un crâne de chien, ce qui pourrait aussi laisser croire à l'aisance des gens qui ont été enterrés à cet endroit. Mis à part les crânes, on a trouvé peu d'ossements canins pour reconstituer des squelettes.

Greenville compte 8 p. 100 de toutes les sépultures préhistoriques – remontant à 5500 ans – actuellement connues, sur la côte de la Colombie-Britannique; on y trouve aussi 70 p. 100 de celles qu'on peut attribuer au Stade évolutif récent – les 1300 dernières années de l'histoire des Amérindiens avant les premiers contacts avec les Européens.

Ces sépultures de dépotoir constituent peut-être l'un des derniers exemples d'une pratique culturelle importante. Cette pratique a été remplacée, tout le long de la côte – peut-être vers 1300 apr. J.-C. –, par celle, historiquement attestée, des tertres funéraires.

Les enfants en bas âge, habituellement nombreux dans les sites funéraires de l'époque historique, ont peut-être été relégués dans des lieux mortuaires particuliers au cours de la période préhistorique. Le nombre supérieur d'hommes retrouvés dans de nombreux sites du nord de la côte pourrait être un indice de l'esclavage des femmes à la suite des guerres du Stade évolutif moyen et, vraisemblablement, à la suite de celles du Stade évolutif récent. La forme des crânes exhumés suggère que les morts de Greenville auraient été biologiquement apparentés à ceux de Prince Rupert Harbour; cela pourrait donc indiquer une ascendance tsimshiane commune vieille de 3000 ans. Cependant, ces deux groupes, ainsi que celui de Blue Jackets Creek (îles de la Reine-Charlotte), vieux de 4000 ou 5000 ans, ne présentent pas les traits d'un bassin humain à parenté biologique commune de la côte nord de la Colombie-Britannique.

Preface

When I began to write this manuscript, my intention was to provide a straight-forward site report, describing the excavation of the Greenville burial ground and the analysis of the materials found therein. As I read over the 60 pages produced with that end in mind, it became apparent that much of what I had written would only have meaning within a broader context of coastal British Columbia mortuary sites and human remains. Also, the relatively unique temporal position of the Greenville site in a heretofore known sphere of Northwest Coast mortuary remains dominated by earlier and later sites suggested that a comprehensive review might be in order. Consequently, I have attempted to pull together a body of information just as relevant to the interpretation of Northwest Coast prehistory as the artifactual remains left by those cultures deemed ancestral to today's native peoples.

As will be apparent in the following pages, there are many gaps in our knowledge of human remains on the British Columbia coast with respect to chronology, mortuary practices, and vital statistics, as well as paleopathology and human biology. I would hope that other investigators would help fill in those gaps, as well as test my resulting speculations, with continuing studies of mortuary remains, new thinking, and new site excavations. I would also hope that this book demonstrates to contemporary native peoples some of the intricacies and relevance of studying the human remains of past populations.

The excavation and analysis of the Greenville site was made possible by the Lakalzap Band Council and the people of Greenville. I hope that our work and this report have done justice to their concerns and foresight. Their support, encouragement, interest, and patience are deeply appreciated. I also thank them for welcoming me into their homes and for giving me an opportunity to share a little bit of their lives and history beyond archaeology. I am indebted to my field crews for their expertise, persistence, and patience: Joanne Curtin, Alan McMillan, Deanna Ludowicz, Arlene Yip, Geordie Howe, David Archer, Monica McKay, Sherry Clark, Alvin McKay Jr., Robert Moore, Alvin Martin, and Elmer Azak. Oscar Swanson, Mitchell Stevens, Paul Foote, and several Greenville school children assisted in the fieldwork and helped us in many other ways.

Following our initial exploration in 1981, the excavation was completed under permits 1982-2 and 1983-13 issued by the Archaeology Branch, Victoria, in accordance with the Heritage Conservation Act of the Province of British Columbia.

Funding was provided by the Canadian Museum of Civilization, by Employment and Immigration Canada through its COSEP Federal Internship Programme, and through a cost sharing arrangement between the Terrace District Office of the Department of Indian Affairs and Northern Development and the Archaeological Survey of Canada's Rescue Archaeology Programme. The Lakalzap Band Council provided additional support during each of the three seasons of excavation.

I am indebted to Darlene Balkwill for her detailed identification and analysis of the faunal remains from the site and extensive contribution to this book; to Gregory Young for his contribution on the preserved wood remains; to Patricia Sutherland for her expert analysis of the Greenville artifacts. Clifford Crompton and Charles Tarnocai, both of Agriculture Canada, Ottawa, took responsibility for the analysis of the elderberry seeds and soils respectively. Other colleagues helped me to unaddle my brains during the writing of this manuscript: Rebecca Wigen of Pacific Identifications, Victoria; Gay Frederick, Peter Macnair, and Richard Hebda of the Royal British Columbia Museum; Philip Hobler and Mark Skinner of Simon Fraser University; R.G. Matson of the University of British Columbia; Larry Newitt of the Geological Survey of Canada, Ottawa; Bryan Gordon and Richard Morlan of the Archaeological Survey of Canada. I am grateful to Richard Morlan and R.G. Matson for their careful reviews of the final draft and recommended changes during its preparation for publication. David Laverie drew the maps and excavation profiles on Figures 1, 2, 5, and 6. All other charts and graphs, including Figure 14, were created with the aid of Software Publishing Corporation's Harvard Graphics. The stylized background map on Figure 3 is a copyrighted product of New Visions Technologies Inc. Last, but not least, I thank George MacDonald, Executive Director of the Canadian Museum of Civilization, for entrusting me with the Greenville project initially and for providing me with the opportunity to see it through, in the face of my other museum duties, to its hopefully contributory end.

Following their analyses at the Canadian Museum of Civilization, the Canadian Museum of Nature, Agriculture Canada, and the Canadian Conservation Institute, all site materials were returned to Greenville for disposition by the Lakalzap Band.

Jerome S. Cybulski

Archaeological Survey of Canada
Canadian Museum of Civilization

Table of Contents

List of Tables

List of Figures

Chapter I

Introduction

This study provides analytical results from an archaeological excavation of a pre-historic burial site in Greenville, a modern Nisga'a Indian community in the Nass River valley of west-central British Columbia.[1] The site was identified late in the summer of 1981 following an accidental discovery of human bones during lot preparation for a housing development. Controlled excavations were carried out for a two-week period and, subsequently, for six weeks in 1982 and four weeks in 1983 under the auspices of the Canadian Museum of Civilization (then known as the National Museum of Man, National Museums of Canada) and the Lakalzap Band Council of Greenville.

The Greenville site, a shallow midden, yielded over 36 human burial features, the skeletal remains of a minimum 57 individuals, 231 cultural artifacts, and 19,389 pieces of non-human bone. Two partial human skeletons were added to the sample from a nearby location in 1984. This assemblage enables a first-look at mortuary practices, skeletal biology, paleopathology, culture content, and subsistence in the Nass River area during the Late Developmental Stage of Northwest Coast prehistory, a period from about A.D. 450 to the time of European contact. Indeed, the Greenville burial ground is the first clearly identified prehistoric site of any type and time period to have been excavated in the traditional territories of the Nisga'a, major contributors to the ethnographic Northwest Coast culture pattern of native North America (Drucker, 1955).

Circumstances of Discovery

The excavation of the Greenville burial site was completed as part of my staff duties with the Archaeological Survey of Canada, a division of the Canadian Museum of Civilization. In Ottawa, on August 13, 1981, I received a telephone call from George F. MacDonald who was directing an archaeological excavation for

---

[1] The terms "prehistory" and "history" have been used for convenience throughout this book to differentiate time before and after the arrival of the first European explorers to the shores of British Columbia. They are terms commonly used in North American archaeology, though obviously from the perspective of the white man. To the Nisga'a, as to all First Nations peoples in the Western Hemisphere, prehistory is history.

the Canadian Parks Service and the Canadian Museum of Civilization at a Skeena River site just east of Terrace, British Columbia. George MacDonald, then Senior Scientist with the museum, informed me that human bones had been discovered in Greenville, some 85 km to the north, as a result of construction activity. He received word of the find from officials of the Archaeology Branch, Province of British Columbia, Victoria, who earlier had been notified by the Lakalzap Band Council. A brief inspection in Greenville by one of George MacDonald's field crew members, David Archer, indicated the bones might be from a previously unrecorded archaeological burial site. Concerned for the human remains and also recognizing a possible heritage significance, the Lakalzap Band Council sought to have the bones identified and expressed interest in having the site of discovery further investigated.

George MacDonald notified me because of my previous experience in cooperative mortuary archaeology with First Nations peoples in British Columbia (Cybulski, 1975a, 1978a) and analytical familiarity with human remains from archaeological sites in the territories of the Coast Tsimshian, close linguistic and geographic neighbours of the Nisga'a (Cybulski, 1974, 1978b, 1988a). Following permission by telephone from the Lakalzap Band Council, I arrived in Greenville with three field assistants on August 23. That evening, we met with the Council for formal introductions, to obtain details on the discovery, and to discuss respective concerns about identifying and analyzing the bones, necessary archaeological work, and potential results. We had funding sufficient for a two-week exploration, during which time we examined the bones already found, established a site grid, collected human remains that had been exposed on the surface by rains, carried out test excavations, identified the presence of an apparently prehistoric midden, and recovered several intact or partly intact human burials. On the basis of our findings, the Lakalzap Band Council agreed that more extensive excavation of the site should be completed, the basis for continued work in 1982 and 1983.

The initial discovery of human bones was made on July 21 and 22, 1981, during excavation of a minor drainage ditch in the area of a new housing development. This work was directed by Willis, Cunliffe, Tait/DeLCan (1982), consulting engineers and planners in Terrace, under contract to the Government of Canada Department of Indian Affairs. Paul Foote, senior technician with the firm, provided details about the find and assisted in locating the discovery site, described as a "low-lying mound." The bones had been collected by local RCMP Special Constable Alex Angus and stored in the Greenville Band Office.

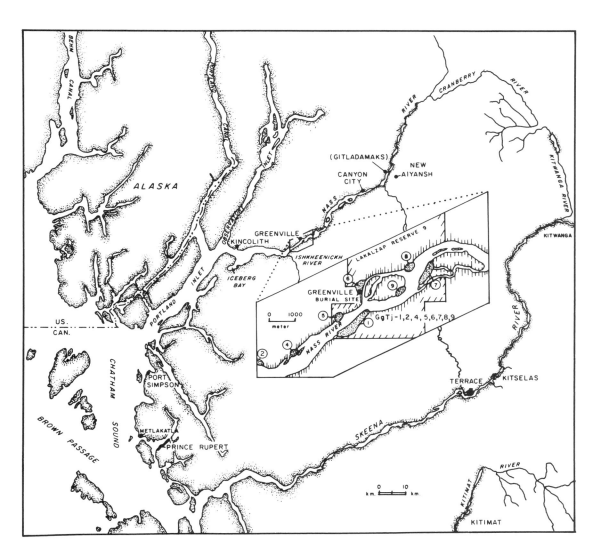

FIGURE 1. *West-central British Columbia including Greenville and environs. (GgTj # locations from B.C. Archaeology Branch site records.)*

Site Location and Historical Context

Greenville (population ca. 400) is on the northwest side of the Nass River about 28 km from its mouth where the river empties into Portland Inlet (Fig. 1). Situated in the Coast Mountains, the village is about 1.5 km below the limit of tidal action in the Nass River estuary. The climate is intermediate between the temperate rain-swept coast and the continental interior of British Columbia. In

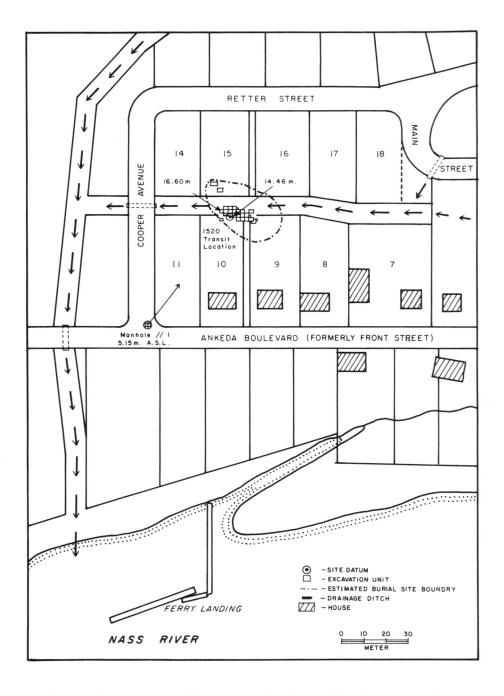

FIGURE 2. Location of burial site in Greenville. (Lot plan after Willis, Cunliffe, Tait/DelCan, December, 1979.)

winter, snowfall is variably heavy and the river freezes for some distance below Greenville; in summer, temperatures may exceed 32° C. The river frequently floods in June, due to heavy runoff from melting mountain snows. Flora in the immediate area of the site include large cottonwood trees, white birch, aspen, alder, willows, skunk cabbage, devil's club, and elderberry.

The burial site was located at 55° 01' 45" N and 129° 34' 27" W in the south end of the village about 135 m from the river bank (Fig. 2). On advice from the British Columbia Archaeology Branch, the Canadian archaeological site designation, GgTj 6, was assigned to the burial site. This designation had previously been given to the whole of Greenville during a 1976 archaeological survey by boat of Observatory Inlet, Portland Inlet, and the lower Nass River (Carlson, 1977). In Greenville, the surveyors were shown stone tools in the possession of residents, reportedly found "some 2'-9' below the surface during house construction," suggesting a prehistoric occupation (ibid., pp. 17, 21; fig. 19).

Greenville, one of four modern Nisga'a villages, the others being Kincolith, Canyon City, and New Aiyansh, was founded as a Methodist mission in 1877 (McNeary, 1976). Aside from the 1976 survey results, there is little archaeological or ethnographic information about its earlier history. Stephen McNeary (ibid., p. 52), citing the work of Franz Boas who recorded Nisga'a oral history late in the 19th century, and unpublished notes by George T. Emmons, another early ethnographer, noted that Greenville stands on the same site as "Laxkaltsap" (*Laxgalts'ap* in current Nisga'a orthography), an "ancient" principal village on the lower Nass that was abandoned for the village of Gitiks. Present-day residents often use the spelling "Lakalzap" ("dwelling place comprised of dwelling places" as written on Council letterhead, or "on the town" in the lexicon of Franz Boas (1916:966)).

We do not know, *a priori*, whether the burial site refers directly to the ancient village or, perhaps, to others in the area that may have been occupied then. The 1976 boat survey also recorded the nearby known historic period villages of Gitiks and Angidaa (GgTj 1 and GgTj 7 on Fig. 1) which had been abandoned by the turn of the 20th century, partly for the newly established mission community at Greenville (McNeary, 1976:52-53).[2] Neither of these sites has been tested for

---

[2] Stephen McNeary (1976:54) wrote that Gitiks may have been located farther down river from Greenville, at Indian Reserve 12, just below the mouth of the Ishkheenickh (*Ksisg'asginist*) River. Roy Carlson (1977) was reasonably certain of its location at GgTj 1 on Figure 1, as were our Nisga'a colleagues at Greenville.

prehistoric occupation, nor did we undertake archaeological work in Greenville other than at the burial site as per agreement with the Lakalzap Band Council.

Aims of Analysis and Comparative Data

The primary purpose of this report is to describe and interpret the Greenville skeletal population and its mortuary environment, and to place these data into the context of Northwest Coast prehistory and history with special reference to the Nass River and the Nisga'a nation. In the broader context, I attempt an interpretive analytical overview of what is currently known about human remains from the British Columbia coast, particularly with respect to mortuary practices, chronology, and vital statistics. The Greenville faunal remains and artifacts are methodologically considered to define the site's context, and some additional comparative data are presented in human biology and paleopathology.

Ethnographically, the Nisga'a formed one of three dialect-based subgroups of the Tsimshian, a major ethnolinguistic division of the Northwest Coast whose territories extended along the Nass and Skeena Rivers and their tributaries, the lakes and plateaus in between, and neighbouring offshore islands (Garfield and Wingert, 1951). Except for sketchy summaries or brief specialist approaches by Franz Boas (1895:569-583; 1902) and Edward Sapir (1915, 1920), there are no published early ethnographic sources exclusive to the Nisga'a. Rather, their history, social organization, customs, traditions, economics, subsistence, and material culture have more commonly been reported as part of Tsimshian ethnography with appropriate Nisga'a citations (Boas, 1916; Garfield, 1939; Garfield and Wingert, 1951; see, also, McNeary, 1976:6-7 for other published as well as unpublished references). Stephen McNeary's (1976) doctoral dissertation, though based on field research carried out in the 1970s, also serves as an important source of information on the traditional economic and social life of the Nisga'a, as does the book by William H. Collison (1981) whose missionary work among the Nisga'a, as well as the Skeena River Tsimshian and Queen Charlotte Islands Haida, resulted in some observations during the last quarter of the 19th century.

As noted earlier in this introduction, there has been no previous substantive archaeological work on the Nass River from which comparisons might be drawn with our work at Greenville.[3] Skeletal remains and mortuary elements are, how-

---

[3] In 1967, a National Museum of Man archaeological crew partly excavated a cave site (GfTj 1) about 1.6 km southwest of the Ishkheenickh River where it intersects with the Nass. Field notes (MacDonald, Clark, and Fladmark, 1967) indicated the presence of artifacts, faunal remains, and human skeletal remains. No analytical report is available.

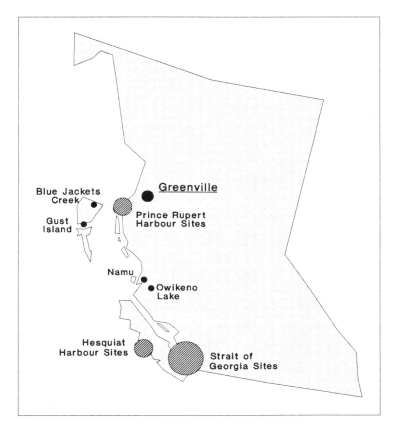

FIGURE 3. Regional locations of British Columbia coast burial sites discussed in the text. (Black circles identify single sites; shaded circles identify multiple sites.)

ever, known from one other Tsimshian subarea, Prince Rupert Harbour, encompassing ten midden sites near the mouth of the Skeena River and neighbouring islands (Calvert, 1968; MacDonald, 1969; Cybulski, 1974, 1978b, 1986, 1988a, 1990, n.d.a; MacDonald and Inglis, 1976, 1981; Simonsen, 1988a). A minimum 288 deceased individuals have now been identified from these sites (Calvert, 1968; Cybulski, n.d.a), and I refer to resultant comparative data where available and appropriate.

Other modern studies of known prehistoric skeletal remains and (or) mortuary elements on the British Columbia coast have been undertaken for the Queen Charlotte Islands (a site at Blue Jackets Creek near Masset: Severs, 1974; J. Murray, 1981), the central coast (a site at Namu near Bella Bella: Luebbers, 1978; Curtin, 1984), and the south coast (17 sites in the Strait of Georgia region: Heglar, 1958; Mitchell, 1971; Gordon, 1974; Seymour, 1976; Beattie, 1976, 1981; Burley,

1980, 1989; Hall and Haggarty, 1981; Trace, 1981; R. Murray, 1982; Bernick, 1983; Conaty and Curtin, 1984; Lazenby, 1986; Cybulski, 1988b, 1991a; Johnstone, 1988; Curtin, n.d.).   Human remains of the historic period are known from modern archaeological excavations at Gust Island Rockshelter on the Queen Charlotte Islands (Cybulski, 1973), Owikeno Lake on the central coast (Cybulski, 1975a), and Hesquiat Harbour on the west coast of Vancouver Island (Cybulski, 1978a), and from early museum collections (Cybulski, 1990).   The locations of all pertinent assemblages revealed through modern archaeological excavations are shown on Figure 3.

On the basis of British Columbia studies, Northwest Coast prehistory has been ascribed to four stages: a Lithic Stage from 10,000 to 5,500 years B.P. (before present in radiocarbon dating terminology); an Early Developmental Stage from 5,500 to 3,500 years B.P.; a Middle Developmental Stage from 3,500 to 1,500 years B.P.; a Late Developmental Stage from 1,500 years B.P. to the time of European contact about 220 years ago (Fladmark, 1986).   Radiocarbon age estimates for the Greenville site (detailed in Chapter II) place it in the Late Developmental Stage, the first British Columbia coast burial site with substantial information to be so positioned, the other prehistoric sites largely pertaining to the Early and, predominantly, Middle Developmental Stages.

Chapter II
Excavations and Chronology

By the time of our August, 1981, arrival in Greenville, the original surface features of the burial site had been obscured by construction activity and no decidedly mound-like element could be recognized. The area west of the minor drainage ditch, formerly a swamp, had been filled and graded, and the area immediately to the east of the ditch, subsequently found to include the major undisturbed portion of the site, was fully covered with overburden from the excavation of the ditch (Fig. 4). In the disturbance of the excavated portion, there were concentrations of finely crushed shells that promised a midden deposit akin to prehistoric shell middens previously excavated on the coast of British Columbia (e.g., MacDonald and Inglis, 1976). Human skeletal elements, exposed by heavy rains, could also be seen on the surface of the overburden on either side of the drainage ditch.

FIGURE 4. Greenville burial site at start of 1982 excavation.
(View northeast from Cooper Avenue.)

Site Plan

Excavation of the site proceeded by 10 cm levels in 2-by-2 m units with appropriate extensions made for exposing and recovering burial features. Altogether, 22 formally identified excavation units were opened, three on the west side of the drainage ditch that proved culturally sterile except for occasional disturbed surface or overburden finds, and 19 on the east side covering an area of approximately 80 m^2. They are shown on the site plan of Figure 5, as are the locations of 27 outlying test pits which were dug to determine the horizontal extent of the site as indicated by the presence or absence of shell. For the most part, shell was not revealed in these pits except for three in the immediate vicinity of the northernmost formal excavation units.

A permanent datum was established using a manhole (5.15 m above sea level) to the southeast of the site at the intersection of Cooper Avenue and Ankeda Boulevard, and the site datum was triangulated to property pins adjacent to the site (details on Fig. 2, Chapter I). Separate datums were established for each excavation unit and related to the permanent datum and as heights above sea level. Finds within each excavation unit were controlled vertically by reference to the unit datum.

The archaeologist's standard tool kit of hand trowel, whiskbroom, and dustpan was used to excavate the formal units and three test pits, those marked on the site plan as "1981 TEST PIT" and test pits 13 and 14. Other test pits were dug with a shovel. Dental picks, grapefruit knives, kitchen spoons, wooden tongue depressors, and small paintbrushes were used for fine detail excavation work on the human burials. In 1981, we took advantage of the construction contractor's offer to remove overburden with a backhoe/front-end loader, limiting this procedure to a 4-by-6 m area to the south and east of Unit 4. In 1982, a similar machine owned and operated by the Lakalzap Band was employed to remove overburden north of Unit 7b. Both operations were carefully monitored resulting in the recovery of disturbed human remains as reported in Appendix A. Backdirt from the excavation units was not screened during the initial two-week exploration period, but was passed through one-eighth inch mesh during the 1982 and 1983 field seasons.

Deposits and Stratigraphy

The depth of the excavation in the main site area (i.e., east of the minor drainage ditch) averaged 1 metre, roughly delimiting the average depth of the overall deposit to its base, a culturally sterile, dense distribution of iron-stained cob-

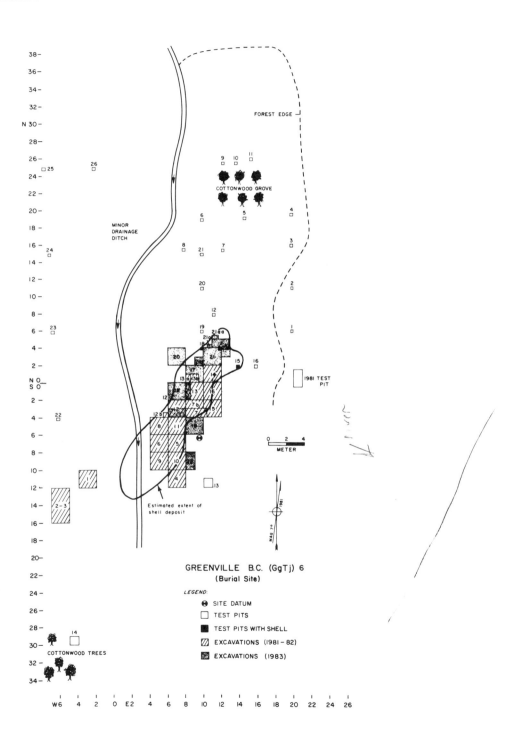

GREENVILLE B.C. (GgTj) 6
(Burial Site)

LEGEND:

⊕ SITE DATUM
☐ TEST PITS
■ TEST PITS WITH SHELL
▨ EXCAVATIONS (1981-82)
▨ EXCAVATIONS (1983)

bles, pebbles, and angularly fractured shale-like rock which was designated as Layer "D." This base was 5.43 m above sea level at points closest to the bottom of the drainage ditch.

Above the base, four apparent stratigraphic layers, including two sublayers, were recognized (e.g., Fig. 6). An uppermost layer "O" consisted of overburden from the construction crew's drainage ditch excavation. It varied from 0.25 m to 0.45 m thick along the east wall limits of Units 10, 5, and 11, and up to 0.50 m thick at Units 7 and 7b. The matrix included a mixture of other, formerly undisturbed layers and materials that had been machine-dug from the bottom to the top of the site, as well as original ground surface deposits.

Layer "A" began with the ground surface beneath the overburden and extended from 0.10 m to 0.40 m deep in different parts of the site. It was divided into two sublayers, "A1" and "A2." The chief distinction was that A1 contained many roots and rootlets, and much modern cultural debris, while A2 was essentially devoid of those elements except for occasional large tree roots. A1 was, in effect, a highly organic humus and root mat layer, while A2 marked a less organic first cultural layer pertaining to the context of the burial ground. It consisted of a darkly colored (black or very dark gray) fine-grained mixed silt and clay matrix with small pebbles, some fire-cracked rock, and some carbon staining. Indicated in this layer were some faunal remains and artifacts, some disturbed human remains, and a number of burial features, most revealed as pits intrusive into the next layer.

Layer "B" represented the main cultural construction of the deposits from which the majority of faunal remains, artifacts, and human remains were recovered. This was a deposit of concentrated, finely crushed shell, mainly composed of blue mussel (*Mytilis*), but also including some clam and barnacle. The layer ranged from 0.10 m to 0.50 m thick in different parts of the site, and its approximate extent relative to the excavated units is shown on the site plan (Fig. 5). The shell usually was thick in quantity along and about the long axis of the illustrated irregular oval and diminished at its periphery, indicating a mound in this context. Mixed with the shell were a black, fine-grained silt-clay matrix, varying quantities of cobbles and fire-cracked rock, occasional flecks of charcoal, and some concentrations of charcoal.

Layer "C", below the shell layer where the latter occurred in most excavated areas, was almost indistinguishable in soil composition from Layer A2. Compared with A2 and B, there was an increase in the number of pebbles and fire-cracked rock, an increase in the size of the rock, a substantial decrease in the amount of faunal remains, and only rare occurrences of artifacts and human bone. Charcoal flecks and occasional concentrations of charcoal were also noted. Layer C varied

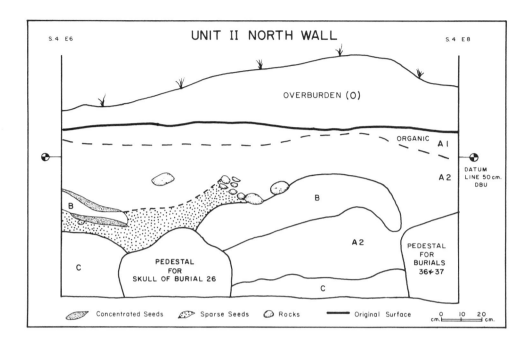

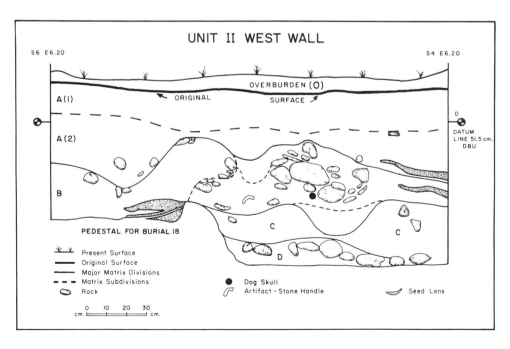

FIGURE 6. North and west wall profiles of excavation unit 11.

TABLE 1. Summary of Greenville individuals

Burial	Sex	Age	Layer	Sequence[1]	Context
1	Female	30-34 yrs	B	M	Burial, greatly disturbed
2	Male	30-34 yrs	B	M	Burial, greatly disturbed
3	Female	45-49 yrs	B	M	Burial, intact
4	Male	12-16 yrs	B	M	Burial, intact
5	Male	48-54 yrs	B	E	Burial, incomplete
6	?	2-4 yrs	A2	L	Burial, intact
7	Female	60+ yrs	B	E	Burial, intact
8	?	9-11 yrs	B	M	Burial, greatly disturbed
9	Male	40-44 yrs	B	E	Burial, greatly disturbed
10	Female	45-54 yrs	B	E?	Burial, incomplete
11	Female	28-34 yrs	B	E?	Burial, partly decayed
12	Female	30-39 yrs	A2	L	Burial, partly disturbed
13	?	9-11 yrs	B	M	Burial, greatly disturbed
14	Female	18-22 yrs	B	M	Burial, partly disturbed
15	Male	22-28 yrs	B	M	Burial, partly decayed
16	Male	50-59 yrs	B	M	Burial, slightly disturbed
17	Male	35-44 yrs	C?	?	Clustered remains
18	Male	35-44 yrs	"A2"	L	Burial, intact
19	Male	20-24 yrs	A2/B	L	Burial, intact
20	Male	22-28 yrs	B	E	Burial, slightly disturbed
21	?	8-10 yrs	B	M	Burial, partly disturbed
22	Female	40-49 yrs	B	M	Burial, intact
23	Male	55-64 yrs	B	M?	Burial, intact
24	Female	60+ yrs	B	M	Burial, intact
25a	?	3-5 yrs	B	M	Burial, partly disturbed
25b	?	3-5 yrs	B	M	Clustered remains
26	Male	17-20 yrs	A2	L	Burial, intact
27	Male	20-24 yrs	B	M	Clustered remains
29	Female	55-64 yrs	B	E	Burial, greatly disturbed
31a	Male	20-34 yrs	B	E?	Clustered remains
31b	Female	12-16 yrs	B	E?	Clustered remains
32	Male	40-44 yrs	A2	L	Burial, intact
33	Male	22-26 yrs	A2	L	Burial, slightly disturbed
34	Male	28-34 yrs	A2	L	Burial, intact
35a	?	8-10 yrs	A2	L	Burial, partly disturbed
35b	?	9-11 yrs	A2	L	Disturbed remains
35c	?	12-16 yrs	A2	L	Disturbed remains
36	Male	40-49 yrs	A2	L	Burial, partly decayed
37	Male	35-44 yrs	A2	L	Burial, slightly disturbed
38	Male	16-18 yrs	A2	L	Burial, intact
39	?	20+ yrs	C	E	Burial, mostly decayed
40	Female	22-28 yrs	B	M	Burial, intact
41	?	2-4 yrs	B	M	Clustered remains

(TABLE 1 continued)

Burial	Sex	Age	Layer	Sequence[1]	Context
42	Female	60+ yrs	A2	L	Burial, intact
43	Female	12-16 yrs	?	?	Assembled remains
44	Female	50-59 yrs	?	?	Disturbed skull
45	Male	30-39 yrs	?	?	Assembled remains
46	Female	40-49 yrs	?	?	Assembled remains
47	Female	18-22 yrs	?	?	Assembled remains
48	Male	60+ yrs	O	?	Clustered remains
49	Male	40-49 yrs	O	?	Clustered remains
50	?	3-5 yrs	O	?	Clustered remains
51	?	9-12 mos	B	M	Isolated skull
52	Male	60+ yrs	O	?	Clustered remains
53	?	12-16 yrs	B	M	Isolated mandible
54	?	Fetus	B	M	Clustered remains
55	?	4-6 yrs	?	?	Assembled remains
56	Male	40-49 yrs	?	?	1984 water-line remains
57	?	8-10 yrs	?	?	1984 water-line remains

[1] Probable sequence of deposition as explained in the text: E = early, M = middle, L = late.

from 0.05 m to 0.65 m in thickness, and blended almost imperceptibly with Layer A2 in those portions of the site where the shell layer was absent.

Human Skeletal Remains

Human skeletal remains were frequently encountered, either as single or grouped disturbed elements or as intact or partly intact burials, throughout the horizontal extent of the site. There had been a great deal of disturbance by the construction activity. Prior to our arrival, 171 skeletal elements had been recovered, including three skulls, parts of two other skulls, and an assortment of postcranial bones and teeth, a minimal equivalent of five deceased individuals. In 1981, we collected 494 additional elements from on and within the site overburden (Layer O) including portions of three skeletons (93 elements). In these instances, it appeared that originally intact burials or segments had been lifted by the construction contractor's backhoe during excavation of the minor drainage ditch and redeposited as part of the overburden. Altogether, over 1,400 disturbed skeletal elements were recovered from the site, including 540 isolated or clustered pieces found within cultural deposits (primarily Layer B) mainly undisturbed in modern times.

Including the disturbed elements and intact or partly intact burials, a minimum 59 individuals were identified in the Greenville skeletal collection following laboratory analysis. They are detailed as to represented remains and archaeological context in Appendix A and summarized in Table 1 by age at death, sex, associated stratigraphic layer, probable sequence of deposition as explained in the section on chronology, and context of identification. All but the last 15 are labelled by burial numbers assigned in the field, the last 15 numbers assigned during laboratory analysis for individuals identified from disturbed elements.

The two finally listed burials, 56 and 57, were not recovered during the 1981-1983 project. They were sent to me early in 1984 following their discovery by the Lakalzap Band during excavation for a water line ca. 35-40 m northeast of the estimated 1983 site boundary. Since the horizontal extent of the burial site appeared delimited, as indicated by the presence or absence of shell, it is possible that Burials 56 and 57 came from another burial ground, an aspect of this study that forms part of the discussion in Chapter VII. However, because of similarities in preservation, there was little reason to suspect that they were not part of the same general temporal population represented in the 1981-1983 project, and I have, therefore, included the remains as part of the overall Greenville sample.

Within the sequence of field-assigned burial numbers, it will be noted that the numbers 28 and 30 are missing. Laboratory assessments showed that the remains assigned those numbers proved to be parts of other burials. In this connection, attempts were made, to a point of diminishing returns, to match disturbed elements to incomplete burial skeletons or to each other. Apparent successes in the latter cases resulted in some individuals identified in Table 1 as "assembled remains." Those identified as "clustered remains" were on-site groupings of unarticulated bones, though in some cases out of the cultural depositional context, i.e., in the disturbed overburden. All those identified as "burials" indicate skeletal remains that were wholly, partly, or at least minimally articulated *in situ*. Further discussion of these various classes of human remains is provided in Chapter III within a broader context of the meaning of disturbed skeletal elements in coastal British Columbia shell middens.

Site Features

Cultural features recorded in the Greenville midden seem to have been exclusively oriented to mortuary purposes and are mainly detailed in the following chapter and in Appendix A. Although some of the faunal data might be interpreted to reflect the remnants of a fish camp (see Discussion section in Chapter IV), there was no concrete evidence that the site was actually lived on in prehistoric times. There were no post moulds or other structural indicators of houses, nor were "living floors" apparent, as might be indicated by hardpan or ash deposits. A probable hearth, the only such feature recorded in the site, was located in the southeast quadrant of Unit 21a. Positioned wholly within Layer B, this was a grouping of large fire-cracked cobbles roughly set in a semi-circle. It measured 60-by-75 cm horizontally and was 25 cm high. In its midst was a large concentration of charcoal weighing 311 g, collected and submitted for radiocarbon dating. The date returned, 1135 ± 120 years B.P. (S-2488), was statistically the same as a collagen-derived radiocarbon date of 1190 ± 80 years B.P. (S-2487) obtained for Burial 40, an intact Layer B interment located about 1.5 m to the west in Units 21 and 21c. It may be that the hearth served as a vehicle for burning food and clothing for the dead, a burial ritual ethnographically reported for the Nisga'a (Boas 1895:573). This might also explain the presence of charcoal elsewhere in the burial site and occasional, apparent concentrations of large cobbles, including fire-cracked examples, commonly referred to as "boiling stones" in the language of Northwest Coast archaeologists (e.g., Mitchell, 1971).

Site Chronology and Burial Sequence

Altogether, 11 bone or charcoal samples were submitted for radiocarbon dating, including human bone from five burial features in addition to Burial 40, a human femur from a disturbed context, and three discrete chunks of charcoal besides that from the hearth feature. The first ten samples were submitted to the Saskatchewan Research Council Radiocarbon Dating Laboratory, Saskatoon, as part of a continuing contractual arrangement with the Canadian Museum of Civilization, while the eleventh sample was submitted to Beta Analytic, Inc., Coral Gables, Florida. The resultant laboratory age estimates are reported in Table 2 and visually represented sequentially on Figure 7 in terms of their means and two-sigma intervals. In the following discussion, the estimates, expressed as radiocarbon years B.P., were converted to calibrated calendar years with two-sigma intervals using the computer program by Minze Stuiver and Paula J. Reimer (1986) for the bi-decadal data curves of Minze Stuiver and Gordon W. Pearson (1986). The calibration curves constitute those recommended by the Twelfth International Radiocarbon Conference (Taylor, 1987) and effectively supercede all those previously proposed (e.g., Damon et al., 1974; Klein et al., 1982).

With the permission of the Lakalzap Band Council, two human bone samples were initially submitted for dating following the 1981 exploratory work in order to confirm the suspected prehistoric context of the remains, to learn what sort of time range was represented, and to examine the relationship between the disturbed bones collected prior to excavation and the *in situ* burials that we had exposed. Additional samples were submitted to the Saskatchewan laboratory following the 1982 and 1983 excavations to test and refine the original age estimates, to investigate the relative ages of specific cultural features, and to investigate potential time differences between the apparent stratigraphic layers. A final sample was submitted to Beta Analytic in 1990 in an attempt to resolve a problematical calendrical calibration from one of the ten previously received estimates and to test a finding of apparent temporal discontinuity between Layers A2 and B (see below).

Although the mean values of laboratory age estimates are often emphasized in archaeological site reports, radiocarbon "dates" do not identify specific points in time. Rather, each estimate is a statistical approximation of a range of possibilities in which the carbon 14 activity of a sample actually lies (Taylor, 1987:125). By convention, a two-sigma range about the mean (usually, and appropriate in the case of the Saskatchewan Research Council and Beta Analytic estimates, twice the $\pm$ figure supplied by a laboratory) affords an acceptable probability statement, roughly equivalent to a 95% confidence interval in a normally distributed statistical curve. Also, while the radiocarbon years supplied by a laboratory might be converted to calendar years using A.D. 1950 as the conventional "present" reference point for 0 B.P., the results are not always accurate. Past fluctuations in the available atmospheric carbon 14 assimilated by the living organism (tree or human in the present case) whose remains ultimately supply the tested sample have a significant bearing on calendrical correspondence. Calibration techniques such as those used here provide more correct ranges for interpretation and correspondences with world-wide events.

The initial estimates confirmed the prehistoric context of the skeletal remains, but also provided two discontinuous time ranges which suggested the possibility of two discrete burial components. One of the bones collected by Constable Angus produced the earliest age estimate of all those eventually obtained, 1585 $\pm$ 110 years B.P. (S-2220) (calibrated maximum range of A.D. 220-660; intercept at A.D. 438), while Burial 3, intact in Layer B, yielded an age estimate of 1045 $\pm$ 105 radiocarbon years (S-2219) (A.D. 729-1220; A.D. 995). Although out of context, the early estimate was not particularly troubling at the time since the disturbed femur, as well as other bones collected prior to our excavation, appeared to have been machine-dug from the lowest levels of the site, represented by the base of the minor drainage ditch.

As shown on Figure 7, subsequent estimates filled in the discontinuity between the first two and extended the range upward, suggesting continuous use of the burial ground for as much as 1,000 years based on the means of the estimates, or

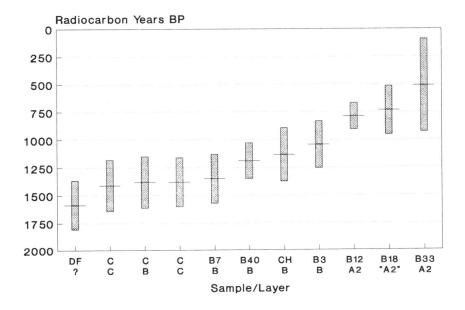

FIGURE 7. Distribution of uncalibrated radiocarbon age estimates from the Greenville site (with two-sigma ranges).

TABLE 2. Laboratory radiocarbon age estimates from the Greenville site (years B.P.)

Estimate	Laboratory number	Sample	Excavation unit	Layer
510 ± 210	S-3001	Burial 33 ribs	21	A2
735 ± 110	S-2332	Burial 18 tibia	11	"A2"
790 ± 60	Beta-39588	Burial 12 ribs	13/13b	A2
1045 ± 105	S-2219	Burial 3 ribs	9	B
1135 ± 120	S-2488	Wood charcoal (hearth)	21a	B
1190 ± 80	S-2487	Burial 40 ribs	21/21c	B
1350 ± 110	S-2333	Burial 7 ribs	7/7b	B
1380 ± 110	S-2330	Wood charcoal	10	C
1380 ± 115	S-2329	Wood charcoal	11	B
1410 ± 115	S-2331	Wood charcoal	10	C
1585 ± 110	S-2220	Disturbed femur	--	--

1,700 years based on the extremes of the intervals. Closer visual and statistical inspection of the estimates and the variable distribution of the site's cultural content by depositional layer, however, indicated that some important refinements and interpretations could be made, particularly with respect to Layers B and A2, but also Layer C.

Burial deposition sequence

Most of the cultural remains recovered from the site that were not disturbed by construction activities were associated with Layer B matrix materials. Table 3 reports the distribution of vertebrate fauna, artifacts, and human remains by associated depositional layer. The fauna and artifact distributions are based on separately counted elements, while the human figures are based on the identified individuals. This was principally the way in which the different materials were found. As for the human component, there would be little to gain in realistic comparative accuracy by breaking down skeletons into individual bones, thereby making this set of data more numerically compatible with the singly counted faunal elements and artifacts. Aside from an occasional hearth or ash deposit containing charcoal, human burials are the most stable datable cultural units in a Northwest Coast midden environment. While there were a number of disturbed human skeletal elements at Greenville, they have effectively been accounted for in terms of individuals.

It was possible to estimate the sequence of deposition for many burials in the site as related in Table 1. Several factors were taken into account. On the broadest level, the burials in Layer A2 were initially assumed to be later than those in Layer B. For Layer B, some burials were resting on or slightly in Layer C, while others were more wholly contained by the shell matrix and, presumably, relatively more recent. In the site as a whole, some burials had been disturbed by later interments, either directly or indirectly as detailed in Appendix A. All of this information, in conjunction with the radiocarbon dates, ultimately resulted in defining a threefold interment sequence for the site: early, middle, and late. The first two groups, perhaps best acknowledged as subcomponents, were associated with the shell deposit, and the last, an apparently discrete component, was associated with the overlying Layer A2 deposit.

Table 3 indicates that very few materials were associated with Layer C, essentially insignificant numbers relative to those for Layers B and A2. As evident on Table 2 and Figure 7, two charcoal samples from Layer C produced radiocarbon age estimates virtually identical to the two earliest estimates for Layer B. One of the latter was based on charcoal and the other on bone collagen from Burial

TABLE 3. Greenville site distributions of vertebrate faunal elements, artifacts, and human individuals by stratigraphic layer

Layer	Faunal elements [1] Number	%	Artifacts Number	%	Human individuals Number	%
A2	1,014	5.35	41	17.75	14	24.56
B	13,177	69.48	143	61.90	30	52.63
C	305	1.61	7	3.03	2 [2]	3.51
Other[3]	4,468	23.56	40	17.32	11	19.30
--------	--------	--------	----	--------	----	--------
Total	18,964	100.00	231	100.00	57	100.00

[1] The lower number of faunal elements reported here than in the introductory chapter excludes intrusive species and "class uncertain" elements as explained in Chapter IV.
[2] This number includes one individual of uncertain association (Burial 17 in Table 1; details in Appendix A).
[3] This category includes disturbed surface and overburden finds, and three artifacts, 439 faunal elements, and one intact human burial recorded in mixed deposits of layers A2 and B, or B and C.

7 which rested in a pit dug slightly into Layer C. The concurrent radiocarbon estimates and the paucity of materials suggest that Layer C did not represent a discrete early cultural component of the Greenville site. More likely, Layer C was a former surface some 1,500 years ago on which shell was deposited as an activity marking the first cultural use of the site. Only one burial, Burial 39, was clearly in Layer C, having been recorded distinctly below the shell layer and below a layer of rocks seemingly intentionally placed. The burial could not be directly dated because it was so poorly preserved there was little substantive bone left to be collected. The comparable radiocarbon age estimates for Layer C and lower levels of Layer B suggest the interment was probably intrusive from earliest Layer B times.

On the subject of "intrusion," it may be noted that no mention of a burial pit is made in Appendix A for the context of Burial 39. As further discussed in the next chapter, this does not necessarily mean that the body wasn't interred in a pit dug from the inferred 1,500-year-old former surface of the site. Pits are difficult to discern in a shell midden and might only be readily detected between or near the junctures of decidedly contrasting stratigraphic matrices, such as from Layer A2 into B or from Layer B into C in the present situation.

Although Burial 39 was very poorly preserved, possible differences in the potential for bone preservation among the stratigraphic layers did not seem to significantly influence their differences in cultural content.   It could be argued that most of the bone from the site came from Layer B because bone might preserve better in shell than in silt and clay.   Shell has basic properties that effectively neutralize the potentially bone-damaging acidic soils of a forest environment and forms a more loosely integrated matrix with potentially better drainage characteristics than a more tightly knit silt and clay matrix.

Soils analysis carried out by scientists at Agriculture Canada in Ottawa yielded pH values of 6.40 to 6.95 for 11 samples from various parts of the site (mean of 6.74, standard deviation of 0.17).   While technically "weakly acidic" values, they also are "high" readings close to the value of 7 which is regarded as chemically neutral, neither unusually acidic nor alkaline (pers. comm., Land Resource Research Centre, Agriculture Canada, 1991).   Although some skeletons in the site were better preserved than others, there did not appear to be any consistent differences between layers.

To further test the possibility that variable preservation may have influenced the distribution of cultural materials among the layers, I compared the stratigraphic distribution of artifacts made from bone as opposed to those made from stone, both of which were represented in the Greenville site collection which is described in Appendix B.   The results are shown on Figure 8.

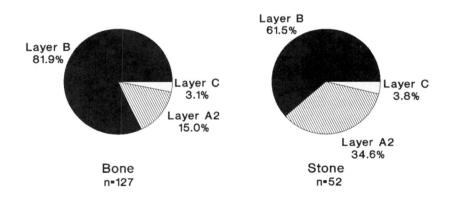

FIGURE 8. Stratigraphic distribution of Greenville site artifacts made of bone and of stone.

The two groups of artifacts were represented at very similar low frequencies in Layer C, indicating that preservation likely had little to do with the very low overall cultural content in this layer.   In fact, there were twice as many artifacts made from bone as from stone (four and two respectively; a seventh artifact was made from an animal's tooth), further suggesting that preservation was not at issue here. It is likely that these few artifacts had been dropped or discarded on the former 1,500-year-old surface and through perturbation processes (e.g., human activities, plant growth, frost-heaving, animal-burrowing, etc.) had become part of Layer C.

One might argue that because of small numbers alone, it would be difficult to detect meaningful preservation differences based on the cultural content of Layer C. This might be supported by the distinct differences in frequencies evident on Figure 8 between layers A2 and B, where more artifacts were available. Proportionally fewer artifacts made of bone than of stone were recovered from Layer A2 than Layer B, a statistically significant difference (chi-square = 8.932, $p < 0.005$). However, further tests strongly suggested that the differences reflected cultural rather than preservation factors. Statistical tests were also carried out to compare the distributions of artifacts versus humans in layers A2 and B. There were no proportional differences shown between the distributions of all artifacts and humans at the conventional 5% probability level (chi-square = 1.764, $p > 0.1$), or between the distributions of stone artifacts and humans (chi-square = 0.182, $p > 0.5$). There was, though, a significant proportional difference between the distribution of bone artifacts and humans (chi-square = 5.478, $p < 0.02$). Relatively more deceased humans and stone artifacts were associated with Layer A2, while proportionally more bone artifacts were associated with Layer B. These differences may have been connected in some way with an apparent temporal gap between the two layers, a possible correspondence which is discussed in Chapter VII.

It may be noted on Figure 7 that the 11 radiocarbon age estimates form three clusters. From earliest to latest, the first five dates appear to form one group, the next three a second cluster, and the last three a third cluster. The significance of the clusters was tested statistically using methods for radiocarbon age estimates described by Albert C. Spaulding (1958) and Austin Long and Bruce Rippeteau (1974). One of Albert Spaulding's methods tests the statistical commensurateness of two dates using the standard normal distribution curve. Austin Long and Bruce Rippeteau provide methods for testing the statistical integrity of groups of radiocarbon dates to allow decisions for averaging, thus improving the precision of dating when a suite of estimates is available for the same archaeological event. As regards the usefulness of a "suite of estimates," R.E. Taylor (1987:105) has noted:

> . . . it is often difficult to evaluate directly the various factors that could influence the accuracy of a single ^{14}C value. For this reason,

little reliance should be placed on an individual ^{14}C "date" to provide an estimate of age for a given object, structure, feature, or stratigraphic unit. A critical judgement of the ability of ^{14}C data to infer actual age can be best made with a suite of ^{14}C determinations on multiple samples drawn from the same context or with multiple ^{14}C determinations obtained on different fractions of the same sample.

In the present situation, it is the stratigraphic unit that is important since the clusters appear to identify two temporal levels with Layer B (the first incorporating Layer C as defined above) and a third with Layer A2.

Using Albert Spaulding's method, no statistically significant differences were found among the radiocarbon dates within each cluster. Nor was a significant difference found between the latest date in the first group (Burial 7) and the earliest date (Burial 40) in the second group, a finding further discussed below. A statistically significant difference was found between the latest Layer B date (Burial 3) and the earliest Layer A2 date (Burial 12; $t = 2.11$, $p < 0.04$).

Application of Austin Long and Bruce Rippeteau's methods identified each cluster as a separate statistically viable unit with the exception of one date, that of the disturbed femur in the earliest group. While "statistically valid" because it did not significantly differ from the next earliest date (or the latest in the group), the date met rejection criteria generated from within the group itself (Long and Rippeteau, 1974:208). Since the sample could not be stratigraphically defined, it appeared best to also reject the date on intuitive grounds. Thus, S-2220 could be objectively as well as subjectively eliminated as having meaningful impact on the site's dating.

Initially, I completed all of these tests and achieved the same results without the Beta Analytic estimate for Burial 12. However, the data at hand for Layer A2, prior to obtaining Beta-39588, could have been interpreted as inconclusive. The estimate for Burial 33 presented an unusually large standard error, and there was some *in situ* contextual uncertainty concerning Burial 18's association with Layer A2 (the reason for the quotation marks in Tables 1 and 2, and on Figure 7).

The 510 ± 210 B.P. estimate for Burial 33 gave four calibration ranges with a maximum two-sigma range of 1200 - 0* B.P. and an upper limit calendar date of A.D. 1955*, the asterisk denoting atmospheric influence by the atomic bomb (Stuiver and Pearson, 1986). The chances of Burial 33 possibly being that recent, or even from the time of the establishment of Greenville in 1877, were quite slim inasmuch as no one at Greenville knew of a modern or older Christian cemetery in the area of the site and the burial was culturally similar to others that had been excavated. Because a sufficiently large sample of bone was submitted for dating, there is reason to suspect that procedural problems in the laboratory may have been responsible for the unduly large standard error, although this could not be verified (cf., Taylor, 1987:125-126).

Taken alone, Burial 18, which was in a discrete box outline, seemed to be associated with Layer B, without clear evidence of a grave pit, resting on Layer C. The excavator, however, recorded two peculiarities that suggested a pit potentially connected with Layer A2. The matrix around the burial was darkly stained for a distance of 10-15 cm beyond the edge of the box outline, and the shell matrix covering the burial was depressed, suggesting that it could have been the fill of a pit (see Fig. 6, west wall). Also, Burial 18 was one of three descriptively similar burials in a 2.5-by-2 m area, which suggested contemporaneity. Each burial was of a male in a discrete box outline of very similar proportions and small size, with each skeleton very tightly compressed in its small space, the skull face down in one corner (see Chapter III and Fig. 14). Burial 26, one of the three, was in a distinct Layer A2 pit deeply intrusive through Layer B and also resting on Layer C. There was no question of its association with Layer A2. The other, Burial 19, adjacent to Burial 18 and also resting on Layer C, was in a mixed A-B depositional matrix. Like Burial 18, it was surrounded by a more darkly stained matrix, albeit with a lighter concentration of shell and greater mixture of silt and clay that suggested fill. In this case, there was no adjacent vertical profile that might have revealed a definite pit outline.

The fact that Burial 18 produced a radiocarbon date significantly different from that of the latest dated known Layer B interment, Burial 3 ($t = 2.04$, $p < 0.05$), and not significantly different from that of Burial 33, further supported its affiliation with Layer A2. The two dates formed a statistically discrete cluster from the others, and calendrical calibrations of the resulting averages suggested a substantial temporal gap between Layers A2 and B. Burial 12 was selected for dating to test this finding. This was a known Layer A2 pit interment that had the added characteristic of a mixed shell and soil fill in the nature of Burial 19, thereby giving credence to the latter burial's association with Layer A2. While nothing could be done about the large standard error of S-3001 short of obtaining a second radiocarbon estimate from Burial 33, the resultant "suite" of dates for Layer A2 tended to lessen its impact in the following interpretation.

Using Minze Stuiver and Paula J. Reimer's (1986) "CALIB" computer program, the three clusters (excluding the earliest date) gave weighted averages of 1379.3 ± 56.2 B.P. years, 1136.4 ± 56.2 B.P. years, and 761.6 ± 51.1 B.P. years (with no error multipliers included in the standard deviations; see Stuiver and Pearson, 1986).

They are the same results obtained by hand calculations using the formula of Austin Long and Bruce Rippeteau (1974) but a lot simpler and faster to achieve. Calibration gave two-sigma calendar ranges of A.D. 566-760 (intercept at A.D. 655), A.D. 770-1010 (A.D. 892), and A.D. 1180-1290 (A.D. 1264). These ranges were used to construct Figure 9 which is an attempt to summarize the overall "final" time frame for the Greenville site. The chart also includes the distribution of deceased humans by age group and sex which were estimated as associated with each interment subcomponent/component. This feature is discussed in the next chapter.

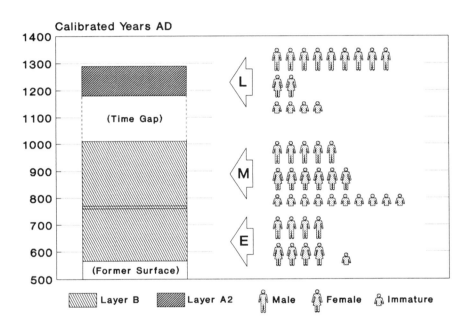

FIGURE 9. Time frame for the Greenville site in calibrated calendar years and distribution of deceased humans per subcomponent (E = early, M = middle, L = late).

Only a minor, ten-year calendrical gap exists between the early and middle sub-components associated with Layer B. As noted above, no statistically significant difference occurs between the latest radiocarbon age estimate of the first cluster and the earliest of the second. Indeed, no significant difference occurs between the date for Burial 7 and that for the hearth charcoal in the middle cluster of estimates. This may be interpreted as evidence for continuity between the two shell groups. At the same time, the fact that the middle cluster forms a statistically discrete group of radiocarbon age estimates provides evidence for the broad 400 years or so time span of interment in Layer B.   Layer B reflects a continuous deposition sequence.   By contrast, the burials in Layer A2 represent a discrete later entity, separated from the burials associated with Layer B by a minimum 170 years.   It seems that the site was abandoned for some reason and then restored to its former use as a burial ground.   The fact that shell was not a matrix feature of this later use further suggests that the presence or absence of shell may itself have been an associated mortuary ritual that varied through time.   These ideas are further referenced in the next chapter and more fully explored in Chapter VII.

Chapter III

Mortuary Practices

Soon after we began to expose a number of burials early in the 1982 field season, an elderly Nisga'a onlooker expressed bewilderment with the discovery, commenting that "long ago we buried our people in trees." Because of the contrariness of what he saw as opposed to what he had been taught of the old ways, he offered that those people in the ground must have died of smallpox as introduced to the native people by Europeans. Historical records show that an initial outbreak of the disease occurred shortly after European contact with Northwest Coast Indians in the 1770s, apparently affecting the entire coast, and that subsequent epidemics occurred on the Nass River, as well as in other areas, in the 1830s and 1860s (Boyd, 1990:137-144). The elder reasoned that the Greenville site deceased reflected hurried burials of people who were "dying like flies;" there simply was no time for the usual ceremony, and burying people in the ground would have helped prevent spread of the disease.

History versus Prehistory

While the decidedly pre-European period radiocarbon age estimates for the Greenville site and burials clearly ruled out "smallpox" to account for most and, quite likely, all of the interments, I was somewhat perplexed by the gentleman's reference to tree burial among the Nisga'a, knowing at the time that this was a method of burial principally reported ethnographically for southern coastal British Columbia groups including those now known as Kwakwaka'wakw and Kwa-giulth (collectively southern Kwakiutl) and Nuu-chah-nulth (north and central Vancouver Island Nootka) (Boas, 1890:839; Drucker, 1951:147-150). Late in the 19th century, however, Franz Boas (1895:582) wrote that many Nisga'a tales mentioned tree burial, "such as is practised by the southern tribes," although he detailed *cremation* as the form of burial actually practiced by the Nisga'a (ibid., p. 573).

The Northwest Coast ethnographic literature is, in fact, cursory and often confusing on the subject of native burial practices with regard to mechanisms for disposing of the dead. Franz Boas did not seem to have actually observed burial or other customs he reported for the Nisga'a, or, for that matter, for the Tsimshian at large, having obtained details through native informants, often in places distant from their home villages. From his writings on both Nisga'a and Tsimshian customs, we are led to believe that cremation was the norm and that it also was common to other northern Northwest Coast groups, including the Tlingit of Alaska and the Kaigani and Queen Charlotte Islands Haida. Specific to the Nisga'a, Franz Boas wrote that all bodies were burned, including those of shamans, though for the Tsimshian, Tlingit, and Haida, he reported that the bodies of shamans were "buried in caves or in the woods" (Boas, 1890:837).

To account for the Nisga'a tales regarding tree burial, Franz Boas "suppose(d) that the custom of cremating the body was borrowed *recently* from the Tlingit," though almost in the same breath he wrote that cremation was prevalent "in olden times" (Boas, 1895:581-582; italics mine). Another 19th century writer, however, indicated that burial practices were varied among the Tlingit with cremation largely a practice of the northern groups, around Sitka, and other modes of burial practiced by the southern Tlingit (Niblack, 1890:351-361). Even so, cremation was "not a universal practice amongst the northern Tlingit, a large proportion of sepulture being by inhumation" (ibid., p. 355).

The same author also wrote that for "the larger portion of the southern Tlingit, Haida, and Tsimshian, . . . sepulture by interment is practised similar to our method of burial" (ibid.). Franz Boas himself, writing about Kwakwaka'wakw and Kwa-giulth customs, noted the "body is placed in a small house similar to those of the Tlingit and Haida" (Boas, 1890:839), seemingly contradicting his earlier statement about cremation being prevalent among the latter groups, not to mention his reference to tree burial among the Kwakwaka'wakw and Kwa-giulth.

Indeed, the ethnographic record indicates there can be no concise statements about the historic and protohistoric periods as to specific forms of burial among different Northwest Coast cultural groups or local subgroups, and this is further supported by actual observation. In the late 1700s (ca. 1785-1795), early explorers such as Dixon, Portlock, and Vancouver, observed some Tlingit grave sites where burial boxes were suspended on long thick wooden poles scaffold-like above the ground and other Tlingit grave sites where burial boxes had been placed in caves (Niblack, 1890:351-353). The boxes contained whole skeletons, partial skeletons, skulls, or ashes. For the British Columbia coast, museum-sponsored expeditions around the turn of the 20th century recorded and collected whole or partial human skeletons and skulls from burial caves, mortuary houses, tree burials, and elaborately carved mortuary "totem" poles, some accompanied by artifacts of European manufacture (Cybulski, 1975b).

Archaeology also portrays a variety of historic period native burial practices on the British Columbia coast. In 1971 and 1973, I was given the privilege of analyzing human remains at Hesquiat Harbour on the west coast of Vancouver

Island (Nuu-chah-nulth territory). Those remains, numbering over 100 individuals and dating to the first few decades of the 19th century, lay exposed in caves and rockshelters, and some may have been secondary depositions after tree burial (Cybulski, 1978a). In 1975 and 1977, I analyzed human remains at a burial ground on Owikeno Lake in the Rivers Inlet region of the central British Columbia coast (Oowekeeno territory of the northern Kwakiutl). The site was greatly disturbed but evidence suggested the remains, dated to the last decades of the 19th century, were originally in small grave houses similar to those still standing or otherwise recognizable elsewhere in the area (Cybulski, 1975a; Seymour, 1977, 1979). In keeping with this "tradition," our Oowekeeno hosts and co-workers constructed a new cedar grave house to contain the remains on site after I had finished my study (Cybulski, 1977a:50-52). Also in the Rivers Inlet - Owikeno Lake region, human remains of the historic period have been recorded in the crevices of rock slides (B. Simonsen, pers. comm., 1975).

During an archaeological survey of Kwakwaka'wakw territory in 1973, Roy Carlson and Philip Hobler (1976) recorded burial sites in Blunden Harbour and Quatsino Sound: burial caves and rockshelters, "burial islands," mortuary houses, and tree burials. On the Queen Charlotte Islands in 1967, George MacDonald excavated a rockshelter holding the skeletal remains of 24 deceased, dating around A.D. 1800 (Cybulski, 1973). In his report on the find, he mentioned other similar sites and above ground methods of disposing of the dead which were practiced historically by the Haida (MacDonald, 1973).

Some elements may be concluded from this discourse on "traditional" native burial practices. Conceivably, the reported and known variations (and apparent contradictions in the literature for the same cultural group) might have been related to class distinctions among the people, a prominent characteristic of Northwest Coast society in other respects (cf. Drucker, 1955). Regardless of this possibility, while there seem to have been a great variety of burial "modes" practiced on the British Columbia coast by the native people, one clearly definable mode widely known to archaeologists is not mentioned in any Northwest Coast ethnography or ethnohistoric document. That is the form of burial shown by the Greenville site, midden burial or, more precisely, shell midden burial, the predominant form known from the prehistoric period.

Appendix C summarizes other prehistoric human remains analyzed for the British Columbia coast. Together with Greenville, the figures identify a minimum 759 deceased individuals representing 30 burial sites from north to south, all of which were shell middens. The figures, while seemingly large, only reflect site data from which I have been able to extract vital statistics (discussed later in this chapter) either through my own analyses or from the reports of other investigators. Additional known prehistoric midden burial sites include St. Mungo Cannery (DgRr 2) in the Fraser River Delta with at least four burials excavated (Calvert, 1970) and two sites at Pender Canal in the Gulf Islands (DeRt 1 and DeRt 2) with as many as 100 deceased represented (Carlson, 1985, 1986; Cybulski, 1991b).   A midden burial site at Tsawwassen (DgRs 2), also in the Strait of Georgia region, revealed an estimated 80 to 100 individuals excavated between 1988 and 1990 (Curtin, 1990).   Computerized records in the British Columbia Archaeology Branch indicate eight additional coastal prehistoric midden sites containing human burials (File BCHH01, October 31, 1990).   With the addition of these remains, the total number of currently known prehistoric deceased approximates 1,000 individuals from 42 shell midden sites.

With one possible exception, no currently known prehistoric human remains from the British Columbia coast are from any other method of burial.   The possible exception is an intriguing cave and rock crevice complex of disturbed skeletal remains on Gabriola Island off the east coast of Vancouver Island near Nanaimo.   Mark Skinner (1989) reported a minimum 12 individuals from this complex (site DgRw 199), some with collagen-based radiocarbon age estimates in the range of 2400 to 2700 years B.P.   The remains of other individuals giving similar bone dates were later recovered by A. Joanne Curtin (pers. comm., 1990). Because of their disturbed nature, it is uncertain whether the bones represent primary burials (individuals whose corpses were placed *in situ* and whose bones were subsequently disturbed) or whether they might have been collected from former midden burials and secondarily placed, possibly as a function of ritual.[4]

Notwithstanding the localized Gabriola Island possibility for above ground disposal of the dead, known human remains from the British Columbia coast indicate a distinct, widespread difference between historic and prehistoric period disposal methods.   In Appendix C, I have also listed historic period burial sites that have been archaeologically excavated and studied in detail.   Represented are 194 individuals from 13 designated sites including the caves and rockshelters at Gust Island and Hesquiat Harbour, and the apparent grave house(s) at Owikeno Lake.   These historic period human remains and sites represent but a fraction of those known from the British Columbia coast.   Elsewhere, I have reported museum-collected remains numbering at least 399 individuals from 34 above ground mortuary locali-

---

[4] The ritual use of corpses, body parts, and human bones on the British Columbia coast is ethnographically known and archaeologically interpretable (Cybulski, 1978b).   R. Schulting and J. Ostapkowicz (1990) more recently postulated ritual to account for unarticulated human bones found in a cave in the Bella Coola valley on the central coast.

ties, including 14 on the Queen Charlotte Islands, two on the central coast, nine along the north and east coasts of Vancouver Island and the adjacent mainland, four along the west coast of Vancouver Island, and five in the vicinity of Victoria (Cybulski, 1975b, 1977b (map of localities on p. 32), 1978a, 1985, 1990). Hence, at least 593 individuals are currently known from 47 historic period above ground mortuary localities throughout the coast. It may be added that none showed evidence for cremation.

The dichotomy between these known historic and prehistoric period corpse disposal methods is not explained by the ethnographic or ethnohistoric record. Alfred P. Niblack, the 19th century writer who summarized the Tlingit burial methods cited above, also wrote that they had "undergone many changes since the advent of the whites" (1890:361), implying that cultural disruptions brought about by European contact may have influenced what we know of Northwest Coast mortuary practices ethnographically. Such possible disruptions, however, do not account for the known prehistoric and historic difference. By the late 1800s, missionary pressures may have been profound with respect to treatment of the dead and such pressures could have been responsible for Niblack's previously cited reference to "sepulture by interment . . . similar to our method of burial" for the Tlingit. Christian methods of burial then called for below ground interment largely as they do today in both white and native society. Yet, missionaries did not begin to have significant impact on the beliefs of the Indians in most areas of the coast until the 1850s and 1860s (Cole and Darling, 1990; see Halpin and Seguin, 1990, for the Tsimshian). Undoubtedly, many of the historic period above ground remains dated earlier (e.g., Gust Island and Hesquiat Harbour), though even under potential missionary influences, above ground disposal of the dead was still practiced by the Ooweekeno late in the 19th century.

Aside from the Tlingit reference, I have been unable to find any other clear reference to below ground burial in the early literature. Indeed, such practices seem to have been unheard of among the native people of the time, as attested to in part by the Greenville elder's comment cited at the beginning of this chapter. On the basis of his 19th century observations of the Haida, William Collison (1981:65) wrote, "They never interred their dead." This was in the context of his discovering outside his Masset lodging one morning,

> . . . a great pile of the remains of the dead, some in grease boxes tied around with bark ropes, some in cedar bark mats which had fallen to pieces, revealing the contents; whilst skulls and bones were scattered around . . . The older men had known that this was the custom (ibid.).

Similarly, the Reverend A.J. Brabant, who in 1875 founded a Roman Catholic mission at Hesquiat on the west coast of Vancouver Island, wrote that "The Indians up to this (time) had never buried their dead under ground" (Brabant in Moser, 1926:59). In this connection, it may be noted that the skeletal remains of a minimum nine individuals, dated to the late 18th century, were recovered in 1966 from a shell midden at Yuquot on the west coast of Vancouver Island (Dewhirst, 1980; Cybulski, 1980) just up island from Hesquiat Harbour. They would appear to contradict Brabant's statement if applicable to other Nuu-chah-nulth. However, the elements were disturbed and very incomplete, and only one individual could be construed as a burial, though without evidence of a grave (Dewhirst, 1980:56). Also, osteological evidence, in the form of cultural head shape modification, suggested the remains may not have been those of local residents and, therefore, were disposed of differently from the preferred custom.

The temporal distribution of prehistoric burials

Conceivably, several centuries could have passed between the time that natives of the British Columbia coast buried their dead in shell middens and the "ethnographic present." It is otherwise strange that no mention should have been made of shell midden burial in the early literature since it was so prevalent in the past. Perhaps, people living in the 19th century simply may not have remembered that far back, or the oral tradition was interrupted for some other reason. In any event, it appears that the last several centuries before European contact witnessed a marked change in the mortuary practices of ancestral Northwest Coast societies.[5]

The observations are plausible in light of Figure 10 and additional data concerning the temporal distribution of human burials from the British Columbia coast. The first three bars in the graph reflect the Early, Middle, and Late Developmental stages of prehistory as defined by Knut Fladmark (1986) and detail the five regions from which prehistoric burials are known. The first, or Lithic Stage of prehistory has not been included since it is currently inconsequential in terms of known human burials and, for the most part, shell middens are not apparent in coastal archaeology prior to 5500 years ago (ibid.). Two of 42 burials from the site of Namu were assigned a broad time range of 9700-5000 years B.P. (Curtin, 1984) and I have included them with the known Early Stage burials from

---

[5] Archaeologists have speculated that some human remains found in middens are, in fact, representative of above ground corpse disposal practices (e.g., Burley, 1989; Johnstone, 1989). The argument is addressed in a later section of this chapter in the context of disturbed skeletal remains, the apparent source of evidence for the speculation.

that site.   The earliest other known burials from the coast, 5,000 to 4,000 years old, mainly represented at Namu and Blue Jackets Creek, are all included in the figure.

The historic period bar reflects the 593 individuals reported above.   The prehistory bars total 745 individuals from 35 midden sites.   In preparing this part of the graph, I was careful to include only those individuals for which temporal information was certain or reasonably certain as regards each stage.   The data were derived from my assessments of the Greenville burials and those of Prince Rupert Harbour and of one Duke Point site (DgRx 5) in the Strait of Georgia region (details in Appendix D), and from the various other sources listed in Appendix C and Appendix D.

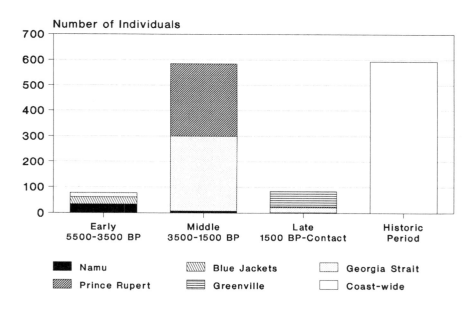

FIGURE 10. Temporal distribution of human burials from the British Columbia coast.   Early, Middle, and Late bars identify B.C. prehistory stages as defined by K. Fladmark (1986).

The prehistoric burials entered into Figure 10 are about 250 short of the known total discussed previously but can be considered representative. If anything, the Middle Stage bar would likely increase substantially in height and the Early and Late Stage bars only slightly if the 250 could be included, the Early Stage bar perhaps more so than the Late. Almost all of the excluded individuals are from the two Pender Canal sites and Tsawwassen for which temporal information was not available at the time of this writing with respect to all of the burials. From

DeRt 2 at Pender Canal, I included 15 individuals that were directly dated by radiocarbon techniques (Carlson, 1986). Seven of the age estimates produced Early Stage figures, six were in the Middle Stage range, and only two reflected the Late Stage. Of 28 total site carbon 14 estimates available for both DeRt 1 and DeRt 2 at the time of this writing, including estimates based on wood charcoal samples, seven were in the Early Stage range, 14 in the Middle Stage range, and seven in the Late Stage range (Mitchell, 1971; Carlson, 1986).

Initial interpretations for the Tsawwassen site suggested the burials would date to the latter part of the Marpole culture phase and (or) the Gulf of Georgia culture type. Marpole is one of two regionally identified culture phases dominating the Middle Developmental Stage of British Columbia coast prehistory in the south, at ca. 2500-1500 years B.P., the other being Locarno Beach at ca. 3500-2500 B.P. (Fladmark, 1986). The Gulf of Georgia culture type is a regional variant of the Late Developmental Stage (ibid.). Radiocarbon dates from the bones of Tsawwassen burials, however, have predominantly identified the Locarno Beach and Marpole phase time ranges (A.J. Curtin, pers. comm., 1990), and a time frame of 4000 to 1100 years B.P. has been suggested for the sample as a whole (Curtin, 1990).

The Pender Canal and Tsawwassen situations represent a departure for "dating" burials from sites in the Strait of Georgia region as both analyses have been relying on radiocarbon age estimates obtained directly from the skeletons. Virtually all of the other Strait of Georgia burials included on Figure 10 have been "culturally," or relatively dated, the traditional approach taken by archaeologists in the region. Marpole, Locarno Beach, and other cultural phases for the region have largely been defined by designated artifact types and their presence or absence in a site component. For the most part, only one or a few wood charcoal samples from a site have traditionally been assessed to "date" the components (cf. Burley, 1989). Burials have then been assigned to the phases by virtue of presumed component or artifact associations. The difficulty here is that artifacts are frequently dislocated and redeposited during construction of a shell midden, and the whole deposit is subject to a variety of perturbation processes. Nearby charcoal samples selected for dating need not be contemporaneous. One might also question the reliance on one or only a few radiocarbon age estimates used to date the sites (see Chapter II).

A.J. Curtin, responsible for the analysis of the burials from Tsawwassen, has noted earlier dates for some than might ordinarily be associated with the Marpole culture phase as interpreted from artifact types. The burial dates are more in tune with radiocarbon estimates that usually identify the Locarno Beach phase, and south coast archaeologists are beginning to agree with such findings as they might apply to other sites (A.J. Curtin, pers. comm., 1990). Another case in point is a multiple burial of ten individuals from DgRx 5, a Duke Point site near Nanaimo. Rebecca Murray (1982), who reported the archaeology and artifact analysis of this site and three others in the area, assigned the burial to the Marpole culture phase apparently because shell disc beads, a presumed diagnostic marker for this phase, were associated with some individuals. This assignment was made despite the fact that a pre-Marpole phase 3080 ± 70 years B.P. (WSU-2229) radiocarbon age estimate was reported by Rebecca Murray for a sample of midden shell 30 cm above the burial. I subsequently obtained a collagen-based radiocarbon age estimate of 3490 ± 125 years B.P. (S-2350) from one of the represented individuals (Cybulski, 1990; see Appendix D for further clarification). Additional evidence that the burial was of pre-Marpole times was that none of the few skulls or skull parts available for analysis showed evidence for intentional head shape modification, a predominantly post-2500 years B.P. cultural phenomenon among coastal British Columbia native people (Beattie, 1985:33-34).

While this discussion indicates that some or, perhaps, many human burials from the Strait of Georgia region may be earlier than originally assessed, changes would largely entail a backward shift from Marpole to Locarno Beach times, as most of the known burials from this region have previously been associated with the Marpole culture phase (e.g., Beattie, 1981). Any changes would not materially alter the distribution pattern shown on Figure 10. What is more important in the context of the chart is that very few currently known burials bracket the 13 centuries between the Middle Developmental Stage of British Columbia coast prehistory and the period of European contact from which information about the "ethnographic present" has largely been derived. Less than 12% of all known midden burials come from the Late Developmental Stage and more than two-thirds of this sample is represented by Greenville. For whatever reason(s), midden interment seems to have diminished substantially as a method of burial in the Late Developmental Stage of prehistory and seems to have entirely ceased by about A.D. 1200-1300 calibrated calendar years. Outside of Greenville, which most significantly provides this temporal information, the latest well dated human midden burial is from Little Qualicum River site (DiSc 1) in the Strait of Georgia region with an associated radiocarbon date of 730 ± 80 years B.P. (GaK-6819; Bernick, 1983) and a calibrated calendar range essentially the same as that of the late burial component at Greenville.

It is interesting to speculate that with the Greenville site, archaeology may be witnessing one of the last examples of midden burial on the coast of British Columbia as a significant cultural practice. The other 25 midden burials from the Late Developmental Stage are from 11 sites, an average of 2.3 burials per site, hardly indicative of large cemeteries in the manner of those known from the Middle

Developmental Stage (e.g., Boardwalk and Lachane at Prince Rupert Harbour; False Narrows, Marpole, and Tsawwassen in the Strait of Georgia).[6] Possibly significant as well, is the evidence at Greenville of an early component of burials distinctly associated with shell as opposed to a later component not so associated. Available reports indicate that virtually all the Middle Developmental Stage burials from the coast are shell-associated, and the early component (early + middle subcomponents) at Greenville would appear to reflect a continuum in a long-standing ritual of shell-related burial that lasted until about A.D. 1000 (calibrated), at which point the practice may no longer have been fashionable.

The data seem to indicate that coastal mortuary practices changed radically during the Late Developmental Stage of prehistory, with the shift to above ground corpse disposal probably finally occurring after about A.D. 1250. This inference assumes, of course, knowledge of above ground disposal of the dead in the 500 years prior to the historic period. That is something we do not have in terms of hard archaeological evidence. In fact, there is relatively little evidence at all of burial in the Late Developmental Stage compared with the earlier Middle Developmental Stage. An interesting corollary is that there is relatively little in the way of other cultural data for the Late Developmental Stage despite inferential writings to the contrary (e.g., Mitchell, 1971; MacDonald and Inglis, 1981; Burley, 1989) so that it is difficult to quantitatively test the validity and significance of the apparent evidence presented here for an abrupt change in mortuary practices. Was there, in fact, an abrupt change in mortuary practices by about A.D. 1300 or are the data presented here simply a reflection of our general lack of knowledge about the Late Developmental Stage in terms of hard archaeological evidence? Are the data presented here symptomatic of a larger sphere of cultural or social change on the coast of British Columbia by A.D. 1300? Was the change in burial practices a unique social element, unrelated to other cultural or social phenomena of the time?

----

[6] The 37 analyzed individuals reported for the Marpole site in Appendix C represent only a fraction of the burials that have been recovered from this site, known in the early days of British Columbia coast archaeology as the Eburne Mound or Great Fraser Midden. According to Owen Beattie (1985:32), 200 human skeletons were excavated in 1931, and some had previously been excavated around the turn of the 20th century. Available archaeological and osteological data on these remains are spotty, and the 1931 collection, originally in the care of the Vancouver City Museum, seems to have since been dispersed to various institutions in North America and abroad (e.g., Bork-Feltkamp, 1960). It is unfortunate that this collection has never been reported in its entirety (we do not know exactly how many individuals were excavated, nor their age at death and sex distribution), but that was generally the case for early burial excavations on the British Columbia coast, as well as elsewhere in North America.

About the only other widespread quantitative archaeological data available for comparison are in the form of radiocarbon age estimates. Figure 11 shows the distribution of "all" radiocarbon age estimates (details in Appendix D) currently available for the coast of British Columbia as represented by the five burial regions. Fifty-three sites are represented whether or not they produced human burials. The exclusion of radiocarbon age estimates from sites outside the five burial areas does not materially alter what may be viewed as a representative pattern for the coast; there are very few sites known outside this sphere. I selected 500-year increments for this chart because of the nature of the data. In terms of the three prehistory stages, 55.5% of the estimates would fall in the Middle Developmental Stage, 22.4% in the Early Developmental Stage, and 22.1% in the Late Developmental Stage. While this is a more equitable distribution than shown by the burials on Figure 10, caution must be used in making too much of the apparent lack of exact conformity to the burial chart since radiocarbon age estimates do not necessarily reflect quantifiable cultural data. In many cases, carbon samples have been collected to "date" potential sites or "horizons" which have not been sampled or adequately studied for quantifiable cultural data. In a number of instances, the interpretive emphasis has been on the "date" itself rather than on the cultural "event" being dated. In the main, the distribution of radiocarbon age estimates broadly mirrors the basic pattern shown on Figure 10 by the distribution of human burials. The broad conformity shows that the burials do not necessarily form an anomalous pattern relative to our overall archaeological knowledge of coastal prehistory.

Disturbed Skeletal Elements

As indicated in Table 1 (Chapter II) and detailed in Appendix A, 36 individuals from the Greenville site were recovered as articulated or partly articulated *in situ* interments. This figure comprised less than two-thirds of the total sample of identified individuals, the rest culled from 1,422 disturbed skeletal elements. While the majority of the disturbed elements appeared to be products of the construction contractor's backhoe, 540 elements, or 38% of the group, could not be directly so implicated.

Human skeletal elements which have variably been described as disturbed, isolated, scattered, disarticulated, or unarticulated occur commonly in Northwest Coast midden deposits, particularly in those where intact or partly intact human skeletons have also been reported. For the most part, these types of remains have not been included in osteological analyses (e.g., J. Murray, 1981), or in archaeological reports where mortuary practices have been discussed, in favour of intact burials. Potentially significant exceptions for archaeological interpretation are the

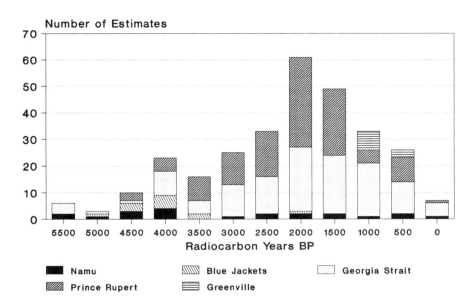

FIGURE 11. Distribution of mean radiocarbon age estimates from the British Columbia coast by burial region.

recent reports on the Strait of Georgia sites at False Narrows by David Burley (1989) and Long Harbour by David Johnstone (1989). In both cases, the authors have speculated that disarticulated or scattered human skeletal elements may represent evidence for above ground disposal of the dead in the prehistoric period (e.g., tree burials, grave houses, platforms, and surface placements similar to those described above by William Collison for the Haida).

In neither case, however, have compelling arguments been advanced. The speculation seems more to have arisen out of a desire on the part of the authors to demonstrate long-standing prehistoric cultural continuity with the historic period (from at least Marpole phase times) than out of a careful appraisal of the purported evidence. David Burley's argument simply consisted of stating that "similar occurrences from other midden excavations are almost always attributed to grave house or tree burials," citing as an example an unpublished doctoral dissertation which was not expressly concerned with the subject (Burley, 1989:56). In an unpublished interim report on the Long Harbour midden excavation, David Johnstone (1989:3) wrote that some scattered human remains "bore moss etches, weathering, or carnivore tooth marks suggestive of their being located at the surface for some time before they became deposited within the midden." It was not stated how many scattered skeletal elements were represented, nor how many were marked, so we have no idea of the statistical significance of the finding. In any event, markings such as those listed may occur on the bones of articulated below ground interments, the "moss etches" represented by rootlet marks on the bone, and the "weathering" by leaching of soils. It is also not uncommon for dogs to dig up and chew human bones from burials, and it is the rare Northwest Coast midden that does not show evidence for dogs in the earlier societies who buried their dead in the middens.

While no data were given in either report on the numbers of disturbed skeletal elements apparent, it is difficult to ignore the fact that in both middens human remains were predominantly portrayed as articulated interments; i.e., the presumptive statistical evidence would point to below ground burial as a significantly dominant practice of the people who constructed the middens. If this was the norm, why should some corpses have been disposed of above ground? In personal discussion, at least one archaeologist suggested to me that above ground disposal may have been allotted high status or high ranking individuals while commoners were buried below ground. Yet, David Burley (1989:59-62) went to great lengths to interpret the presence of both upper and lower class elements among the interments at False Narrows based on the occurrence and distribution of "grave goods." On the broader geographic front, one would also have to conclude from the archaeologist's reasoning that virtually all historic deceased known from the British Columbia coast were upper class individuals and virtually all prehistoric deceased were lower class persons, a conclusion that would seem highly improbable (see, also, later discussion in this chapter).

It is also difficult to ignore the fact that prehistoric shell middens are not undisturbed deposits, or that they would not have been culturally or naturally disturbed during their apparent hundreds or thousands of years of use, resulting in the disturbance or potential disturbance of intact burials, thereby producing scattered skeletal elements. While I cannot argue for this observation from the perspective of the False Narrows and Long Harbour sites (information in the reports is unavailable for inferences like those below), there is evidence from other midden sites to conclude that what we today observe as loose human skeletal elements come from disturbed formerly intact interments.

At the Greenville site, only 14 interments were not disturbed to any degree and most of the site's skeletons lacked one or more bones or parts (details in Appendix A). The incomplete nature of four burials could largely be attributed to the processes of natural decay. For one of them, root growth was also responsible for disturbance and it was likely entirely responsible for the greatly disturbed and incomplete nature of Burial 8. Five or, possibly, six burials were disturbed by modern activity, principally by the construction activities that prompted excavation of the site but also, in two cases (Burials 12 and 13), by localized digging which had taken place some time before the excavation of the minor drainage ditch.

More to the point, though not necessarily exclusive of other factors such as the growth of roots or animal activity (burrowing animals as well as dogs), eight burials, and possibly two others, had been directly or indirectly disturbed by subsequent interments. The most obvious examples were Burials 5 and 9. The upper body of Burial 5 had been truncated and largely lost by the later interment of Burial 4; only the lower limb skeleton and a few lower vertebrae were left articulated. In the case of Burial 9, only one lower limb was left articulated, the rest of the skeleton scattered by a shallow pit dug for the interment of Burial 3. Burial 29 also lacked many parts, including a skull, and there was evidence to conclude that it had been disturbed by the interment of Burial 20.

These examples illustrate that humans were, indeed, *buried* in the midden and that subsequent interments (also buried individuals) disturbed earlier interments. I emphasize these points not only to account for scattered skeletal elements but also to acknowledge below ground burial in the absence of structural evidence in the deposits for burial pits. My reading of many archaeological reports is that if structural evidence for a burial pit is not apparent, then a conclusion is reached that an individual was deposited on the surface of the midden and through some natural(?) means later subsumed into the midden. As noted in the previous chapter, the presence of structural evidence for a pit may well depend on its occurrence between or near the juncture of decidedly contrasting stratigraphic layers. On the other hand, a certain stretch of logic would be necessary to conclude that burial pits had not been dug in cases of truncated or otherwise disturbed skeletons partially or wholly superimposed by others.

Another way of investigating the issue of disturbed skeletal elements is to note their distribution in a site. Some data are presented in Table 4 which provides excavation statistics for the midden at Greenville and for those of Boardwalk and Lachane in the Prince Rupert Harbour region.[7] In each case, the excavated volume of the midden is reported, as are the number of burials (articulated or partly articulated skeletons), the number of disturbed skeletal elements, and the number

---

[7] This and most other information on the Prince Rupert Harbour sites presented in this monograph is based on my analysis of the skeletal remains and relevant field records in the collections of the Canadian Museum of Civilization (Cybulski, n.d.a). Comprehensive archaeological reports are not yet available for these sites, although many facets of the Dodge Island excavation have been detailed by Patricia D. Sutherland (1978).

of "people" present, that is, the minimum number of individuals figured from both types of remains as represented in the site.

TABLE 4. Midden site excavation statistics with respect to human remains

Site Segment[1]	Excavated volume[2]	Burials	Disturbed elements	People[3]	•Per cubic metre• Elements	People
Greenville	144	36	1,422	57	9.88	0.40
Boardwalk[4]	1,041	95	1,281	120	1.23	0.12
Area A	186	43	972	60	5.23	0.32
Area C	177	42	208	48	1.18	0.27
Other areas	678	9	79	11	0.12	0.02
Lachane[4]	976	36	1,780	62	1.82	0.06
Area E	104	10	1,154	23	11.10	0.22
Other areas	872	26	624	38	0.72	0.04

[1] Boardwalk site Areas A and C identified "back ridge" or "shell-dump" areas as opposed to "front platform" or "living" areas (see text). Similarly, Area E at Lachane was designated a "shell-dump."
[2] Volume expressed in cubic metres.
[3] People = minimum number of deceased per site or segment.
[4] This line includes remains from unknown site locations.

Boardwalk and Lachane were the largest Prince Rupert Harbour sites excavated in terms of area and volume, and in terms of recovered human skeletal remains. Boardwalk was largely undisturbed historically or by modern activity. This contrast with the Greenville site is apparent in the marked difference between the densities of disturbed skeletal elements recovered from each site. The Lachane site was historically disturbed by railway construction, the building of squatters' cabins, and second world war military training encampments (cf., Inglis, 1974), and also suffered some disturbances during its 1973 excavation, the source of the data provided in Table 4. This is partly reflected in the large number of disturbed skeletal elements reported in Table 4, and, to some extent, in the overall site number per cubic metre when compared with Boardwalk. Other factors, however, also need to be considered in the interpretation.

The Boardwalk and Lachane sites were regarded as large winter village middens by the archaeologists responsible for their excavation (MacDonald and Inglis, 1981). As part of their field strategy, they delineated both sites into areas of excavation. At Boardwalk, six areas were designated. Areas A and C, separately reported in

Table 4, were identified as "shell-dumps" at the back of the site next to the forest, while the other areas, nearer the sea, were mainly identified as "living" areas. The shell dumps appeared to have been just that: depositional ridges of almost vertically continuous whole and crushed shell up to 2 m deep in places, without significant internal evidence for house floors or other indications that people actually lived in these areas (though there was some such evidence for an earlier occupation beneath the shell dumps or in areas where shell had been culturally cleared). On the other hand, the living or "front platform" areas of the site were formed of deposits earmarked by compressed layers of shell or mixed soil and shell, and definable "house" outlines. As indicated in Table 4, human remains were recovered from both types of areas, but almost 90% of all burials from the site were concentrated in the shell dump areas, as such, definable cemetery locations.

Seven excavation areas were designated during the Lachane site project. They did not correlate as well as the Boardwalk areas with definable cultural "use" areas of the site with one exception. Like Areas A and C at Boardwalk, Area E at Lachane was specifically defined as a shell dump and appeared similarly constructed. Correspondingly, human burials were highly concentrated in this area, though they only formed about 28% of the total burials recovered in 1973. It is noteworthy, however, that a later, 1987 excavation (Simonsen, 1988a), which was concentrated in Area E, produced an additional four articulated or partly articulated *in situ* interments and 11 individuals overall including disturbed skeletal elements.

Overall, the Lachane site excavation produced a lower density of human remains than did the Boardwalk site excavation. However, at both sites there were clearly definable cemetery areas of articulated or partly articulated interments, and those areas, in contrast to other areas of the middens, produced the highest numbers of disturbed skeletal elements. It does not take much imagination to conclude that the scattered skeletal elements likely came from disturbed, formerly intact burials. In the case of Area E at Lachane, which produced an inordinately dense distribution of disturbed elements, most of the disturbance could be attributed to the presence of a military training trench that had been dug through the deposits during the second world war. At Areas A and C of the Boardwalk site, there were clear indications that burials had been disturbed by subsequent interments and by non-burial pits that had been dug in both areas during prehistoric times, possibly to clear areas of the site for habitation or to retrieve buried remains for ritual purposes (Cybulski, 1978b). Indeed, only 43 of the 95 recovered burials at Boardwalk had not been disturbed to any degree, and cultural factors could be involked to account for most disturbances in the remaining 52 interments. Other factors, such as root growth, tree falls, and natural midden erosion, were also responsible for burial disturbances at Boardwalk and at other midden sites in the Prince Rupert Harbour region.

I would suggest that at other midden sites on the coast of British Columbia, some attention be given to the integrity of articulated interments and their distribution before far reaching cultural inferences are made concerning disturbed or "scattered" human skeletal elements. In this connection as well, those types of remains form an integral part of the burial population and must be considered in osteological analyses in order to present comprehensive demographic profiles. This is not necessarily a straightforward task, however, as disturbed elements may be missing parts of partly intact interments and care must be taken to avoid duplication of individuals. From the standpoint of archaeological interpretation, care must also be taken to accurately describe the contexts of disturbed remains in an objective manner without immediate recourse to cultural inferences such as automatically assuming that a group of unarticulated bones represents a secondary burial or reburial. It may represent a formerly intact burial that had been greatly disturbed even if the source of the disturbance is not immediately apparent. It is for this reason that I have used the contextual identifiers for individuals in Table 1: "burial" only for those individuals articulated or partly articulated in situ; "clustered remains" for groups of closely situated unarticulated bones; "disturbed remains" for the unarticulated bones of an individual distributed over a wider area; "assembled remains" for individuals formed in the laboratory of differently catalogued disturbed bones; "isolated (bone name)" for an individual represented by a single disturbed element in a portion of the site.

Vital Statistics (Age and Sex)

Sex and age at death determinations for the deceased individuals from Greenville are reported in Table 1 (Chapter II) and Appendix A. The determinations of sex were drawn from pelvic and cranial indicators (e.g., Krogman and Iscan, 1986) and related elements of size and robustness in other skeletal parts. Age at death estimates were derived from study of the pubic symphysis (Todd, 1920; McKern and Stewart, 1957; Gilbert and McKern, 1973), ilium auricular surface (Lovejoy et al., 1985), cranial suture closure (Montagu, 1960; Meindl and Lovejoy, 1985), epiphyseal union in long bones, claviculae, vertebrae, and innominata (McKern and Stewart, 1957; Ubelaker, 1978), dental development (Ubelaker, 1978), sacral development (McKern and Stewart, 1957), and, where present, degree of ossification of the thyroid cartilage (Krogman and Iscan, 1986:127-129). The degree of occlusal tooth wear and the variable presence and extent of degenerative changes in each person were also taken into account. All of the criteria were considered comparatively within the Greenville group and individuals seriated to arrive at the age ranges shown.

Of the total 59 individuals in the series, 25 were identified as male and 17 as female, a ratio of 1.47:1, or 147 males per 100 females. Included in this group were three adolescents (12 to 16 years). There were two adolescents and one adult (20+ years) unidentifiable as to sex. In addition to the adolescents, there were six juveniles (8 to 11 years), six children (2 to 6 years), and two infants including a fetus. Altogether, the ratio of adults (16-18 years and older) to immature was 2.11:1, or 67.8% adults relative to the total series. Exclusion of the two individuals found elsewhere in 1984 does not appreciably change this information for the site itself.

A low proportion of immature, especially infants (3.4%), in the Greenville series is a feature that has been reported for other prehistoric sites on the coast of British Columbia. For example, there were no infants (individuals less than 2 years) in a sample of 28 individuals from Blue Jackets Creek on the Queen Charlotte Islands and only one or, possibly, two children (J. Murray, 1981). A.J. Curtin (1984) reported two infants (4.8%) and four children in a sample of 42 individuals from Namu, and Owen Beattie (1981) reported only ten infants (8.7%) and four children among 115 individuals from eight sites in the Strait of Georgia region. Ten Prince Rupert Harbour sites yielded similarly low proportions of infants (23) and children (10) in a sample of 288 individuals (Cybulski, n.d.a; see also Appendix C, Table 14).

As ably discussed by A.J. Curtin (1984) for Namu, the very low representation of infant remains in these series would not appear to be an accurate reflection of low infant mortality for the prehistoric period. She noted that taphonomic factors and potential biases in recovery might have been responsible, but that even when such potential influences are offset by careful osteological assessment, the representation of infants still appears much lower than expected for a demographically stable and stationary prehistoric population. A.J. Curtin suggested instead that selective burial practices may have been operating in earlier Northwest Coast societies, though also noting that the archaeological evidence for such a conclusion was largely negative in osteological terms rather than positive in cultural terms.

To address this issue on a broader scale, I have detailed in Appendix C (Table 14) the numbers of individuals in each of five age groups for the prehistoric samples currently known from the coast of British Columbia as well as for the historic samples. A synoptic representation of these data is shown on Figure 12 which indicates a consistently low proportion of infants (and related low overall proportion of immature) in the five regional prehistoric groups when compared with the historic group.

It is tempting to interpret the chart as a reflection of increased infant mortality in the historic period. That could very well have been the case since the span of time represented by the historic samples (ca. late 18th to late 19th centuries) was a period that saw widespread epidemics of European-borne infectious diseases on the Northwest Coast (e.g., smallpox, as noted at the beginning of this chapter). However, the immature proportions of the coastal British Columbia historic series closely match those of prehistoric sites elsewhere in North America (cf., Cybulski, 1978a:57-59). What we may, in fact, be witnessing in the historic data is a disruptive cultural consequence of generally high mortality at that time, mortality having been so high and rapid in the historic period that an earlier proscribed burial tradition may no longer have been tenable.

A possibility for archaeologically recognizable selective burial practices in the prehistoric period was offered by Owen Beattie (1981) in his osteological assessment of eight Strait of Georgia sites. He wrote that "all the individuals" recovered from excavations at the Glenrose Cannery site (DgRr 6) were "either females or infants, and apparently originate(d) from areas of the site set aside for these segments of the population" (ibid., p. 38). Unfortunately, no contextual details (or cited reference) were given for the remains within the site. An appendix (ibid., pp. 240-253) described a child, four juveniles, two adolescents, and five adults of indeterminate sex in addition to the females (6) and infants (4). Thus, the site data portrayed in the text were incomplete, leaving the significance of Owen Beattie's inferential statement uncertain.

Nonetheless, a site by site inspection of the known deceased population samples from the prehistoric and historic periods suggests selective burial practices in the prehistoric period. With respect to the proportions of infants, there would appear to have been greater variability by site in the prehistoric group than in the historic group (see Appendix C, Table 14). The total proportion of infants in the historic series was calculated at 21.1% with a comparable 20.3% average per site. In the prehistoric series, the overall proportion was 8.6% with an average 12.9% per site. The greater variation in the prehistoric series could, of course, be a reflection of its greater geographic spread, although this by itself may say something for greater cultural variation inherent in the prehistoric assemblage. For example, the Strait of Georgia group is much more variable in its sites' representation of infants and composed of a more widely dispersed assemblage of sites than Prince Rupert Harbour.

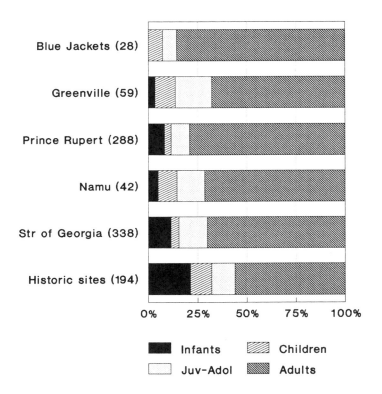

FIGURE 12. Distribution of human remains (individuals) from the British Columbia coast by age group. (Figures in parentheses denote sample sizes.)

However, some sites in both groups appear to have more than their share of infants when compared with others. The total number of individuals from Dodge Island and Parizeau Point represents only 11.1% of the total Prince Rupert Harbour series but accounts for 43.5% of the total infant sample. Likewise, Long Harbour and the Hill site account for 14.04% of the total Strait of Georgia series, but their samples contain 42.1% of the infants. Long Harbour is particularly noteworthy because of its very high proportion of infants (9 of 10 immature, or 56.2% of the site's total). It may be significant that the two sites were closely situated, both located on one of the Gulf Islands (Saltspring).

The possible connection between infants and females in selective burial practices offered by Owen Beattie may also hold some truth. For Long Harbour, 4 of 6 individuals identified by sex reportedly were females. A like situation is apparent for Parizeau Point in the Prince Rupert Harbour group.

Perhaps it is also significant that although males outnumbered females in the Dodge Island site, where 6 of 20 individuals were infants (30%), all five females were young adults, between 16 and 34 years, consistently of child bearing age (Cybulski, n.d.a). The mean female age at death was 23.7 years (standard deviation of 5.7). At Greenville, where only two infants were evident, the adult female sample (15 persons) ranged from 18 to 60+ years, with a mean age of 43.7 years (standard deviation of 16.0) and 60% of the women older than 40 years.[8] On the whole, the concept of selective burial practices in the prehistoric period with respect to age at death and sex is worth further exploration in future studies of coastal British Columbia populations given the potential patterns observed here. Also, attention might be given to the age at death and sex distribution of remains within midden sites and between closely situated sites to assess whether concentrations of certain individuals existed.

A more lucid pattern of vital statistics is apparent for the coast of British Columbia in terms of adult sex ratios. The Greenville series presented a notably unequal sex ratio in favour of males. As indicated on Figure 13, this is a finding that appears consistent for all prehistoric north coast sites currently known, contrasting with the more equivalent sex ratios evident in the central (Namu) and south coast (Strait of Georgia) series.

The data entered into the chart are detailed in Appendix C, Table 14. The chart includes only those adults (16 years and older) identified as to sex or possible sex. Jeffrey Murray (1981) reported a more equitable sex distribution for the Blue Jackets Creek site than indicated on Figure 13 and in Table 14. The data here are based on my own study of the remains for a comparison of non-metric morphological cranial variants with Greenville (see Chapter V). We disagreed on the sex identifications of four adults, and I identified one male skeleton whose sex Jeffrey Murray left unassigned. I cannot explain the discrepancies other than to say I am reasonably confident of my identifications.

With the exception of 20 individuals identified through my own studies as listed in Table 13 and some adjustments to the Crescent Beach data based on a recent study of the remains for another purpose (Cybulski, 1991b), the sex identifications for the Strait of Georgia series were taken from the literature as reported by others. In this connection, the sex of approximately 18% of all reported adults is

---

[8] All mean ages calculated in this study assume an upper limit of 69 years for those aged 60+ years. Conventional osteological techniques generally do not allow age estimates beyond about 60+ years. From the standpoint of longevity, it is entirely possible that some individuals assigned this age range actually lived to 70, 80, or even 90+ years.

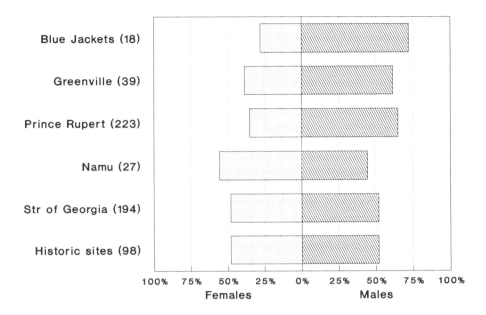

FIGURE 13. Distribution of human remains (adult individuals) from the British Columbia coast by sex.

unknown, a substantially higher proportion than for the other series shown on the chart with the exception of Blue Jackets Creek. Conceivably, identifications of these unknowns could alter the relative proportions shown on Figure 13, but it is only possible to work with the information that is available.

Elsewhere, I suggested for the prehistoric period that the marked differences in sex ratios between the larger (than Namu and Blue Jackets Creek) and, therefore, more statistically valid samples from Prince Rupert Harbour and the Strait of Georgia regions more likely reflected population composition and socially selective mortuary practices than they did differential mortality (Cybulski, 1990). A possible explanation for the favoured buried male proportion at Prince Rupert Harbour was "that slaves cyclically made up a substantial portion of the adult female population and, because of their lack of social status, were not buried in the same sites as the other population" (ibid., p. 58).

This explanation was founded in part on an ethnographic observation by John Adams (1973) that women were favoured as an important resource among some Tsimshian groups, perhaps an earlier motivation for frequent intertribal warfare in the Prince Rupert Harbour region as evidenced by trauma in the sample of skeletons (Cybulski, 1990:58). An assessment of reports for the currently known Strait of Georgia series, as well as my own observations, indicates appreciably less evidence for skeletal trauma which might be attributed to warfare as well as little evidence for socially selective burial practices by sex (i.e., it portrays a nearly equal sex ratio). In prehistoric times, the populations of these two regions may have been very dissimilar in their social and cultural dynamics.

There was some evidence for warfare-related injuries in the Greenville series (Chapter VI), also from a traditionally Tsimshian enclave. By the same token, it may again be noted that the majority of women identified in the buried sample were older than younger. Possibly, young women were favoured to be taken as resource-related captives in intertribal conflicts. In this connection, older women also outnumbered younger women in each of the two largest skeletal assemblages of Prince Rupert Harbour, Boardwalk and Lachane (Cybulski, n.d.a).[9]

As noted above, the historic data may have been influenced by the disruptive consequences of European contact. However, except for the small Gust Island Rockshelter sample from the Queen Charlotte Islands, no north coast groups are represented and it is of interest that the sex ratio is consistent with those of Namu and the Strait of Georgia. Neither the Owikeno Lake or Hesquiat Harbour series, which form the bulk of the historic skeletal collection, demonstrated warfare-related injuries to any appreciable extent (e.g., Chapter VI). Namu, however, is problematical to the thesis since it presented a pattern of skeletal trauma similar to that of Prince Rupert Harbour (Cybulski, 1990:58; see also Curtin, 1984).

Demographic assessments like those presented here effectively compress time. Depending on the sample, a thousand or more years are represented (about 700 years in the case of Greenville). Presumably, the patterns would not occur if the conditions which brought them about were not fairly consistent over these periods of time. Unfortunately, it is difficult to actually test the constancy of the patterns because the current temporal knowledge of, particularly, the larger samples from Prince Rupert Harbour and the Strait of Georgia, each representing up to 2,000 years, is insufficient to break down the samples into workable analytical units.

The data of Greenville, where at least two discrete time-related burial components are known, suggest a possibility of demographic variation through time. As

---

[9] On average, the Boardwalk and Lachane females were a bit younger than those from Greenville with means of 41.3 years (standard deviation of 12.5; sample of 33 persons) and 39.4 years (standard deviation of 12.5; sample of 21 persons) respectively. In the Boardwalk series, 72.7% of the adult females were aged at 35-44 years or older; in the Lachane series, this group comprised 57.1% of the adult female sample.

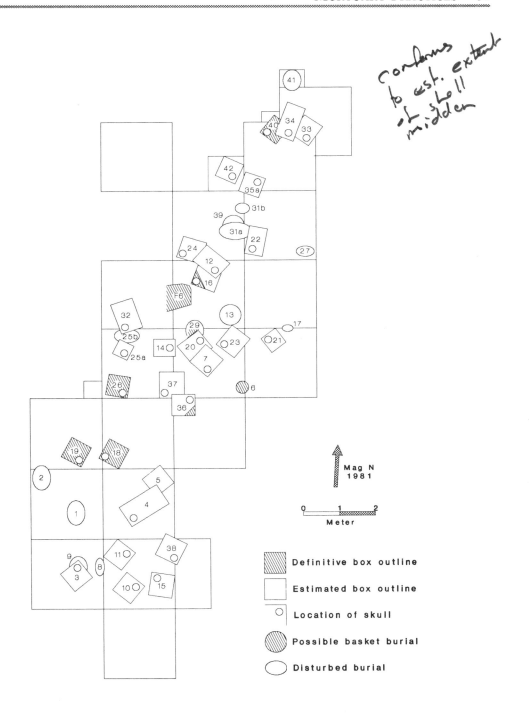

FIGURE 14. Greenville site cemetery plan.

illustrated on Figure 9 in the previous chapter, a demographic contrast is apparent between the shell (early + middle) and soil (late) components of the site. The shell component presented a nearly equal distribution of adult males (9) and females (10), whereas the soil component was dominated by males, nine as opposed to only two females. As well, the majority of immature from the site were associated with the more equivalent adult sex distribution of the shell component, 11 individuals as opposed to four in the soil, or, late component. The small sample sizes preclude meaningful statistical assessments, but it may be of interest that the dominant male segment of the late period presented a younger age profile (mean of 30.9 years; standard deviation of 10.8) than the male segment of the shell component (mean of 37.6 years; standard deviation of 14.4). The male segments within each shell subcomponent were reasonably consistent with means of 36.2 and 38.6 years. Hence, the late component of the Greenville site, stratigraphically and temporally discrete from the shell component, appears to have been dominated by males, in particular, males appreciably younger than those in the shell component where the sexes were more equitably distributed.

Burial Boxes, Elderberry Seeds, and Rocks

Figure 14 is a plan of the Greenville burials superimposed on the excavation grid of the main site area east of the minor drainage ditch (cf., Fig. 5, Chapter II). The burial plan differs from those usually shown for archaeological sites in that I elected to illustrate the individual burials by "coffins" with skull locations rather than skeletal stick figures (e.g., Gordon, 1974), circles (e.g., Curtin, 1984), or approximately accurate anatomical figures (e.g., Larsen, 1990). It is highly likely that burial boxes were used for most of the deceased at Greenville. All of the archaeologically recovered intact or partly intact skeletons (36 individuals) were flexed.[10] In almost half the cases, the degree of flexure was extreme and this seemed to relate to the size and shape of the container used for burial, a small square box. Wood was preserved with eight individuals. Distinct, nearly square outlines, measuring 58 cm to 65 cm per side, were apparent for four burials (those fully shaded on Fig. 14). In one case, Burial 40, a young adult female in the Middle (upper shell) subcomponent of the site, the outline was, in fact, formed by the variably preserved sides and bottom of a nearly square box, 59 cm x 64 cm. Within the box, the skeleton was very tightly flexed on its front and left side, head

---

[10] Details on flexure and other mortuary elements discussed in this and subsequent sections of this chapter are reported for each individual in Appendix A.

in one corner (roughly west relative to grid north) and pelvis in the opposite corner (east) (Fig. 15).

The more poorly preserved sides and bottom of a square box, 58 cm x 60 cm, were recorded for Burial 26, an early young adult male in the Late (soil) subcomponent. In this case, the skeleton was also very tightly flexed on its front and left side with its skull and pelvis in opposite corners (grid southeast and northwest respectively).

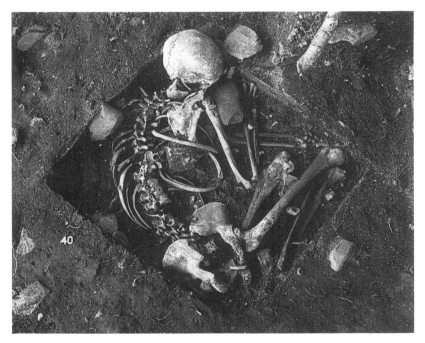

FIGURE 15. Burial 40 in square box.

Very thin, friable fragments of wood were recorded underneath the skeleton of Burial 18, a middle-aged male likely affiliated with Layer A2. The integrity of a square configuration, 60 cm x 61 cm, was maintained by an outline of small rocks and a dense concentration of seeds subsequently identified as elderberry (*Sambucus racemosa* L.) by botanists at Agriculture Canada in Ottawa (Fig. 16). The skull was in the west corner of the box and the pelvis in the east corner. There also were rocks on top of the skeleton, possibly placed originally to secure a lid which had subsequently decayed.

The fourth skeleton demarcated by a square outline was Burial 19, a young adult male associated with the Late subcomponent of the site. All elements noted

FIGURE 16. Elderberry seeds with Burial 18 (a) and Burial 36 (b).

FIGURE 17. Square box skeletal outline of Burial 38.

with Burial 18 were also present, including a thin layer of wood in one corner of the outline. The box outline, formed by rocks, measured 63 cm x 65 cm. The skull was in the southeast corner of the configuration and the pelvis in the northwest corner.

There were two burials with elderberry seeds that formed partial box outlines. Burial 29, in the Early (lower shell) subcomponent, featured a concentration of seeds immediately above the pelvis. The concentration had a straight edge apparently formed by a box used to contain Burial 20 which had been interred at a later time, probably disturbing Burial 29 (see Fig. 14). Burial 36 in Layer A2 featured a thick corner-shaped concentration of seeds upon initial exposure of a femur (Fig. 16 B). Burial 16 in Layer B (Middle subcomponent) featured a corner-shaped concentration of small rocks, evidently indicating a once intact box. No seeds were found with this person's skeleton.

It seems reasonable to conclude that most of the site's individuals in all three subcomponents were placed in boxes prior to burial. In addition to the definitive outlines and the preservation of wood in some cases, the outlines of the flexure of most skeletons could be interpreted as square or rectangular (e.g., Figs. 17 and 18). Interestingly, however, only six individuals appeared to have been placed in rectangular boxes, the majority of those identified being square or nearly square (22

FIGURE 18. Rectangular box skeletal outline of Burial 22; note rocks on skeleton, possibly used to weight a lid.

persons).   One child's skeleton, Burial 6 in the Late subcomponent, presented a distinctly circular configuration which suggested that a woven basket rather than box might have been used to contain the corpse (Fig. 19).

It is intriguing that square boxes would have been used for burial, since it is customary to associate burial with rectangular "coffins" (see additional discussion below).   A possible explanation is that boxes commonly used to store provisions in a village served another function in time of need. Historically for the Nisga'a, the most common type of box used to store food inside a house "was about two feet tall and had a square base" (McNeary, 1976:80).   "Two feet" translates to about 61 cm in the metric system, matching or very close to the box or outline measurements shown at the Greenville site.

Another potential indicator for the use of food storage boxes was the presence of elderberry with 16 individuals in the form of preserved seeds.   In eight cases, there were heavy concentrations, in the manner of Burial 18, measuring up to 20 cm thick.   Perhaps, the seeds represented the remains of stored food, though other explanations for the presence of elderberry are possible as discussed in a later section of this chapter.

A ninth wood-related feature, identified during the excavation as Feature 6, materialized in the western one-quarter of Unit 13, Layer B, initially as a large, nearly square concentration of elderberry seeds 60 cm x 70 cm (shown as "F6" on Fig. 14). Excavation of the seeds revealed two or three wood planks evidently forming the bottom of a box. Some poorly preserved pulpy bone, a portion of which was identified as part of a human pelvis (innominate), rested on the end of one of the boards. This may have been a food storage box that had secondarily been used to contain one or two skeletal elements accidentally unearthed elsewhere on the site and reburied during Layer B times.

FIGURE 19. Possible basket burial skeletal outline of Burial 6.

According to Stephen McNeary (1976:80), "cedar" was the wood of choice traditionally used by the Nisga'a for making boxes. Three samples of wood from the site were submitted to the Canadian Conservation Institute, Ottawa, for possible identification. They are reported as Floral Samples #8, #19, and #21 in Appendix E by Gregory S. Young. Sample #8 was collected from the coffin of Burial 18, sample #19 from Feature 6, and sample #21 from the box associated with Burial 40. As detailed by Gregory Young in his report, poor preservation of the micro-anatomy of the samples precluded specific identifications, but as a group the samples were narrowed to three taxonomic possibilities at the level of genus. Among them was *Thuya*, a group that includes western red cedar and northern white cedar.   Western red cedar is, perhaps, the most likely candidate for the Greenville remnants since this tree is common in the Nass River valley (McNeary, 1976:48).   In a personal communication (1991), Dr. Richard Hebda, a Royal British Columbia Museum specialist on the native use of cedar, suggested to me that Alaskan yellow cedar, in a second group portrayed by Gregory Young (genus *Chamaecyparis*), might be another good possibility for the Greenville boxes, but that Pacific yew, an example of Gregory Young's third group *(Taxus)*, is unlikely as it is only practical for working very small items.   Both of these trees would also have been accessible to local peoples who might have buried their dead at the Greenville site.

Boxes for burial do not seem to have been reported for other prehistoric sites on the British Columbia coast, although their use in some middens has been assumed from the tight flexure of skeletons (MacDonald, 1969:251) or from the presence of rocks on top of skeletons, presumed to have weighted lids (Burley, 1980:29).

At three Prince Rupert Harbour sites near the mouth of the Skeena River, the skeletons of eight burials were situated within partial or complete whitish clay outlines likely indicating the one-time presence of boxes (Cybulski, n.d.a).   Each clay line was about 2.5 cm wide and possibly also indicated the use of food storage containers for these Middle Developmental Stage burials in traditional Coast Tsimshian territory.   In later times, Tsimshian peoples on the Skeena River reportedly used clay to seal the seams of boxes used to store meat (Robinson, 1962:41).   In addition, five other Prince Rupert Harbour burials included preserved pieces of wood.

While food storage boxes may have been used for burial at prehistoric Prince Rupert Harbour, the majority of burial boxes in those midden sites, unlike Greenville, appear to have been rectangular.   For the most part, this conclusion stems from my study of the degree of flexure of the skeletons and the outlines they presented.   Also, the one complete clay outline in the series was rectangular, measuring 91 cm x 53 cm, and two partial clay outlines intimated horizontal box dimensions of 91 cm x 53 cm and 97 cm x 51 cm.   These measurements are about the sizes of the boxes deduced for Burials 12 and 32 at Greenville from their flexed skeletal outlines (e.g., Fig. 14).   Only one partial clay outline at Prince Rupert Harbour suggested a horizontal square, possibly one end of a rectangular box containing a so-called "seated" burial, an individual who had been flexed in a box which was then positioned upright in the burial midden.   The skeleton appeared articulated as if the progressively decaying body had collapsed in a very small space demarcated by its partial clay outline. In only a very few instances at these sites could skeletal outlines, in the absence of definitive evidence for boxes, be interpreted as square.

There is little ethnohistorical information available on the shape of boxes used for burial on the northern Northwest Coast, possibly because of the literature emphasis on cremation. However, Alfred P. Niblack, who described Tlingit burial practices based on the observations of late 18th century explorers in Alaska, cited three cases where skeletons had been found in square boxes, the smallest "about 3 feet square and $1\frac{1}{2}$ feet deep" (91 cm^2 and 46 cm deep) (Niblack, 1890:352). Noting that these were not numerous, the explorers at one location concluded "that only 'certain persons' were thus entombed" (ibid.).   At other Tlingit burial locations, bodies were reported in "oblong" chests and heads were occasionally found separately in small square boxes.

Rock associations

As noted above, rocks were associated with some Greenville burials, but, overall, such associations were uncommon. Only nine skeletons, or a quarter of the sample of those found intact or partly intact, were recorded with rocks. Generally, the rocks were cobble-size and indistinguishable from similar materials distributed throughout the site.   None were of the large boulder or slab-like varieties reported with midden burials in the Strait of Georgia region and none could be construed to reflect burial cairns (cf. Mitchell, 1971; Hall and Haggarty, 1981; Burley, 1980).

All three subcomponents were represented among the nine Greenville burials with rocks. It is interesting to note, however, that rocks formed perimeters around male skeletons in four instances, abutting or probably abutting their boxes, but not in four female instances. They were only on top of the female skeletons, or, in the case of Burial 40, scattered within its box. Whether any significance can be attached to this apparent distinction by sex is unclear. In the case of the females, the rocks may have served to secure lids, though rocks on top of three male skeletons probably served the same purpose.

At Prince Rupert Harbour, rocks usually much larger than those at Greenville (in some cases, boulders or large slabs) were associated with 49% of 219 burials for which information of this type was available. In most instances, the rocks rested on the skeletons and may have been used to secure lids (with no sex differences indicated). In some instances, the rocks above were separated from the skeletons by soil and may have been used to mark graves that had been accidentally unearthed or opened intentionally.[11]   In at least three cases, rock associations likely represented cairns.   The exclusive representation of cobble-size rocks at Greenville may have been due to cultural differences in the way the dead were treated, but the apparent contrast could also reflect the fact that larger rocks simply were not available in the immediate area of the site.   Certainly, no boulders or large slabs were encountered near or in the site during the excavation.

The association of rocks with midden burials appears to have been a long-standing "tradition" on the coast of British Columbia.   Both cobbles and boulders were reported with burials excavated at Namu, many dating to the Early Developmental Stage of British Columbia coast prehistory (Curtin, 1984:20).   In view of the temporal position of Greenville, the fewer rock associations there, relative to those at Prince Rupert Harbour, may have reflected a waning, formerly widespread coastal custom, corresponding with the eventual abandonment of below-ground midden burial during the Late Developmental Stage.

Flexed and Extended Burials

"Flexed burial," exclusively the position of corpse disposal in the Greenville site, seems to have been the norm on the prehistoric Northwest Coast (e.g., Burley, 1980:28-29).   The fact that bodies were flexed may have been related to the use of small burial (a.k.a. food storage) boxes, as in the cases of Greenville and Prince Rupert Harbour, although other explanations have been suggested.   For Namu, where there was no solid evidence for boxes, A.J. Curtin (1984:19) wrote that the tight flexure of certain skeletons may have indicated the bodies were bound or wrapped prior to interment.

While flexed body positions appear to have been the norm, bodies in extended positions (legs-to-torso angle at 180°) are not unknown, if infrequent among coastal midden burials.   Four of 22 studiable burials (18.2%) were extended skeletons at Namu (Curtin, 1984:23) and six of 163 skeletons (3.7%) were in fully extended positions at Prince Rupert Harbour (Cybulski, n.d.a).[12]

---

[11] Graves may have been intentionally opened to obtain human bones for ritual purposes (Cybulski 1978b).

[12] Over one-third of the total sample of individuals (288) in the Prince Rupert Harbour sites were represented as greatly disturbed burials or as clustered, disturbed, or assembled remains according to the definitions given for the Greenville individuals and explained in Chapter II.   In a few additional cases, no information on position of the skeleton was available in the field record.   Those seem also to have been the circumstances for almost half the sample of individuals at Namu according to A.J. Curtin's report.

A.J. Curtin (1984:23) explained that three of the four persons in extended positions at Namu were parts of multiple interments and that the latter possibly reflected shared unusual circumstances surrounding the deaths of the persons buried together (ibid., p. 26-27). At a Duke Point area midden on the south coast of British Columbia, at least five of ten persons in a multiple burial were in extended body positions, and all ten may have shared a common disease process skeletally demonstrable in six of them (Cybulski, 1991b).

However, the six extended bodies at Prince Rupert Harbour were single interments at three different middens. The one other contextual element they shared was that each was early in the overall sequence of burial at these and other sites in the series, dating between 2800 and 3500 years B.P. (Cybulski, n.d.a). As well, three of the extended Namu burials were early, dated at 5000-4000 years B.P., while the fourth was dated at 2000 to 3000 years B.P. (Curtin, 1984). As mentioned earlier in this chapter, the Duke Point mass grave was dated at 3490 ± 125 years B.P. All told, of 18 known extended burials in coastal British Columbia midden sites (including three reported for the predominantly Marpole period Strait of Georgia site at False Narrows (Burley, 1989:55)), 13 have been dated at 3000 years or more. Possibly, mortuary practices on the British Columbia coast were much more variable with respect to position of the body prior to that time than they were later, or maybe food storage boxes were not as commonly used then for burial. Flexed burials are also known in the early Prince Rupert Harbour sequence, as they are at Namu (Curtin, 1984) and in the Early Developmental Stage series at Blue Jackets Creek (Severs, 1974:193).

Compass Orientations

Compass orientations with respect to the lay of a body have been investigated in prehistoric burial sites on the assumption that earlier societies may have attached some significance to the direction in which the deceased would face or head (in terms of axial orientation) when buried.

For the burials at Blue Jackets Creek, Patricia D.S. Severs (1974:193) stated that "Most individuals were found in varying degrees of flexion resting on their right side with the facial region of the cranium roughly north . . ." More details were given for the burials at Namu by A.J. Curtin (1984:23-25) who reported that compass orientations were "extremely variable" overall but possibly related to the sex of a person. Five of seven males were axially oriented so that they headed northeast, north, or northwest, whereas eight of ten females were headed southwest or south.

At Greenville, 12 of 32 skeletons were headed southwest, six southeast, and four south. Four other compass headings were also represented, excluding north. Hence, 22 individuals, or 68.8% of the observable sample, were heading in some directional variant of south. There was no distinction according to sex.

To some extent, this potential pattern of orientation is visible on Figure 14 which includes the locations of the skulls in the boxes. But it is not so much the orientation of the skeletons that seems significant as it is the orientation of the boxes in which the deceased were placed, if my interpretations of the skeletal outlines are correct. Most of the boxes were oriented northeast-southwest according to the direction of magnetic north in 1981 when the site plan was initiated. Indeed, the entire site, as earmarked by the shell deposit, was oriented northeast-southwest according to its long axis (see also Fig. 5). In 1981, true north was about 26° west of magnetic north in this geographic area. Hence, the long axis of the site was directed east-west relative to true north, as were most of the boxes within, perhaps significant in terms of the rising and setting sun. The lack of precision as regards the boxes may, in part, be due to my interpretations of the outlines formed by the skeletons. However, the actual box containing Burial 36 was not so precisely positioned as indicated by its corner of preserved seeds. In any event, if there was an orientation pattern in death at Greenville, it did not seem to involve the bodies per se but the boxes in which they were placed and, perhaps, more importantly, the cemetery as a unit.

Grave Goods, Dogs, Labrets, and Food for the Dead

In studies of Northwest Coast prehistory, archaeologists have traditionally focussed on the presence or absence of grave goods with human burials as potential indicators of the relative social rank or status of the deceased in life (e.g., Burley, 1989:59-62). In this sense, the phrase "grave goods" has commonly been reserved for cultural artifacts and possible classificatory distinctions, by ethnographic parallel, according to wealth objects, ritual objects, and utilitarian items.

At Greenville, there was only one burial with a presumably associated artifact. A large cobble tool made of schist, 13.9 cm long x 8.0 cm wide x 1.8 cm thick, rested on the anterior lower spine of Burial 11, a late young adult female in Layer B. The significance of this lone association may only be guessed at, but the artifact may have represented a favoured chopping or scraping tool, a utilitarian item used, perhaps, to prepare animal skins for clothing, traditionally the work of women among Nisga'a (Nisga'a School District 92, Bilingual-Bicultural Department, 1981). The anatomical location of the find suggests that the tool originally rested on the person's belly.

The Greenville site appears unique on the coast in not having had any burials associated with objects of personal adornment, the most common form of artifact association with midden burial, some possibly indicating associations of rank or status.   For example, shell disc beads and (or) dentalia, representing necklaces, bracelets, ear ornaments, or headband inserts, have been reported with Marpole phase burials in the Strait of Georgia region (Haggarty and Hall, 1981; Burley, 1989:59-62), while shell or amber beads were found with six burials at Namu (Curtin, 1984:25).   Articles of personal adornment, made of shell, amber, and (or) copper, were recorded with five human skeletons at Prince Rupert Harbour.   Two others featured associated animal teeth probably representing a bracelet in one case and a necklace in the other, and stone labrets (lip plugs) were recorded with five people.   Altogether, 22 deceased at five Prince Rupert Harbour middens had definite artifact associations and 14 of them featured items of personal adornment.

While the burials of Greenville lacked items of personal adornment and only one had a manufactured item of any type, some had other forms of cultural associations as described in the following sections.

Dogs

The head of a domestic dog, represented by an articulated skull and mandible, was "cradled" by the upper right arm and chest of Burial 4, an adolescent male in Layer B (Fig. 20).   In a study of the faunal remains from the site (see Chapter IV), Darlene Balkwill estimates the weight of this dog at 28 lb. (12.6 kg), a dog of medium size by modern standards.   One other burial, Burial 9, a middle-aged male in Layer B, *may* have had an associated dog's head or skull.   Burial 9 was greatly disturbed by the interment of Burial 3 and, therefore, the association, represented by a right frontal and a maxilla collected with the few bones remaining of Burial 9, was very uncertain.   These bones, estimated to be from a dog much smaller than the one with Burial 4, could have represented disturbed midden elements as a fairly large number of dog and *Canis* sp. skeletal elements, as identified by Darlene Balkwill, were recovered from the site.   Altogether, 35 dog bones were counted, another bone was identified as dog or coyote, and 35 skeletal elements were attributed to *Canis,* the genus which includes dogs, wolves, and coyotes (discussed in Chapter IV).

Domestic dog remains are often found in coastal British Columbia shell middens which served as human burial grounds, either as disturbed bones or teeth, or as intact or partly intact skeletons (R.J. Wigen, pers. comm., 1990).   Specific references are available for Namu where, in addition to disturbed dog bones, three fully articulated skeletons were excavated by University of Colorado archaeologists

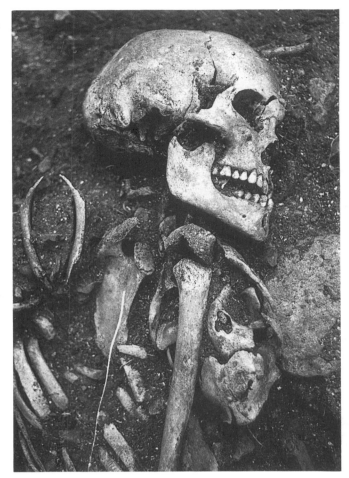

FIGURE 20. Dog skull and mandible with Burial 4.

in 1968-1970 (Conover, 1978:84-85) and for the Pender Canal sites where "most canid remains were associated with human burials and rock features" at DeRt 2 (Digance, 1988). *Canis* remains, without reference to species, have also been reported for Blue Jackets Creek (Severs, 1974:198).

Where such information is available, there seem to be temporal and spatial correspondences between the presence of dog remains and human burial. Most of the human remains reported for Namu came from the 4000 to 5000 years B.P. levels of the site, as did most of the canid remains reported by Kathryn Conover (1978:84). At Boardwalk, the only Prince Rupert Harbour site for which a comprehensive faunal analysis has been completed (Stewart, 1977), 245 dog bones or teeth and seven complete skeletons were collected, 77% of the disturbed elements and all the skeletons in two of six excavation areas where human remains were the dominant finding (see Table 4 references to Areas A and C earlier in this chapter). Judging from the descriptions in Frances Stewart's report (ibid.) and the site records available to my investigation of the human burials, at least some of the complete dog skeletons represented intentional separate interments. One other was directly associated with a human burial, the flexed corpse of a middle-aged male whose out-stretched right arm cradled the carcass of the dog, each skeleton facing the same direction and sharing the same axial orientation (Cybulski, n.d.a).

Unarticulated dog bones also appear to have been associated with six other human burials at Boardwalk and one at the Lachane site. In the Lachane case, the field record identified the dog bones as those of an essentially complete, though extensively disturbed skeleton. Altogether, the eight human burials with associated dog remains included four adult males, an adolescent male, two probable adolescent females, and a child of indeterminate sex.

All of this information seemingly indicates that dogs were given special treatment in death, relegated to the same burial grounds as their human masters and mistresses. Traditionally among Tsimshian peoples, dogs were used in hunting (to drive goats and mountain sheep, and find bear dens), as pack animals (to pull sleds), and as pets (Boas, 1916:402; Garfield, 1939:310). Even unarticulated dog skeletal elements in middens may have come from formerly intact burials (Stewart, 1977:84) as suggested earlier in this chapter for scattered human skeletal elements.

What is difficult to explain, however, is why only a dog *head* was buried with one or, possibly, two humans at Greenville. Indeed, as reported by Darlene Balkwill in Chapter IV, canid skeletal elements other than skull were greatly underrepresented in the Greenville faunal assemblage. For Namu as well, Kathryn Conover (1978:85) reported that canid "head bones outnumber(ed) limb bones three to one and other body parts fifty to one." Even at the Boardwalk site where there did not seem to be any significant difference in the distribution of *Canis* sp. anatomical parts, one excavation trench in Area C and an identified feature elsewhere in this area yielded unusual concentrations of cranial elements attributed to *Canis familiaris* or *Canis* sp. (Stewart, 1977:86, 88).

From the ethnographic record for the Nisga'a, we know that wolves, coyotes, and foxes, the latter also taxonomically assigned to Canidae (but not *Canis*), were trapped for their fur (McNeary, 1976:106) or to occasionally make leather (wolf and coyote) (Nisga'a School District 92, Bilingual-Bicultural Department, 1981:22). Quite possibly, the underrepresentation of canid postcranial skeletal parts in some midden sites or segments could indicate that the animals were processed elsewhere for their skins and furs, and the leg and, especially, torso bone remains discarded then.

This still, of course, does not explain why skull, jaw parts, or teeth should have specifically been brought to the human burial places. Also, it is highly likely on technical, geographic, and cultural grounds that most of the bones attributed to *Canis* sp. in these sites would have been domestic dog rather than wolf or coyote (Stewart, 1977:126-127). No elements of the latter two animals were specifically identified for Greenville and only two elements (out of 1,639 attributed by Frances Stewart to *Canis* sp., coyote, wolf, or dog (less the seven skeletons)) were identified to those two species at Boardwalk.

It might be concluded that dog heads (or parts thereof) held some special cultural significance, perhaps ceremonial in nature, to, at least, the people who buried their dead in the Greenville site. Viola Garfield (1939:305-312; see, also, Garfield and Wingert, 1951:45, 57; Shane, 1984:161) described the *nulim*, or "Dog Eaters" secret society among the Coast Tsimshian and Nisga'a. Membership in the society was open to any Tsimshian who had the wealth necessary for an initiatory ceremony and both boys and girls were eligible. Might the boy represented in Burial 4 have been a Dog Eaters society initiate? Might that also have been the case with the man represented in Burial 9 and those individuals with associated dog remains in the Prince Rupert Harbour sites?

Viola Garfield (Garfield and Wingert, 1951:45, 57), citing Franz Boas, wrote that the Dog Eaters secret society was acquired by the Coast Tsimshian from northern Kwakiutl, mainly Heiltsuk and Haisla, and in turn passed on to Nisga'a. The burial site at Namu, where "canid" cranial parts greatly outnumbered limb and other body parts (cited above), is in the traditional territories of the Heiltsuk (Bella Bella). While Viola Garfield's citation might suggest a relatively recent acquisition of the Dog Eaters society by the Coast Tsimshian and Nisga'a, in the sense of the familiar ethnographic present, the potential archaeological "evidence" presented here suggests that it or a related ceremonial may have had considerable time depth on the central and northern coasts of British Columbia, on the order of 4,000 to 5,000 years at Namu through 1,400 to 900 years ago at Greenville. Given that the chronological progression from Namu to Greenville is consistent with the order of the Dog Eaters society's reported transmission for the native groups traditionally represented in those territories, it would be interesting to investigate a Middle Developmental Stage burial site on the Nass River and an Early Developmental Stage burial site in the Prince Rupert Harbour region if such sites exist. Though quite probably a statistical artifact given the relatively small number of human burials associated with dog remains at Prince Rupert Harbour, it may be pertinent that none of the burials known to be early in the sequence (ca. 2800 to 3500 years B.P.) were associated with dog remains (Cybulski, n.d.a).

For Greenville, the Dog Eaters society analogy might be taken one step further by noting Darlene Balkwill's observation in Chapter IV that three *Canis* bones exhibited cut marks suggesting "evidence that dogs were eaten." Wolves, coyotes, and foxes were not considered edible historically by the Nisga'a (McNeary, 1976: 106) and there is, thus, no reason to suspect that dogs might have served as dietary items in the past. On the other hand, Viola Garfield (1939:310) recounted a Dog Eaters tale where "partaking" of dogs was part of the ritual.

Labrets

The custom of wearing labrets is well known historically among northern Northwest Coast peoples (Niblack, 1890:256-257). As noted above for Prince Rupert Harbour, labrets have occasionally been recorded with prehistoric burials. However, there is reason to suspect from the archaeological record that some people who wore labrets in an earlier time were not buried with them. As well, dental evidence indicates that those people who wore labrets, possibly a hallmark of status (Collison, 1981:175-176), may be recognized in archaeological burial sites even though the artifacts are missing.

Three so-called "medial" labrets made of stone were recovered as part of the artifact assemblage at Greenville (Fig. 21), but none were associated with human burials.[13] However, abrasion facets from wearing labrets, previously identified and illustrated for skeletons from north coast British Columbia middens (Cybulski, 1974), were present on the lower anterior teeth of nine skeletons, all adult female.

Included in the group were Burials 3, 11, 12, 22, 24, 29, 40, and 42. All three burial subcomponents were represented. In terms of total teeth, eight central incisors, eight lateral incisors, and four canines were involved (Table 5). A coincident observation was that five females with labret abrasion also exhibited ante mortem loss of one or more lower anterior teeth, suggesting that labret use was responsible, perhaps encouraging localized periodontal disease. For all adult Greenville females, there were 62 anterior tooth sites observable for labret abrasion or tooth loss. Twenty teeth featured labret facets (32.3%) and 15 teeth were lost ante

---

[13] The term "medial" is somewhat anatomically inaccurate in the present sense but has been proposed in the archaeological literature to identify singularly worn labrets positioned in the facial midline just below the lower lip, to contrast with "lateral" labrets worn in the cheeks on either side of the mouth (Keddie, 1981:61). A physical anthropologist colleague suggested to me that the terms "labial" and "buccal" (identifying anatomical positions toward the lip and toward the cheek respectively) might more correctly be used to distinguish the two styles (M. Skinner, pers. comm., 1991).

mortem (24.2%). For the adult Greenville males, none of whom exhibited labret wear, none of 85 anterior tooth sites showed evidence for ante mortem loss.

FIGURE 21. Stone labrets recovered from the Greenville site.

From these data it might be concluded that Burial 7, an old woman with five of her six lower anterior teeth lost before death (Table 5), also wore a labret

TABLE 5. *Labret abrasion facets and mandibular tooth loss in adult Greenville females*

Burial	Mean Age	Right teeth[1]								Left teeth[1]							
		M_3	M_2	M_1	P_2	P_1	C	I_2	I_1	I_1	I_2	C	P_1	P_2	M_1	M_2	M_3
3	47.0	o	o	o	o	o	o	o	A	x	o	o	o	o	o	o	o
7	64.5	x	o	x	o	o	x	x	x	x	x	o	o	o	o	-	x
11	31.0	o	o	o	o	d	o	d	A	o	o	d	d	d	d	o	o
12	34.5	o	o	o	o	o	o	o	A	A	o	o	o	o	o	o	o
14	20.0	o	o	o	o	o	o	o	-	-	-	o	o	o	o	o	o
22	44.5	o	o	o	o	o	o	A	x	x	A	o	o	o	o	o	o
24	64.5	x	x	x	x	o	o	A	x	x	-	A	-	o	x	x	x
29	59.5	o	o	o	o	o	A	x	x	x	x	A	o	o	x	o	o
40	25.0	o	o	o	o	o	o	A	A	A	A	A	o	o	o	o	o
42	64.5	o	o	o	o	o	o	A	x	-	A	o	o	o	o	o	o
46	44.5	o	o	o	o	o	o	o	A	A	A	o	o	o	o	o	o
47	20.0	-	-	-	-	-	o	-	-	-	-	-	-	-	-	-	-

[1] M = molars; P = premolars; C = canines; I = incisors; subscripted according to position in jaw. A = tooth abraded by labret; x = tooth lost ante mortem; o = tooth normal and unaffected by labret abrasion; d = tooth damaged and unobservable for labret abrasion; - = tooth missing postmortem.

during life. Indeed, two other, much younger women in the Greenville sample might also have worn labrets. In these cases, Burials 14 and 47 on Table 5, some or most of the anterior teeth necessary for observation were missing postmortem. Given the prevalence of women in the site with labret facets, quite possibly all the females buried in the site may have worn labrets. In addition to Burials 14 and 47, who could not completely be tested for abrasion facets, there were three identified adult females who lacked lower jaws.

Tooth abrasion facets from labrets have previously been reported for skeletons from Prince Rupert Harbour (Cybulski, 1974), Blue Jackets Creek (Severs, 1974), Crescent Beach (Percy, 1974; Beattie, 1981; Conaty and Curtin, 1984), the Hill site (Hall and Haggarty, 1981), Namu (Curtin, 1984), Pender Canal (Weeks, 1985, 1986), and site DgRq 18 at White Rock, British Columbia (Lazenby, 1986). Those at Blue Jackets Creek and Namu involved molars and premolars (e.g., Severs, 1974: Plate 18), consistently indicating the use of lateral or buccal (cheek) labrets. All of the other examples, like Greenville, consistently suggested the use of medial or labial (lip) labrets.

In connection with another Northwest Coast archaeological project (Matson, Pratt, and Rankin, 1991), I recently reexamined all of the extant Crescent Beach remains, including some not previously reported, 22 individuals from Pender Canal, and the purported case from White Rock. This study was expressly directed toward an investigation of dental labret abrasion and its spatial and temporal occurrences and distributions by sex in prehistoric coastal British Columbia sites. Methodological procedures and details of the results of this investigation have been reported elsewhere (Cybulski, 1991b), but some pertinent results may be summarized here (Fig. 22).

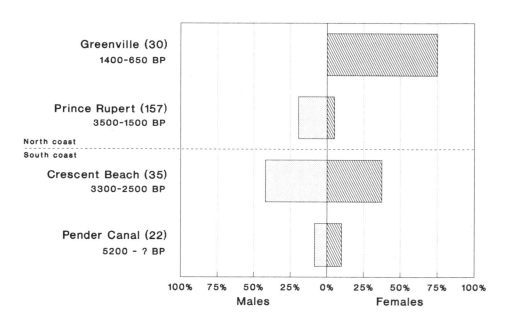

FIGURE 22. Frequencies of occurrence by sex of individuals with dental labret abrasion in four coastal British Columbia series.

Dental abrasion facets suggest that the use of medial or labial labrets was the dominant mode in prehistoric coastal British Columbia, with lateral or buccal labret facets so far found only at Blue Jackets Creek and Namu. While the practice of wearing labrets was only known historically in the northern half of the coast (among Haida, Tsimshian, and northern Kwakiutl), in the prehistoric period, labrets were worn by people on both the north and south coasts, extending to the Strait of Georgia region. In the south, medial labrets may have been worn as early as 5000 or more years ago based on a radiocarbon date for a Pender Canal skeleton with dental labret abrasion reported by Roy L. Carlson (1986), but probably not much more recently than about 2000 years B.P. based on all other findings to date (see Cybulski, 1991b, for details on chronology; also Keddie, 1981:66 for time estimates previously derived from the evidence of artifacts). Excluding the case from White Rock, which in its original report had been misidentified as an example of labret abrasion (Cybulski, 1991b), and only a single example from the Hill site, Greenville and Namu are the only local prehistoric series so far known in which the phenomenon appears to be sex-limited (three males at Namu; Curtin, 1984:105). At Prince Rupert Harbour, Crescent Beach, and Pender Canal, both men and women apparently wore medial labrets.

The Greenville data by sex are consistent with historic knowledge of labret use on the northern Northwest Coast. Only women reportedly wore labrets in ethnographic times. The Greenville data suggest that this north coast pattern began with the onset of the Late Developmental Stage of prehistory about 1,500 or 1,400 years ago. Both sexes wore labrets prior to that time, notably in the Tsimshian territorial enclave defined by Prince Rupert Harbour, but also at Blue Jackets Creek (J. Murray, 1981). If, indeed, labret use was a mark of rank and status, this information could indicate that north coast social patterns may have undergone some change between the Middle and Late Developmental stages.

It should be noted that the data for Pender Canal shown on Figure 22 are based on an incomplete sample, perhaps only one-third of the series of lower jaws potentially available from these sites. A comprehensive study of dental labret abrasion in this series is being undertaken by Simon Fraser University researchers (R.L. Carlson, pers. comm., 1991). This may account for the much lower frequency of occurrence of dental labret abrasion at Pender Canal (9.1% of both males and females) than at Crescent Beach (37.1%), although temporal or other factors, perhaps interpretable in terms of social patterns, might also be involved.

Overriding this observation for the moment is that the two south coast series show an almost equal distribution of labret wear for the sexes, while Prince Rupert Harbour gives a different pattern. Males clearly dominate the Prince Rupert Harbour picture, and this is in marked contrast to the historically expected north coast pattern presented by Greenville.

Partly based on a tentative record of dental labret abrasion reported for Crescent Beach by Richard Percy (1974), R.G. Matson (1989:10) touched on the idea that individuals with "ascribed" or "achieved" status might be recognized among the site's burials. While he did not explain or elaborate on the concept, presumably, the first type of status would be attained through heredity via kinship, while the second would be attained through acquired wealth, as suggested by the Northwest

Coast ethnographic record.   It is interesting to note that among the Coast Tsimshian and Nisga'a, in whose traditional territories the Prince Rupert Harbour and Greenville sites are located, social units were based on matrilineal descent (Halpin and Seguin, 1990), while among the central Coast Salish, in whose traditional territories Crescent Beach and the Pender Canal sites are located, descent was reckoned bilaterally (Suttles, 1990).   In the latter case, it could be assumed that either sex would expectedly attain ascribed status with equal probability, and there is an almost 50-50 sex distribution of individuals with dental labret abrasion.

The Greenville situation, on the other hand, might fit a model of ascribed status based on matrilineal descent, expected if the site's burial population were ancestral Nisga'a.   Interestingly enough, this "Tsimshian" model does not appear to extend further back in time to the Prince Rupert Harbour sites.   Does this mean that the people buried in the Prince Rupert Harbour sites were not ancestral to the Coast Tsimshian?   Quite possibly, though it could also mean that the largely male-related occurrences of dental labret abrasion were indicators of achieved status.

If one assumes that all, or nearly all occurrences of dental labret abrasion, and, therefore, the wearing of labrets, were indicators of ascribed status in the prehistoric groups, then the dental data would identify a bilateral descent system for the south, a matrilineal system for Greenville, and a patrilineal system (inheritance through the male line) for Prince Rupert Harbour.   While the last inference would conflict with ethnographic information about Coast Tsimshian and, therefore, possibly preclude ancestral connections, the attribution of ascribed rather than achieved status to the Prince Rupert Harbour males with labret wear is not far-fetched.   First, males clearly dominate the business of labret abrasion; only three female skeletons showed indications of labret abrasion as opposed to 19 males (in total, five of eight sites in the series featured persons with dental labret abrasion).   Secondly, only two of the individuals with labret abrasion were accompanied in burial by the artifacts themselves.   Indeed, few labrets found in coastal British Columbia middens are actually associated with burials.   This may indicate that in most cases, labrets were heirlooms removed from the deceased prior to burial to be retained as hereditary family objects.   Only in those instances where labrets may be found *in situ* with a skeleton, might they be interpreted as wealth objects and indicators of achieved status.   Otherwise, it seems highly unusual that, for example, labrets were not present with the nine Greenville females who showed distinct signs of dental labret abrasion of long-standing duration.

In the section of this chapter on vital statistics, the Prince Rupert Harbour burial population was noted to be heavily skewed in favour of males.   A possible explanation was that slaves cyclically formed a substantial segment of the general female population and were not buried in the sites. This might account for why so few females in the sites exhibited dental labret abrasion. Otherwise, a more nearly equal sex ratio of affected males and females might have been the case as at Crescent Beach and Pender Canal, perhaps denoting a similar bilateral descent system. Overall, I suspect that males with either ascribed or achieved status might be recognized in the sites based on the "heirloom" hypothesis noted above. Two Prince Rupert Harbour males with tooth abrasion had definitely associated labrets, and three additional males without evidence for dental consequences had been buried with labrets. In two cases, the lower jaws were missing (the burials had been partly disturbed) and could not be studied for labret abrasion. In the third male skeleton, three of the six lower anterior teeth were missing postmortem.

None of the individuals with tooth abrasion marks at Crescent Beach and Pender Canal appear to have been buried with their artifacts. At Crescent Beach, no burials recorded *in situ* (Percy, 1974; Conaty and Curtin, 1984) had associated labrets, though there were many disturbed burials. Sylvia Weeks (1985, 1986) reported five individuals with labrets at Pender Canal. This would suggest only ascribed status for labret-related individuals at Crescent Beach and either ascribed or achieved status for such individuals at Pender Canal.

A final observation can be made with respect to Greenville, potentially significant for social interpretations about the site's use. Seventy-five percent of all observable females in the site exhibited dental labret abrasion facets and, as argued above, all the females buried there might actually have worn labrets. Assuming that labrets were worn as indicators of status, the situation could indicate that the burial site was limited to high status individuals in the society, and that commoners or low status people were buried elsewhere. This possibility is further discussed below.

Food for the dead

As noted in Chapter II, a single hearth recorded in the Greenville site might have been used to burn food and clothing for the dead, a reported Nisga'a mortuary ritual. Radiocarbon estimates from charcoal in the hearth and from bone in a nearby burial suggested contemporaneity. Elderberry seeds with 16 individuals might also have reflected burial-related food offerings, though the presence of these seeds could have been a secondary result of the use of food storage containers as burial boxes or, possibly, a symbol of Nisga'a mythology.

According to Franz Boas (1916:62; 663-664), elderberry held mythological significance for the Tsimshian, including the Nisga'a, and was associated with mortality. An origin myth, the setting of which is the Nass River, involves a quarrel between Stone and Elderberry Bush as to who should give birth first. Elderberry Bush won the argument and "For this reason the people die soon, and elderberry bushes grow on their graves." There were were only sparse concentrations of seeds with eight burials, possibly reflecting one-time growth of elderberry bushes on the graves. In those cases with thick concentrations, elderberry may have been packed in the boxes with the deceased as part of the burial ritual. Hence, the elderberry seeds in the Greenville site are potentially important insofar as their presence may substantiate a deeply rooted oral tradition which in itself appears to refer to a time when below ground burial was the norm.

A possibility that the elderberry seeds may, instead, have represented food for the dead is also of interest. Elderberry was traditionally regarded as "rich food" by the Nisga'a and other Tsimshian (Boas 1916:406). Could the elderberry associated with the Greenville burials, like the prevalence of dental labret abrasion in the women, be an indication that only high status individuals were buried in the site? Another indicator for "rich food" in the site, as suggested by the analysis of the faunal remains (Chapter IV), was the presence of seal and sea lion "flippers." However, there were no concentrations of these bones which might suggest that "flippers" were intentionally placed with burials.

Possibly, the clearest indications of intentionally placed food for the dead were afforded by four concentrations of eulachon vertebrae in the site, as argued in the Discussion section of the next chapter. One relatively small cluster of vertebrae, minimally representing six or seven fish, was found in the depositional matrix around Burial 29 and may have been associated. In the context of the argument for the seasonal occurrence of eulachon presented in Chapter IV, one might wonder, given the advanced age at death of the woman represented in Burial 29, whether she might not have died of starvation when winter provisions had been depleted in her village.

Chapter IV

Faunal Remains

by Darlene Balkwill and Jerome S. Cybulski

The fauna recovered from the Greenville burial site comprised a large body of vertebrate skeletal elements and some invertebrate specimens. All vertebrate material, with the exception of one type of fish bone, was identified by one of us (D.B.) by direct comparison with reference specimens in the collections of the Zooarchaeological Identification Centre, Canadian Museum of Nature, Ottawa. An arrowtooth flounder pterygiophore was identified by Rebecca Wigen, Pacific Identifications, Victoria, using the reference collection in the Royal British Columbia Museum. The small amount of invertebrate material was identified (by D.B.) using keys and illustrations in the text by E.N. Kozloff (1987).[14]

Identifications were taken to the lowest taxonomic level possible. In most cases, this was the species, genus, or family, but some fragments could only be assigned to an order or class. Whenever possible, the name of the species, the element, the side, the part of the body, and the age at death were recorded for each bone or tooth, along with any evidence of modification, such as cut marks, burning, gnawing by carnivores or rodents, pathology, or changes related to the production or use of items as artifacts. This information was recorded on data cards, then entered into the Zooarchaeological Identification Centre's AlphaMicro computer using a customized database programme, Curator, developed by Linnaean Systems of California.

Age at Death Estimation

Based on the degree of epiphyseal fusion, some skeletal elements could be assigned to broad age classes, defined as follows: adult (epiphyses fully fused); young adult (epiphyses partially fused, fusion line visible); immature (epiphyses unfused, porous cortex confined to epiphyseal ends); juvenile/fetal (epiphyses

---

[14] Brenda Dowling meticulously and efficiently handled all the data entry and retrieval for this project. Wendy Dion, a museum volunteer, carefully weighed the two large samples containing eulachon bones, then patiently counted all those tiny vertebrae in the 10-gram subsamples. She also packed up all the faunal material when the analysis was finished. We are very grateful to Rebecca Wigen for identifying a puzzling fish bone.

unfused, porous cortex over all or most of the bone). These age classes refer only to the bone, not necessarily to the animal itself. Different bones and, indeed, different ends of the same bone fuse at different stages in an animal's life. For example, the distal ends of the humerus and tibia of a two-year-old sheep will be fused, but the proximal ends will be unfused, as will the distal end of the radius and both ends of the femur and ulna. However, for some species, an element can give more precise information on the age at death of the animal. In this study, canids were aged using epiphyseal fusion data for domestic dogs given by E. Schmid (1972:75); mule deer were aged using tooth eruption and wear data given by G.E. Connolly (1981), epiphyseal fusion data for the tibia (Purdue, 1983), and comparison of antler development with known-age reference specimens of white-tailed deer; harbour seals were aged using published data for epiphyseal closure of the humerus (Cox and Spiess, 1980).

Reporting Methods

The faunal data were quantified by the number of individual specimens (NISP) and the minimum number of individuals (MNI) for each taxon, and by the percentage of the total identified bone for each taxon which qualified as "identified." An identified bone is defined here as one which could be assigned to the taxonomic level of species, genus, or family; those bones for which only the class or order could be determined were not included in the identified category.

The NISP figures were based on simple counts except for the eulachon family, Osmeridae, where the figure was based on an estimate. Most of these bones occurred in two dense clusters which also contained considerable quantities of tiny pebbles and rootlets. Each cluster was weighed, then three 10-gram samples were extracted. The fish bones in each sample were counted, and the average of the three samples was determined. The number of bones in the cluster was estimated by extrapolating from the average count of the samples. For example, one cluster had a total weight of 118 g; the average bone count for its 10-gram samples was 330, and the number of bones in the cluster was estimated at 3,894.

In most cases, the MNI count for each taxon was calculated using element side, size, and age criteria. However, the MNI counts for two fish taxa were calculated on the basis of known vertebral counts for the species. Vertebral counts for fish of the family Osmeridae range from a low of 55 to a high of 72; the eulachon is in the upper part of the range with counts of 65-72 (Hart, 1973). Since one eulachon has a maximum 72 vertebrae, it would take at least 85 individuals to account for the 6,078 Osmeridae vertebrae in the sample. A similar approach was used for salmonids. The median figure in the range of vertebral counts given by J.L. Hart (1973) was used for each of the nine species included in the *Oncorhynchus/Salvelinus* complex. The sum of these values was then divided by 9 to give a weighted average of 64.8 for *Oncorhynchus/Salvelinus.* The MNI count for the bones identified as *Oncorhynchus* was 33 (calculated on the basis of basipterygia), and the average vertebral count for the five species of salmon was 66. Therefore, a total of 33 salmon would have, on average, 2,178 vertebrae. A total of 6,874 vertebrae were identified as *Oncorhynchus/Salvelinus;* 2,178 of these could be accounted for by the 33 *Oncorhynchus* individuals. This leaves 4,696 extra vertebrae. When this figure is divided by the average value of 64.8 for the complex, the result is 72.5. Thus, a minimum of 73 *Oncorhynchus/Salvelinus* individuals would be necessary to account for the 4,696 extra vertebrae.

MNI was calculated for the entire site as a unit. An attempt was made to compare species distributions for the different stratigraphic levels, but this proved rather fruitless because the provenience information did not contain a specific cultural layer designation for almost 24% of the material, and because 91% of the material that was designated was associated with the shell layer. No obvious differences were noticed.

Overview

Appendix F lists the common and scientific names of all the vertebrates and invertebrates recovered from the site. Table 6 shows the relative abundance of the vertebrates, in terms of NISP, MNI, and the percentage of identified bone, while Table 7 gives only the NISP figures for the invertebrate taxa. Two abbreviations used in the appendix and tables should be explained. First, the slash mark between words or taxa should be read as "or;" for example, "black/grizzly bear" means black bear or grizzly bear. Second, "cf." should be read as "probably." For the statistically oriented reader, the confidence limit for "cf." is 95%.

Both NISP and MNI are commonly used to quantify and compare zooarchaeological data, although both are flawed by inherent limitations. MNI counts are directly affected by the way the sample is subdivided into analysis units; this measure tends to overemphasize the importance of animals represented by only one or two bones. Since there is only one analysis unit in this study, the bias is such that the MNI counts will underestimate abundance. NISP counts can be inflated for certain elements of large mammals, such as metatarsals which are often highly fragmented but still retain identifying features.

Most of the invertebrate sample was made up of snails and bivalves, with a few fragments of barnacle and one piece of crab. All snails belonged to the top

TABLE 6. *Vertebrate species abundance for the Greenville site* [1]

Species	NISP	Per cent	MNI
Mammals:			
snowshoe hare	3	0.02	1
groundhog	94	0.59	3
beaver	12	0.07	1
Peromyscus sp.	29	0.18	9
meadow vole	10	0.06	8
long-tailed vole	1	0.01	1
Microtus sp.	18	0.11	1
Microtinae	49	0.30	7
Cricetidae	5	0.03	--
porcupine	8	0.05	1
small rodent	218	--	--
Delphinidae	1	0.01	1
Cetacean	1	0.01	--
dog	35	0.22	3
coyote/dog	1	0.01	1
Canis sp.	35	0.22	2
Canidae	2	0.01	--
black bear	4	0.02	1
black bear/grizzly bear	6	0.04	1
marten	2	0.01	1
ermine	1	0.01	1
striped skunk	1	0.01	1
sea otter	8	0.05	2
Mustelidae	1	0.01	--
domestic cat	1	0.01	1
Carnivora	6	--	--
northern sea lion	44	0.27	3
Otariidae	29	0.18	1
harbour seal	34	0.21	2
Phocidae	5	0.03	--
horse	5	0.03	1
pig	1	0.01	1
mule deer	27	0.17	4
moose	3	0.02	1
caribou/moose	3	0.02	--
caribou/mule deer	3	0.02	--
Cervidae	3	0.02	--
mountain goat	1	0.01	1
domestic sheep	1	0.01	1
Artiodactyla	2	--	--
unidentified mammal	895	--	--

(TABLE 6 continued)

Species	NISP	Per cent	MNI
Birds:			
Diomedea sp.	2	0.01	1
Phalacrocorax sp.	1	0.01	1
green-winged teal	1	0.01	1
greater scaup	2	0.01	1
surf scoter	1	0.01	1
common/Barrow's goldeneye	1	0.01	1
Anatinae (large duck)	2	0.01	1
bald eagle	9	0.06	1
turkey	1	0.01	1
Grus sp.	1	0.01	1
black-bellied plover/surfbird	1	0.01	1
cf. whimbrel	1	0.01	1
mew gull	18	0.11	5
herring/Thayer's gull	1	0.01	1
glaucous-winged gull	4	0.02	1
glaucous-winged/glaucous gull	4	0.02	--
Larus sp.	24	0.15	1
black-legged kittiwake	2	0.01	1
Laridae	13	0.08	--
common/thick-billed murre	2	0.01	1
great horned owl	1	0.01	1
raven	3	0.02	1
cf. varied thrush	1	0.01	1
Turdinae	1	0.01	--
unidentified bird	89	--	--
Amphibians:			
western toad	53	0.33	4
Fish:			
spiny dogfish	7	0.04	1
Oncorhynchus sp.	89	0.55	33
Oncorhynchus/Salvelinus	6,878	42.81	73
Salmonidae	54	0.34	--
Osmeridae	6,078	37.83	85
walleye pollock	1,227	7.64	40
walleye pollock/Pacific cod	527	3.28	--
Gadidae	273	1.70	--
Scorpaenidae	1	0.01	1
arrowtooth flounder	213	1.33	6
arrowtooth flounder/petrale sole	74	0.46	--

(*TABLE 6 continued*)

Species	NISP	Per cent	MNI
(*Fish continued*)			
cf. flathead/sand sole	1	0.01	1
cf. Pacific halibut	6	0.04	2
cf. starry flounder	2	0.01	1
Pleuronectiformes	22	--	2
unidentified fish	2,058	--	--
Totals:			
Mammals	1,608	3.03	62
Birds	186	0.60	25
Amphibians	53	0.33	4
Fish	17,510	96.04	245
Class uncertain	32	--	--
All vertebrates	19,389	100.00	336

[1] Includes intrusive species; NISP is the number of individual specimens; MNI is the minimum number of individuals; Per cent is the percentage only of those specimens which could be identified to the level of species, genus, or family as explained in the text.

shell family (Trochidae), and the only identifiable bivalve shell was from a butter clam. The rest of the shell fragments could only be described as unidentifiable bivalve or mollusc. All the identified invertebrates were of marine origin. Because the invertebrates made up such a very small portion of the faunal sample, the focus of discussion will be on the vertebrates.

As can be seen from Table 6, the vertebrate material was dominated by fish bones, which made up 90.3% of the total sample of elements, while mammalian elements were a very distant second at 8.3%. Less than 1% were bird and amphibian. The material was very well preserved, with the result that 83% could be identified as to family, subfamily, genus, or species. The level of diversity was moderately high with 55 species represented, including 24 mammal, 21 bird, one amphibian, and nine fish species.

Figure 23 provides an overview of the relative vertebrate abundance for the identified material in terms of MNI counts for birds, land mammals, sea mammals, and fish. The dominant fish segment is further detailed by subgroup. Certain taxa have been omitted in this and subsequent graphs. All small rodents (voles and mice) and toads were omitted on the assumption that their presence in the assem-

TABLE 7. *Invertebrate sample abundance in the Greenville site faunal assemblage*

Species	NISP[1]
Gastropoda:	
Solariella/Margarites	36
cf. top shell family	1
Pelecypoda:	
butter clam	1
unidentified bivalve	24
Unidentified mollusc	39
Cirripedia:	
barnacle	11
Malacostraca:	
true crab family	1
----------------------------	-----
Totals:	
Gastropods	37
Bivalves	25
All molluscs	101
Arthropods	12
----------------------------	-----
All invertebrates	113

[1] NISP is the number of individual specimens.

blage was not due to human efforts and, therefore, not pertinent to cultural interpretations for the site. They are burrowing animals who often find their way into prehistoric deposits where they may expire and, thus, intrusively become part of the faunal assemblage. Domestic sheep, cat, horse, and pig, as well as one moose bone with saw cuts, were omitted because they were historically deposited.

Following is a species by species account of the vertebrates present in the faunal material, beginning with the mammals, then proceeding through the birds and amphibians to the fish. Where appropriate, comments are made on present-day occurrence of the species in the site area, habitats, element distributions, modifications, ages of the animals at death, pathology, and other points of interest.

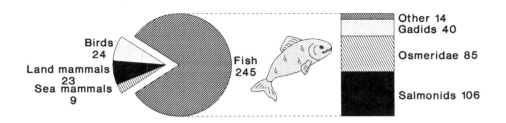

FIGURE 23. *Relative vertebrate abundance at the Greenville site based on MNI counts of nonintrusive species.*

Mammals

Both marine and terrestrial mammal species were present in the faunal sample, although the ratio was 2:1 in favour of the land mammals in NISP terms and 3:1 in MNI terms. A total 122 bones, only 0.76% of the identified bone, came from marine mammals (northern sea lion, harbour seal, sea otter, and porpoise in descending order of abundance). Four species of large terrestrial mammals were identified, with mule deer being the most common, followed by bear, then moose and mountain goat. A variety of smaller land mammals were also identified, several of them furbearing. Small rodents made up the largest component of the mammal assemblage but were assumed intrusive. In addition to the dog, four other domestic mammals were represented, cat, horse, pig, and sheep. Four of five horse bones were found in the disturbed overburden (Layer O), while the fifth, and the pig and cat bones were found in Layer A, which included the original, present-day ground surface beneath the overburden. A tooth from a domestic sheep was recovered at a very shallow depth (7 cm below datum) in excavation Unit 17.

Canidae (dogs, wolves, coyotes and foxes)

The only species in this family definitely known in the faunal sample was the dog; some bones could only be identified as *Canis,* the genus which includes wolves, dogs, and coyotes. The present distribution of the wolf covers the Nass River area, but it is difficult to be sure about the coyote as authorities do not seem to agree. The source books of E.R. Hall and K.R. Kelson (1959) and A.W. F. Banfield (1974) both show a strip along the British Columbia coast as not containing coyotes. However, the coyote distribution map in the handbook by I.M.T. Cowan and C.J. Guiguet (1978) includes the site area, and they describe the range as "westward through the Coast Range in the valleys of the Skeena and Bella Coola and other large rivers possibly to the salt water" (p. 280). A.W.F. Banfield

(1974:289) writes: "Between 1829 and 1907 coyotes extended their distribution northward from the fifty-fifth parallel of latitude to embrace southern Alaska, Yukon Territory, and Mackenzie District." This information is not especially helpful since the site is on the 55th parallel. However, it seems unlikely that coyotes were present in the area in prehistoric times.

Remains of at least three dogs were recovered from the site. E.S. Wing (1978) established the following regression equation which correlates the height of a dog mandible at the first molar with the weight of the dog (correlation coefficient of 0.9808): $\log y = 2.2574(\log x) + 1.1164$, where y is the body weight and x is the mandible height.

An almost complete dog skull and mandible were recovered from Unit 5, positively associated with Burial 4, a teenage boy. The height of the mandible of this dog was 21 mm. Applying E.S. Wing's regression equation, the dog weighed 12.6 kg, or approximately 28 lb., the size of a modern cocker spaniel. A second dog, represented by an almost complete skull recovered from Unit 11, was about the same size. Height measurements were taken on ten dog mandibles found in Middle to Late Woodland period deposits (A.D. 100-700) at the Apple Creek archaeological site in Illinois; the range extended from 18 mm to 24 mm, with a mean of 20.8 mm (Parmalee et al., 1972). Thus, two Greenville dogs were very similar in size to the Apple Creek Woodland dogs.

The bones of a much smaller dog were found in Unit 9, collected with the remnants of Burial 9, a greatly disturbed adult male interment. The weight of this dog could not be estimated because it was represented only by a right frontal and a maxilla fragment with the first premolar. Reference material showed that it was considerably smaller than a dog recovered from the Kirche archaeological site (BcGr 1) in Ontario, attributed to the Huron Indians. A fourth animal, identified as dog/coyote, was represented by a lower first molar the same size as that of the Huron dog.

Some canid bones were modified. One dog radius was gnawed by a carnivore. Suggestive evidence that dogs were eaten was provided by cut marks on three *Canis* bones: a rib was chopped through and had knife cuts on the medial surface; a metatarsal had been chopped through the tip of the proximal articular process during removal of the hind foot; a femur had several meat-removal knife cuts on the shaft. No bones were burned. Three apparent instances of pathology were noted: the head of a rib fused to a thoracic vertebra; a right mandible missing sockets for the first premolar and third molar; a left mandible missing a socket for the first premolar. The two mandible halves may well have been from the same dog. Whether the teeth had been lost during life is uncertain, particularly in the cases of the first premolar. Absence of this tooth in aboriginal dogs has been noted in other studies, including those by G.M. Allen (1920), H.S. Colton (1970), and P.W. Parmalee et al. (1972), suggesting, perhaps, a developmental variation like third molar agenesis in humans (see Chapter V).

Seven of 35 dog bones found in the site could be assigned to broad age classes on the basis of epiphyseal fusion; three vertebrae and three paw bones were fully fused and were classified as adult, but the phalanges and metapodials of dogs fuse early in life, at six months of age. An additional vertebra had a partially fused epiphysis, allowing more precise age estimation of the animal rather than the element; this vertebra came from a 20-24-month-old dog.

Five elements identified as *Canis* could be aged. Two indicated a puppy less than four months old, while another two were less specific. A vertebral epiphysis from a canid younger than 2 years and an unfused calcaneum from one younger than 1.25 years could have come from the same animal. A well worn canine tooth came from an old dog, wolf, or coyote.

Study of all canid elements showed that all regions of the body except the head were underrepresented. This was particularly noticeable for three regions, including the trunk (ribs, sternum, and vertebrae other than caudal), the extremities, and the tail. With at least four animals present (three dogs and one dog/coyote), recovery of the complete skeletons would have yielded 416 extremity bones and 256 trunk bones. Instead, there were only 14 from the extremities and nine from the trunk. Eight trunk bones were vertebrae. Only one rib was found, yet a living dog has 26 ribs. No tail vertebrae were found at all. Although other factors may have been involved, this suggests the head was disposed of in a manner different from the rest of the dog carcass. It is of interest that dog skulls or parts were found with the remains of two human burials, perhaps reflecting selective mortuary ritual practices relating to dogs as discussed in Chapter III.

Otariidae (eared seal family)

This family includes the northern sea lion, northern fur seal, and California sea lion, all of which are found in British Columbia waters, although the last is found only as far north as Vancouver Island. A total 73 bones from this family were present in the faunal assemblage. Forty-four were northern sea lion, but a lack of northern fur seal reference material necessitated identification of 29 elements simply as Otariidae. Size differences and habitat preferences indicate that these probably were northern sea lion bones.

The northern sea lion is the largest of the eared seals, with males reaching 11' (3.4 m) long and 2200 lb. (998 kg); females weigh less than half as much. Sea lions frequent isolated offshore islets during the pupping and mating season in June and July, and during the fall and winter are found in bays, river estuaries, and channels all along the coast (Cowan and Guiguet, 1978). A large rookery was once located on North Danger Rocks in Hecate Strait (Pike and MacAskie, 1969). The northern fur seal is considerably smaller, with males 7' (2.1 m) long and 600 lb. (272 kg), and females 5' (1.5 m) long and 120 lb. (54 kg) (Cowan and Guiguet, 1978). Fur seals are more pelagic than sea lions, although they winter in protected coastal waters:

> A wintering population of mature females occurs in northern Hecate Strait. They do not normally come ashore, but juveniles born the previous summer may strand and die on exposed ocean beaches, especially during winters characterized by intense storms. (Pike and MacAskie, 1969).

For the sake of simplicity, the northern sea lion bones and those identified only as Otariidae are both referred to as sea lion in the following discussion.

Sea lion remains at the site included 26 flipper bones, ten head elements (two mandibles, one hyoid, and seven teeth), 13 limb bones, one scapula, and 23 trunk bones (mostly vertebrae and sacrum). There was a slight preponderance of front flipper bones (14) over those from the hind flipper (9). No skull bones and only two rib fragments were recovered.

Cut marks were noted on 11 sea lion bones. An axis vertebra and sacrum were chopped parallel to the body axis, indicating that the spinal column was split during butchering of an animal. An astragalus, calcaneum, and metapodial showed cuts which probably also occurred during butchering, specifically to remove a hind flipper. Several shallow knife cuts were observed on a cervical vertebra, lumbar vertebra, and sternum; these would have been made when meat was cut away from the bone. Similar but deeper chop marks along the edge of the shaft of a tibia were also classified as meat-removal cuts. Several shallow knife cuts on the anterior edge of the ventral surface of an atlas vertebra may have been meat-removal cuts, but it is more likely that these cuts indicate the head was chopped off.

Of 37 ageable sea lion bones, 26 (70.3%) were immature, four were young adult, and only seven (18.9%) were adult. This suggests preferential killing of immature sea lions.

Sea lion bones may have been fairly popular with dogs, as nine (12.3%) showed gnawing by carnivores. Only one abnormality was noted, a tooth with a twisted root. None of the bones showed signs of burning.

Harbour seal

The harbour seal is abundant in coastal waters and on shore, sometimes ascending large rivers (Pike and MacAskie, 1969). Thirty-four harbour seal bones, plus five identified only to family level (Phocidae) were recovered from the site. The harbour seal is the only species of small seal found along the British Columbia coast in modern times. The five Phocidae bones (fragments of vertebrae, a tooth, auditory bulla, and a phalanx) seemed too small to belong to the elephant seal, so they were most likely harbour seal.

At least two animals were represented; one was older than 2.5-3.5 years at death on the basis of a fully fused humerus. The second seal was younger, and was represented by unfused metatarsals and tibiae. Bones from the flippers were more abundant than those from other body regions, with nine limb and 12 extremity bones, comprising 54% of the seal bones. Hind flipper elements (12) were more common than those from the front flipper (3). The only bones known to be part of the front flippers were two humeri and a radius; six phalanges could have come from either front or hind flippers.

Cuts were observed on three bones; these included meat-removal cuts on a rib, an ischium chopped through (removal of the hind flipper), and shallow knife cuts near the distal end of the humerus (removal of the tip of the front flipper from the meatier base). Carnivore gnawing was present on three bones (a fibula, humerus, and tibia), fewer than for the sea lions. No signs of burning or pathology were noted.

Sea otter

In earlier times, sea otters were distributed all along the British Columbia coast, inhabiting offshore kelp beds and rocky islets (Cowan and Guiguet, 1978). They spend most of their time at sea, which may help to explain why so few sea otter bones were found at Greenville. Only eight were recovered, representing two animals, one of whom was male. The eight bones included a baculum, two left mandibles, two skull fragments, two teeth, and a metatarsal. Another skull fragment, part of a premaxilla, could only be identified as large mustelid, but was probably sea otter. No ribs, vertebrae, or limb bones were recovered; in other words, no meat-bearing bones were present. The head, extremities and baculum might very well have been left in the pelts after skinning. This skewed element distribution suggests that only pelts, rather than whole otters, were brought to the site.

The only modified bone was a mandible that appeared to have the coronoid and condyle cut off, probably during skinning. There was no sign of burning or carnivore gnawing on the sea otter bones.

Skunk

Neither striped nor spotted skunk are present in the Greenville area today; the distribution extends westward only as far as the east slope of the Cascade Range (Hall and Kelson, 1959; Banfield, 1974; Cowan and Guiguet, 1978). However, part of a striped skunk skull (the left temporal with part of the auditory bulla) was recovered from the overburden surface of the site. A few skunk bones were also found at the Boardwalk site in Prince Rupert Harbour (Stewart, 1977). The presence of skunk bones in coastal northern British Columbia archaeological sites may indicate a more extensive distribution in prehistoric times, but it is possible that the skunk bone arrived at Greenville via trade with tribes to the east.

Bears

Both black and grizzly bears are present in the area today. Four bear elements (fragments of a humerus and maxilla, a whole adult phalanx 2, and a second molar) were identified as black bear on the basis of size. Another six elements could only be identified as black/grizzly bear. On the basis of element age, there were at least two animals represented, an old adult black bear shown by the presence of two very worn second molars, and a fetal or newborn black/grizzly bear represented by two ribs and a scapula. A femur which could only be identified as carnivore was also fetal or newborn and the proper size to belong to the black/grizzly.

Modifications were noted on four bones. A black bear proximal humerus fragment had three butchering cuts plus several shallow knife cuts, probably a result of disarticulating the upper foreleg from the shoulder; the bone had also been chewed by a carnivore. Five shallow parallel knife cuts along the posterior edge of a black bear maxilla fragment probably occurred during skinning. One bone, a black bear phalanx 2, was calcined. A black/grizzly bear tooth (fourth premolar) appeared polished.

Snowshoe hare

Modern distribution maps of the snowshoe hare show its presence in the Greenville area. I.M.T. Cowan and C.J. Guiguet (1978:102) say that hare "were and still are to a certain extent an important item in the diet of native peoples." However, only three bones were recovered from the site. There were no cut marks on these bones, so it is impossible to determine whether this animal was taken for its fur, as a source of food, or both.

Beaver

Twelve beaver bones were present in the faunal sample, a mandible, nine loose teeth, a caudal vertebra, and a rib. Although beaver may very well have been eaten, all of these elements, with the exception of the rib, could have been left in the pelt after skinning. No cut marks were noted on the bones. Three loose teeth were incisor fragments; the presence of fine transverse striations at the end of one indicated its use as a tool.

Marten and ermine

These two small furbearers were not well represented in the faunal sample, although distribution maps show their ranges include the Greenville area. The marten is found in coniferous forests from sea level to the tree line at all times of the year, though in the summer it is more often found at higher elevations. The ermine's habitat is more varied and includes the edge of the coniferous forest, rock slides, stream banks, and sea beach debris (Cowan and Guiguet, 1978).

Only two marten bones (auditory bulla and distal tibia) and one ermine bone (whole humerus) were found. No modifications were noted.

Delphinidae (dolphin family)

Only two whale bones were recovered. One was a fragment that could only be identified as cetacean; the other was a lumbar vertebra from a member of the dolphin family. Nine species of this family are found off the coast of British Columbia, but several could be ruled out as represented by the vertebra. The harbour porpoise, which is the only species present in the Zooarchaeological Identification Centre reference collection, was eliminated on morphological grounds. Of the remaining eight possibilities, three (killer whale, pilot whale, and grey grampus) were too large, and two others (the common dolphin, *Delphinus,* and *Stenella*) were less likely, based on habitat and present distributions (Banfield, 1974; Pike and MacAskie, 1969).

On a trip to Washington, D.C., one of us (D.B.) was given an unexpected opportunity to examine some known dolphin vertebrae in the Marine Mammal section of the Smithsonian Institution. Although the archaeological specimen was not directly compared, *Delphinus* and *Stenella* did not appear morphologically correct, but *Phocaenoides dalli* was a good match. *Lagenorhynchus* could not be discounted, although the base of the transverse process seemed too thick. *Lissodelphis borealis* was not examined.

The most likely choices, therefore, were *Lagenorhynchus* (white-sided dolphin), *Phocaenoides* (Dall's porpoise), and *Lissodelphis* (northern right-whale dolphin). The first two are common in the area and are found inshore; *Lissodelphis* is, perhaps, less probable as it is "primarily a deep-water offshore species" (Watson, 1981:247) and has been rarely sighted in British Columbia waters, although A.W.F. Banfield (1974:260) states that it is "probably a normal visitor off our British Columbia coast." In the 19th century, C.M. Scammon (1968:101) reported seeing this species "as far south as San Diego Bay, on the California coast, and as far north as Behring Sea."

Butchering cuts were observed on the lumbar vertebra; the neural arch had been cut off and one or, possibly, both transverse processes appeared to have been cut.

Deer

The deer found in the Greenville area is a small subspecies, *Odocoileus hemionus sitkensis* (Sitka black-tailed deer), thought to have developed from deer that moved into north coastal British Columbia after the last glaciation (Wallmo, 1981).

A total 27 deer bones were identified, most of them (74%) from the head and extremities. Only five were limb bones, all lower elements, including three distal tibia fragments, a midshaft ulna, and a proximal radius fragment. The trunk was greatly underrepresented; there was only one rib, a distal fragment, and the only vertebra was from a tail. The element distribution was skewed in favour of those bones which have little meat on them and which would normally be discarded during butchering. The head elements were mostly mandibles and loose lower teeth; only one skull fragment was found, and that came from a young deer, 6-8 months old. While deer mandibles and extremity bones have a high marrow content which may serve as a source of food, they may also serve as raw material for tools (metapodials) and charms (teeth). According to Nisga'a informants, deer teeth were traditionally used in ceremonial rattles.

A minimum four deer were represented. The age at death of three could be estimated, one at 6-8 months (frontal with developing antler), one at 15-18 months (partially erupted lower third molar), and one at approximately 30 months (lower second premolar with very little wear). Since fawns are generally born in June (Cowan and Guiguet, 1978), these three deer were all killed in the fall or winter.

Several deer bones showed modifications. Cuts were found on seven of them; disarticulation cuts on a carpal and three distal metapodials were probably a result of chopping off the feet. A mandible fragment had been cut through transversely and had several superficial knife cuts on the outer surface near a chop mark; they may have resulted from skinning or tongue removal. The ulnar midshaft fragment had been chopped at one end. One of the distal tibia fragments had been ringed. A groove was cut around the shaft, then the distal end was snapped off. This bone also showed evidence of carnivore gnawing, so it may have been debitage possibly tossed to dogs. Only one pathological element was noted, a mandible with an open area in the bone resulting from an abscess. One bone, a tarsal, was charred.

Moose

Distribution maps in the books by A.W.F. Banfield (1974), E.R. Hall and K.R. Kelson (1959), and I.M.T. Cowan and C.J. Guiguet (1978) all show moose absent from the site area. A.W.F. Banfield (1974:397) states they "occur westward to the Coastal Range," while I.M.T. Cowan and C.J. Guiguet (1978:380) write that in the coastal regions of British Columbia moose occur "chiefly along the summit and east side of the Coast Range" although they "are sometimes seen at the heads of the longer coastal inlets." In his Nisga'a treatise, Stephen McNeary (1976:102) wrote that "before the influx of moose in about 1920, large herbivores were not common in Niska territory," implying that moose were not present in the Nass River valley until 1920.

Three bones were identified as moose, including a scapula, astragalus, and tibia. All were found on the surface of the site or in the disturbed overburden, thus precluding any clear definition of the bones as prehistoric. The tibia exhibited saw cuts, certainly relegating it to more recent times, as saws were not used to cut meat until after the late 18th century (Deetz, 1977).

Caribou

There are no caribou in the Greenville area today but they do occur at that latitude on the east side of the Coast Range (Cowan and Guiguet, 1978). In the faunal assemblage, no bones were definitely identified as caribou. Three antler fragments were from either caribou or moose, but the porous texture more closely resembled that of moose antler. Fragments of a metapodial, a femur, and a tooth could only be identified as caribou/mule deer, and three other fragments (hyoid, mandible, and rib) could only be taken to the family level, Cervidae.

Mountain goat

Mountain goats occur in the general area today, although they are undoubtedly rare in the lower Nass valley near Greenville itself. The animal inhabits very rugged terrain, generally at altitudes above the tree line. "In the Coast Range deep snows may force it to sea-level during the winter months" (Cowan and Guiguet, 1978:389). This species was represented in the faunal sample by only one bone, a tarsal (the lateral malleolus). Because of a small amount of distortion caused by slight osteophytosis, the identification was considered probable rather than definite.

Porcupine

Porcupines occur in the area, although I.M.T. Cowan and C.J. Guiguet (1978: 246) say they are "rare in the coast forest." Eight porcupine bones were recovered, including a mandible, three teeth, two ribs, and two extremity bones. The mandible was heavily gnawed by a small rodent and a calcaneum was calcined. No cuts or pathology were apparent.

Small rodents (voles and mice)

A total 330 bones from at least three species, representing a minimum 26 individuals, were present in the faunal sample. The identified taxa included meadow vole, long-tailed vole, and *Peromyscus.* Forty-nine bones were identified to subfamily, five to family, and 218 simply as small rodent. All parts of the body were represented and these animals were probably intrusive. No modifications were noted.

The bones called "small rodent" were not randomly distributed in the site; 199 of them (91.3%) were found in two clusters. The majority were recovered with Burial 18, Unit 11, while 51 bones were found inside the skull of Burial 16, Unit 13. Both *Peromyscus* and *Microtus* are known to burrow, although this habit appears more common in meadow voles than in deer mice. Grassland forms of *Peromyscus* often nest in short burrows constructed by other species, and meadow voles construct "short shallow burrows" (Banfield, 1974:209) and a complicated system of surface runways which may "connect with an underground labyrinth" (Cowan and Guiguet, 1978: 217). The bones were likely *Peromyscus,* since eight mandibles in the first cluster and two mandibles and a skull in the second were

so identified.   No *Microtus,* Microtinae, or Cricetidae bones were identified in
either of these units.

Peromyscus (deer mice). -- Of 29 bones identified as *Peromyscus,* all were head
elements, including 17 mandibles, ten skulls, and two loose teeth.   Although the
species could not be determined, it may have· been *Peromyscus maniculatus,* the
deer mouse, as this is the only species present in the area today and, perhaps, for
the last 12,000 years.   *P. oreas* (cascade deer mouse) is thought to have been
confined to southern Washington during the last glaciation and then to have expanded its range northward only as far as Rivers Inlet in British Columbia (Banfield,
1974).   *P. sitkensis* (the Sitka mouse) is now confined to the outer Queen Charlotte
Islands but may have inhabited the mainland after the last glaciation.   A.W.F.
Banfield (ibid.) suggests that *sitkensis* reached the islands on floating tree trunks
after landslides deposited sections of forest in the sea and was supplanted on the
larger inner islands by the more competitive deer mouse.   Certainly, habitat preferences seem to point to either *P. sitkensis,* which is found in "the dense, moss-hung
Sitka spruce-western cedar forests," or *P. oreas,* which "prefers the deep, damp,
subalpine forest," whereas *P. maniculatus* "seldom occur in low, wet habitats" (ibid.,
pp. 166, 171-170).

Voles. -- The long-tailed vole, *Microtus longicaudus,* is the only species of field
vole *(Microtus)* that is definitely known to occur in the Greenville area today.
Authorities disagree about the presence of the meadow vole, *Microtus pennsyl-
vanicus,* along the northern British Columbia coast.   According to A.W.F. Banfield
(1974) and I.M.T. Cowan and C.J. Guiguet (1978), meadow voles are not found
west of the Coast Range.   However, E.R. Hall and K.R. Kelson (1959) disagree.
On the basis of specimens collected in British Columbia at Sawmill Lake near
Telegraph Creek, Atlin, and Hazelton, and in Alaska at Fort Wrangell and Taku
River, they extend the range of the meadow vole right to the coast from Hazelton
northward, thus taking in the Greenville area.   The Greenville specimens support
this distribution.   On the basis of teeth, specifically the upper second molar, eight
skulls and two loose upper second molars were identified as meadow vole, and one
skull was identified as long-tailed vole.   An additional 14 mandibles, one skull
missing the second molar, two isolated lower first molars, and a whole femur were
identified only as *Microtus.*

Groundhog

As with the meadow vole, authorities disagree about the presence of the
groundhog in the Greenville area.   E.R. Hall and K.R. Kelson (1959) include
Greenville in its range, although they do not show specimens actually collected

there. A.W.F. Banfield (1974) and I.M.T. Cowan and C.J. Guiguet (1978) show the westward extent of the range stopping east of Greenville, in the upper Nass valley, although Cowan and Guiguet mention that further collecting may widen the known distribution.

A total 94 groundhog bones from at least three animals were recovered. Seventy-four (78.7%) were found clustered in the south half of Unit 12, Layer B. They appeared to represent an almost complete skeleton of one immature groundhog. None of the bones showed signs of modification. A probable explanation is that the groundhog died in its burrow, although it is possible that the animal was either cooked whole or skinned for its pelt, with the carcass discarded virtually intact.

Unidentified mammal

A total 895 fragments could only be identified as mammalian. Eight had been gnawed by carnivores, 25 showed cut marks, and 27 were burned (18 calcined and nine charred).

Birds

Albatross

The faunal sample contained two albatross bones, a distal humerus and a proximal radius. The radius had several shallow knife cuts at the distal end and looked chopped through. Because of a shortage of reference material, identification could not be taken to the species level.

Albatrosses are sea birds, coming ashore only to nest. Three species occur in British Columbia waters, Laysan, black-footed, and short-tailed, though none are known to have nested in Canada (Godfrey, 1986; Guiget, 1978). Although an early 19th century naturalist reported that short-tailed albatrosses nested in the Aleutians, particularly on Umnak Island (Yesner, 1976), the lack of very young individuals in almost 400 albatross bones from archaeological sites on southwest Umnak Island (ibid.) calls this observation into question. Present-day nesting occurs on Pacific islands such as Torishima, Iwo Jima, Bonin, Marshall and the Hawaiian Islands. Short-tailed albatrosses occurred commonly off the coast of British Columbia until the end of the 19th century (Godfrey, 1986); they were heavily hunted for feathers on the main breeding islands, almost causing extinction (Guiguet, 1978). The black-footed albatross and the Laysan albatross are fairly common non-breeding visitors to offshore British Columbia waters, especially during the summer months, and occur casually at other times of the year (Guiguet, 1978; Godfrey, 1986).

There are some behavioural differences among the three species. The black-footed albatross is more gregarious than the Laysan, and tends to feed more in turbulent waters such as channels between islands (Miller, 1940). The short-tailed albatross "occasionally follows vessels for the purpose of picking up what scraps are thrown overboard" (Bent, 1922:8), whereas the Laysan is more solitary, less prone to following boats, and tends to feed farther out to sea (Fisher, 1972; Sanger, 1974). D.R. Yesner (1976:277) suggests that "albatrosses were hunted at sea, in all probability where they congregated in nutrient-rich upwelling waters in interisland passes, and while following boats engaged in other hunting activities."

Cormorants

Only one cormorant bone, a midshaft two-thirds of an ulna, was found. Because of a lack of reference specimens of Brandt's cormorant and the pelagic cormorant, this bone was not identified to species. It seemed slightly smaller than the ulna of a double-crested cormorant. Brandt's cormorant is the same size as a double-crested cormorant, and modern distribution records show it only in southern coastal British Columbia (Guiguet, 1978; Godfrey, 1986). The double-crested cormorant nests and is a winter resident near Vancouver Island, although it occurs casually in southern Yukon (Godfrey, 1986) and southwestern Alaska (Guiguet, 1978). The pelagic cormorant is the smallest and most abundant of the three species found in British Columbia, breeding along the entire coast (ibid.). Thus, the combination of size and modern distribution suggests that the ulna was probably from a pelagic cormorant.

The bone had been chopped through, with knife cuts at both the proximal and distal ends, a heavy gouge near the distal end, and a series of fine knife cuts in the middle of the shaft.

Ducks

Although there were only seven duck bones in the faunal sample, they repre-sented a minimum five individuals from four genera and at least five different species. Four species were identified, green-winged teal, greater scaup, goldeneye, and surf scoter. A fifth species, represented by the proximal third of a carpometa-carpus, could only be described as "large duck" but appeared to be about the size of a mallard or white-winged scoter. Each species was represented by a single ele-ment, with the possible exception of the scaup. The elements included four wing bones, two leg bones, and one quadrate.

Green-winged teals are found on the British Columbia coast during the winter (Guiguet, 1978). The greater scaup is common along the coast in late fall and winter (October through March) but is not known to breed in the site area. There may have been two bones from this species, a tarsometatarsus identified as greater scaup, and a phalanx identified only as "medium duck, size of scaup." Common goldeneyes migrate along the coast in October and November to southern wintering grounds. Barrow's goldeneye winters on the coast, but is less common than the common goldeneye. Both species migrate along the coast north to breeding grounds starting in February (ibid.). They are not known to breed on the northern coast of British Columbia, although they breed inland in the Peace River and Cariboo parklands. Surf scoters winter along the coast from southern Alaska to California; they do not breed in the site area.

Bald eagle

Bald eagles breed in the site area and are very common along the coast. Nine bones were identified, six from the wing and three from the leg. Cuts were noted on one wing bone and one leg bone. There were several superficial knife cuts on the proximal end of the shaft of a carpometacarpus, and the trochlea for digit 2 of a tarsometatarsus had been cut through, with shallow knife cuts showing in the intertrochlear notch.

Turkey

One domestic turkey vertebra, obviously historically intrusive, was recovered from the disturbed surface matrix of Unit 1.

Crane

Only one crane bone (a pollex) was present. It was simply identified as *Grus* sp. because of a lack of reference material for the whooping crane. The bone was probably from a sandhill crane, which breeds in the Queen Charlotte Islands and on the mainland coast, but the past distribution of the whooping crane is not well known. Whooping cranes may once have bred over a wide area of northern Canada, as R. Macfarlane (1891) mentioned seeing whooping cranes on the Mackenzie River near the Arctic Ocean every spring between 1862 and 1865, and there are two nesting records for the vicinity of Great Slave Lake in the 1860s (Greenway, 1958).

Shore birds

One bone was identified as either black-bellied plover or surfbird. Black-bellied plovers are found along the British Columbia coast during spring and fall migrations; surfbirds are common along the coast during migration, but may be found in summer or winter months as well (Godfrey, 1986).

One bone, an almost complete carpometacarpus, was identified as "cf. whimbrel." Morphologically, the match was excellent for whimbrel. However, oystercatchers are approximately the same size as whimbrels, and lack of a reference specimen of oystercatcher meant that it could not be ruled out. Whimbrels are common along the coast during spring and fall migrations (ibid.).

Gulls

The faunal sample held 66 gull bones from at least nine different birds. Although this made up only 0.42% of the identified bone, gulls were by far the most common avian group. Four species were identified (mew, herring/Thayer's, glaucous-winged, and kittiwake) with a fifth species present but not determined. The fifth species, represented by a quadrate, was probably Sabine's gull, *Xema sabini,* as the bone was smaller than the quadrates of the kittiwake and Franklin's gull, but larger than that of the black tern. Sabine's gull occurs regularly on the British Columbia coast during the autumn migration (Godfrey, 1986). Unfortunately, a lack of reference material for *Xema* meant this bone could only be identified as "small gull."

The mew was the most abundant gull in the faunal assemblage; there were 18 bones from at least five individuals. This small gull breeds in the site area (ibid.). One bone was identified as coming from either a herring or Thayer's gull. Neither species is known to breed in the area, but the herring gull occurs during migration and winter along the British Columbia coast, and Thayer's gull also winters on the coast (ibid.). The glaucous-winged gull, which breeds and winters in the area, was represented by four bones, plus another four identified as either this species or the glaucous gull, found on the British Columbia coast during winter (ibid.). The black-legged kittiwake does not breed in the area, but is a transient and winter resident on the coast; immature kittiwakes "occur in large numbers around the Queen Charlotte Islands during the summer months" (Guiguet, 1978:25).

Twenty-four bones could only be identified as *Larus* sp. All but four were from large gulls (larger than herring gull), and were probably either glaucous-winged or glaucous gulls. The four exceptions were from medium gulls, probably Thayer's or herring.

Thirteen bones could only be identified as Laridae (gull family). One was the size of a medium gull, but the others were all small, with seven the size of a mew.

Considering all 66 gull bones, the distribution was biased against elements of the torso. Only seven came from the head (four mandibles, one quadrate, one skull, and one upper beak), five from the trunk, six from the pectoral girdle, and two from the pelvis. Vertebrae were conspicuously absent. Although bird vertebrae are not easy to identify, the "unidentified bird" category contained only one, so this was not a case of gull vertebrae not being recognized. While taphonomic factors may have been involved (vertebrae and sternum are more fragile than limb bones), differential preservation could not have accounted for all of the bias; the quadrate and scapula are fairly robust bones, but were also underrepresented, whereas a fragile skull survived. There appeared to be selection in favour of wings and legs, with wing bones more common. Twenty-eight of all gull bones (42.4%) were wing elements and 18 (27.3%) were leg. The only modifications noted were cut marks on one Laridae and two *Larus* bones; these included disarticulation cuts on the carpometacarpus when the tip of the wing was cut off, and transverse chops through two ulnae near the proximal end, one of which also had several knife cuts.

Murre

Two bones from either a common or thick-billed murre were recovered from one excavation unit. Neither species is known to breed in the area. The common murre winters on the coast from the Bering Strait south to California; the thick-billed murre is less common but "may winter regularly in northern British Columbia waters" (Guiguet, 1978:80). Represented were the posterior half of a mandible and a whole phalanx 1 digit 2, neither of which was modified.

Great horned owl

This bird, which breeds and is a year-round resident in the site area, was represented by a single bone, the proximal third of a radius. No modifications were noted.

Raven

Three raven bones were identified, two wing elements and one leg bone. A carpometacarpus had been chopped through and showed two superficial knife cuts just below the chop mark. An ulna and a tarsometatarsus were unmodified. The raven is a year-round resident in the site area.

Thrushes

There were two bones from this group. One, a complete humerus, was thought to have come from a varied thrush. It was a perfect match morphologically for this species, but the reference collection lacked a Townsend's solitaire, which is the same size. The other bone was part of a skull (a nasal and premaxilla), identified only to the thrush subfamily (Turdinae), but it was the size of a varied thrush. Robin, hermit thrush, varied thrush, and Swainson's thrush breed in the area today; Townsend's solitaire breeds not too far away (Godfrey, 1986).

Unidentified bird

Eighty-nine fragments could only be identified as avian. A few might have been gull, including fragments of a carpometacarpus and a furculum, a phalanx (size of kittiwake), an ulnar midshaft fragment, the centrum of a vertebra (possibly medium-large gull), and a limb bone fragment the size of a small to medium sized gull radius. No modifications were noted on any of the unidentified group.

Fish

Spiny dogfish

There were seven bones from this species, all vertebrae. Spiny dogfish frequently swim at the surface in pursuit of small fish such as herring (Lamb and Edgell, 1986). The flesh is edible and the skin can be used as sandpaper. The liver is rich in oils and vitamins; large livers from old dogfish are richer in Vitamin A than smaller ones. Mature dogfish are available only during the summer months in Hecate Strait and Dixon Entrance, although immature dogfish are available year-round (Hart, 1973).

Salmonidae (salmon, trout and whitefish family)

The family Salmonidae includes three subfamilies: Salmoninae (salmon and trout), Coregoninae (whitefish and cisco), and Thymallinae (grayling). A recent revision of Salmoninae (Smith and Stearley, 1989) moves west coast *Salmo* (rainbow and cutthroat trouts) to *Oncorhynchus* (salmon). The salmonid group was obviously important to the Greenville site people, as 7,021 bones (44.2% of the non-intrusive identified bone) came from fish belonging to this family. Most, if not all, of the bones were from the Salmoninae subfamily; no Coregoninae or Thymallinae were identified. A total 6,878 bones were identified as *Oncorhynchus /Salvelinus,* 89 as *Oncorhynchus,* and 54 only as family Salmonidae.

The 54 bones identified to family level were mostly spines, with a few fragments of basipterygia. It was impossible to distinguish between Coregoninae and Salmoninae for these elements. The bones identified as *Oncorhynchus* were two first vertebrae and elements of the pectoral and pelvic girdles, mostly basipterygia. All but three *Oncorhynchus/Salvelinus* bones were vertebrae; the exceptions included fragments of a cleithrum, mesocoracoid, and postcleithrum 2, all of which are pectoral elements found just posterior to the gills. No cranial elements were present.

Some modifications were noted. Eighty-two vertebrae had cut marks; all were chopped transversely through on a diagonal. Eight vertebrae were charred, and two calcined. The only pathology noted was in six vertebrae from one catalogue number; the vertebrae were fused in three groups of two each, perhaps from the same fish.

Following the revised taxonomy, seven species of *Oncorhynchus* are found in the site area, including five salmon (pink, chum, sockeye, chinook, and coho) and two trout (rainbow and cutthroat). All the salmon are anadromous. The two trout species occur as both freshwater and anadromous forms; the sea-run forms are known as steelhead trout and coastal cutthroat trout. Cutthroat trout spawn mostly in February and March; some steelheads enter fresh water in winter, and others in summer.

Chinook (spring salmon) is the earliest salmon to reach the Nass River, arriving in April (McNeary, 1976). They come in several waves, with peak catches from mid-June to the end of July (Aro and Shepard, 1967). Chinook is the largest of the five species; some individuals weigh more than 100 lb. (45 kg), but most are about 20 lb. (9 kg).

The Nass River is an important spawning area for sockeye (Hart, 1973). They run early, and peak catches are made in the last week of June and first week of July. Most weigh 5-6 lb. (2-3 kg) (McNeary, 1976).

Pink (or humpback) salmon is the most abundant species in British Columbia. Spawning normally takes place in late August and early September in northern areas. In the Nass River area, the largest catches are usually made in late July and early August (Aro and Shepard, 1967). Pink salmon are, on average, a little smaller than sockeye (McNeary, 1976).

Chum (or dog) salmon arrive after the humpbacks; the run occurs in August and early September, and lasts about a month. Chum salmon are larger than pink and coho salmon (Aro and Shepard, 1967; McNeary, 1976).

The most widespread British Columbia salmon species is coho. Spawning occurs later than for the others, mostly in October and early November, but may continue on into December (McNeary, 1976). According to Aro and Shepard (1967), the peak catch is from the third week of July to the first week of September in the Nass River area, although McNeary (1976) puts it considerably later, with the greatest numbers caught in November.

Osmeridae (eulachon and smelt family)

The other major fish group in the faunal sample was the family Osmeridae, which includes eulachon, surf smelt, capelin, night smelt, and longfin smelt, all found in the area. A lack of reference material for the latter two species, plus the small size of all members of this family (none exceed 9" (23 cm); Hart, 1973) precluded identification to species level.

A total 6,078 Osmeridae bones were recovered, all vertebrae except for ten cranial and pectoral elements. Some vertebrae were found scattered throughout the site's deposits in small quantities, but most occurred in four separately catalogued concentrations: 190 vertebrae in one, 491 in another, an estimated 1,375 vertebrae in a third, and an estimated 3,894 vertebrae in the fourth. The last two groups were adjacent clusters in Unit 8, Layer B, accounting for 5,269 bones, or 86.7% of the total sample of Osmeridae.

Gadidae (cod family)

This family contains four species in the area, walleye pollock, Pacific cod, Pacific tomcod, and Pacific hake. The faunal sample contained 2,027 bones from this family (12.62% of all identified bone). Only one species was definitely identified, the walleye pollock (also known as whiting or bigeye), with 1,227 bones and a MNI count of 40 (on the basis of fifth vertebrae). Another 527 bones were identified as walleye pollock/Pacific cod, and 273 bones were taken simply to family level.

Walleye pollock and Pacific cod are tricky to distinguish, requiring careful examination under a microscope for most of the cranial elements. Even with this procedure, it was difficult to distinguish between the two species for some elements, mainly the articular, ceratohyal, preoperculum, and supracleithrum. The post-temporal also gave some difficulty, with 16 identified as pollock and 13 as cod/pollock. Most other cranial elements could be identified to species if the right part was present. For the vertebrae, the first three were quite difficult, while the fifth was easiest. Vertebrae generally were found to be "simpler" in pollock, a bit more complex along the sides, with more "in-filling" in Pacific cod. All gadid elements that could be identified to species were walleye pollock; no Pacific cod were identified. This is in sharp contrast with fish remains from the Boardwalk site at Prince Rupert Harbour, where Pacific cod was the only gadid fish identified (Stewart, 1974). As pointed out by the investigator, reference material was rather limited; it is not clear from her report whether walleye pollock was one of the available reference specimens.

Walleye pollock and Pacific cod have many similarities in habitat. J.L. Hart (1973) mentions that walleye pollock occur from California to the Bering Strait, where they are found in shallow to moderate depths, from the surface down to 386 m, generally on a sandy or muddy bottom. Pacific cod are also found from California to the Bering Strait; they are "mostly benthic but occasionally taken in quite shallow water" (ibid., p. 223) where the substrate is sandy or muddy (Lamb and Edgell, 1986). Both species school. With 527 bones identified as walleye pollock/Pacific cod, it is puzzling that no Pacific cod were identified. The answer may lie in niche specification. Pacific cod normally are found close to the bottom, while walleye pollock are found more often in the middle and upper part of the water column (Allen and Smith, 1988). Thus, walleye pollock may have been more readily caught than the bottom-dwelling Pacific cod, especially if nets were used.

The element distribution for the gadids by region of the body was quite different from that for the salmonids, as may be seen on Figure 24. The figure draws a comparison between all the bones from the walleye pollock, walleye pollock/Pacific cod, and Gadidae categories, as opposed to all the bones from the salmonids (*Oncorhynchus, Oncorhynchus/Salvelinus,* and Salmonidae categories). The most striking difference was in the head region. Cranial elements made up 20% of the gadid bones but were completely absent in the salmonids.

Modifications on the gadid bones included three charred (supracleithrum, vertebra, and maxilla), and two pathological vertebrae. Cuts were noted on several bones, most commonly on parasphenoids; one cleithrum, one premaxilla, one vertebra, and ten parasphenoids were cut. The parasphenoids were chopped transversely and in three cases longitudinally as well. The parasphenoid is a long narrow bone in the head that extends almost the length of the neurocranium. Transverse cuts at the narrow part of the parasphenoid mean that the pollock heads were cut across slightly in front of the gills; in some cases the head was split down the middle as well. However, it is often difficult to detect cuts on fish bones because of the texture of the bone; occasionally, marks due to breakage will mimic the sharp edges made by cutting. In the case of the parasphenoids, definite cut marks were noted in only two instances; there was a slight element of doubt in the the other eight examples, and they were described as "appears cut."

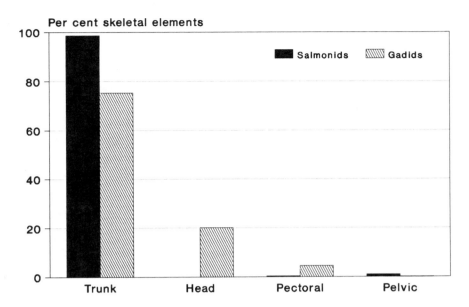

FIGURE 24. Skeletal element distributions for salmonids and gadids by region of the body.

Scorpaenidae (rockfish family)

There are two genera and at least 37 species of the rockfish family in British Columbia waters. Only one bone, the anterior half of a large premaxilla, was present in the faunal sample. The various species of rockfish are extremely difficult to distinguish osteologically, and reference specimens were not available for many of them. Therefore, no attempt was made to take the bone to genus or species level.

Flatfish (flounders and halibut)

This group was represented by 318 bones from at least four species. Most of the bones (67%) were identified as arrowtooth flounder, which is abundant along the northern part of the coast. It occurs in depths to 730-900 m (Hart, 1973) and "only rarely invades depths as shallow as 20 m" (Lamb and Edgell, 1986:202). At least six arrowtooth flounders were present, based on six "atlas" vertebrae. Cranial elements were rare; only one quadrate and one operculum fragment were present. The other 211 bones were vertebrae. No modifications were noted on any of the bones.

Another 74 bones, all unmodified vertebrae, were identified as arrowtooth flounder/petrale sole. Petrale sole occur along most of the British Columbia coast, at depths from surface to 550 m. Concentrations are found in Queen Charlotte Sound, Hecate Strait, and Dixon Entrance, especially after spawning in late winter and early spring (Hart, 1973).

One bone, a vertebra, was identified as flathead/sand sole. Most flathead sole along the British Columbia coast are found at depths between 275 m and 366 m, but they sometimes occur in water as shallow as 5 m. Sand sole are found in shallow water, usually on sandy bottom. Both species spawn in April in northern British Columbia (Hart, 1973; Lamb and Edgell, 1986).

Six bones (three vertebrae and three branchiostegal rays) were identified as Pacific halibut; no modifications were noted. Based on vertebral size differences, at least two individuals were represented. One vertebra was approximately half the size of a 128 lb. (58 kg) reference specimen; the other two were considerably smaller. Halibut are found from near the surface to depths of 1100 m, most commonly between 55 m and 422 m. Most halibut along the British Columbia coast are immature; the older, larger fish are found in deeper water. Spawning occurs from November to January at depths of 275-412 m. The average landed halibut in modern times is about 35 lb. (16 kg), although halibut weighing over 475 lb. (215 kg) have been caught (Hart, 1973). Based on rough size estimates, both halibut in the faunal sample were immature and were probably taken in the 55-422 m depth range.

The only other flatfish species which could be determined was the starry flounder, represented by two vertebrae. Starry flounders are common along the British Columbia coast, usually in shallow water, but they occur as deep as 275 m. They are more tolerant of low salinity than other British Columbia flatfish, and young are often taken in the Fraser River. Spawning occurs in shallow water from February to April (ibid.).

Twenty-two bones, all vertebrae, could only be identified as Pleuronectiformes, the taxonomic order which includes two families of flatfish. Three were from the same undetermined species, species A, while another two were species B; neither was represented in the reference collection which narrowed the possibilities from 17 to eight (ignoring hybrid sole whose taxonomic status is unresolved). Of the eight possibilities, two were unlikely; the roughscale sole is rare, with only two records in the eastern Pacific, while the deepsea sole is a deep-water fish, occurring at depths from 320-1370 m and mostly below 730 m. However, the other six species are fairly common in shallow water on the British Columbia coast. The butter sole, for example, is "abundant in summer in shallow silty depressions in northwest

Hecate Strait, and as a spawning concentration in late winter in Skidegate Inlet" (ibid., p. 620). The most likely possibilities for species A and species B are the following: speckled sanddab, Pacific sanddab, yellowfin sole, c-o sole, slender sole, and butter sole.

Unidentified fish

A total 2,058 bones could only be identified as fish, most of which were vertebral fragments. Two vertebrae were charred. No other modifications were noted.

Amphibians

Fifty-three western toad bones were recovered. At least four animals were represented, with elements from all body regions. The bones were thought intrusive, unrelated to human activities at the site. Most occurred in clusters: 30 bones were found in the baulk wall area of Unit 5, seven were found inside the skull of Burial 38, five in Unit 9, and five in Unit 11. Toads have projections on their hind feet which they use like spades to burrow into the ground, sometimes to a considerable depth (Cook, 1984). Most likely, the presence of the bones was due to the natural deaths of toads in their burrows.

Discussion

Faunal assemblages from archaeological sites are usually valued interpretively for the light they might shed on the food resources of earlier human populations. Indeed, archaeologists often emphasize "subsistence strategies" in their attempts to explain prehistoric cultural dynamics. For the Northwest Coast, the premise derives from the fact that shell middens are invariably assumed to reflect habitation refuse, effectively the "garbage" of past villages or camps that has accumulated over centuries or ·millennia. Northwest Coast ethnographic sources, however, indicate that animals were used for a variety of cultural purposes, in addition to food, and there is little reason to suspect that such uses, aside from the obvious artifact indicators, would not also be reflected in archaeological faunal assemblages. The Greenville site adds another dimension in that it appears primarily as a burial ground, rather than habitation site, in spite of its "kitchen midden" nature.

If one were to interpret the Greenville site faunal assemblage as an indicator of ancestral Nisga'a dietary practices, it would not be surprising, perhaps, that fish were so prevalent, accounting for over 97% of the identified non-intrusive bone and over 81% of the associated MNI count (Fig. 23). Fish were, historically, the staple

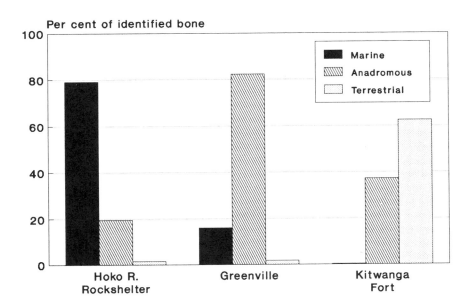

FIGURE 25. Archaeological site distributions of marine, anadromous, and terrestrial vertebrate resources.

food of the Nisga'a, the most important being the anadramous salmon (all five species) and eulachon (McNeary, 1976:86). Appropriately in this context, salmonids and Osmeridae made up the bulk of the identified fish bone, almost 85% in NISP terms and just under 78% in MNI terms.

The faunal assemblage also provides a "correct" ecological orientation for the Greenville site in terms of food resources potentially available to its location irrespective of ancestral implications. This is demonstrated on Figure 25 which compares the Greenville vertebrate fauna with those from two other Northwest Coast archaeological sites in terms of marine, anadromous, and terrestrial proportions. The two sites are Hoko River Rockshelter, an 800-year-old habitation site near the mouth of the Hoko River on the Olympic Peninsula of Washington (Wigen and Stucki, 1988), and Kitwanga Fort, a fortified settlement on the Kitwanga River near its confluence with the Skeena River approximately 100 km due east of Greenville, occupied during late prehistoric and early historic times (Rick, 1989). These sites were chosen for comparison because of their decidedly coast and inland locations and also because they are among only a very few Northwest Coast archaeological sites from which faunal assemblages, like that of Greenville, seem to have been recovered without selection bias.

The marine species represented on Figure 25 include all sea mammals, sea, pelagic, and shore birds (including gulls, ducks, and geese), and all fish except salmonids and Osmeridae (the anadromous quotient), as identified in this and the two other studies. The terrestrial species include all land mammals except those assumed intrusive, and eagles, hawks, grouse, cranes, raven, owl, and songbirds. Canids were included because of the cut marks on some of the Greenville elements suggesting the animals might have been eaten. Canid elements were also represented at Hoko River Rockshelter (0.18% of the identified bone), but not at Kitwanga Fort.

The three sites are clearly differentiated by their dominant faunal groups, marine at Hoko River Rockshelter, anadromous at Greenville, and terrestrial at Kitwanga Fort. The Hoko River Rockshelter orientation is not startling given its position virtually on the shores of Juan de Fuca Strait, near the open Pacific. Kitwanga Fort is an upland site in the Hazelton Mountains, far removed from the Skeena River estuary and tidal limit. Greenville is in a lowland riverine environment intermediate between these two situations.

It is interesting to speculate that the portrait shown on Figure 25 might be simulated for the Nass River itself if refuse deposits were to be excavated at Kincolith *(Gingolx)*, at the mouth of the Nass, and the old upriver Nisga'a village of Gitladamaks *(Gitlaxt'aamiks)*(locations on Fig. 1, Chapter I). Stephen McNeary (1976) spoke of the "coast-interior dimension" of Nisga'a ecology, noting that those upriver had ready access to large herbivores, bear, and grouse, while those down river had easier access to marine resources and the spawning grounds of anadromous fish. McNeary's study focussed on the upriver Nisga'a and, therefore, few details were supplied for Greenville, although he did point out that the people of the lower Nass heavily depended on trade for inland and upland food resources and animal skins for clothing.

That anadromous species formed a significant, if not dominant, proportion of the fauna at Kitwanga Fort (salmonids only) can be attributed to its location near the Skeena River and related cultural ecological factors. The site is in the territories of the Gitksan who formed one of the three dialect-based Tsimshian subgroups and held lineage-based rights to fishing grounds on the Skeena (Adams, 1973). Salmon was a prized food resource for all Tsimshian (the "decisive" one in the words of Viola Garfield (Garfield and Wingert, 1951:13)), including those on the coast who formed the third subgroup, Coast Tsimshian. Reference has been made in this chapter to faunal remains from the prehistoric Boardwalk site located in Coast Tsimshian territory, and the reader may rightly question why this site was not chosen as a coastal anchor for comparison on Figure 25. Such a comparison may have given more insight into the three subareas than ethnographically acknowledged, particularly in quantitative terms, since they are commonly lumped in Northwest Coast discussions of subsistence and ecology involving the Tsimshian (e.g., Fladmark, 1975). Unfortunately, there was heavy selection bias in the recovery of faunal remains from the Boardwalk site (Stewart, 1974, 1977), the only one of several excavated in the Prince Rupert Harbour region (MacDonald and Inglis, 1981) for which comprehensive faunal identifications are available.[15]

Despite the appropriate broad brush ancestral dietary and ecological portraits painted by the faunal assemblage for the Greenville site, there are peculiarities of detail that need to be considered. Some of them involve the fish and their relative proportions.

While not specifically identified because of an incomplete reference collection for the family, the tenor of this analysis has been that the Osmeridae represented in the Greenville fauna were eulachon. The Nass, from a Tlingit word signifying "food depot" (Collison, 1981), was virtually synonymous with eulachon to all northern Northwest Coast Indians, having the richest runs in the area. Eulachon were very important to the Nisga'a, both as a source of food and as a commodity for trade with outer coast and inland peoples. In the 19th century, William Collison (ibid.) wrote that eulachon were taken literally by the tons ("five to ten tons" per household) during their ascent of the river in mid-March. Some were roasted or boiled and eaten fresh, or smoked and dried for later consumption, but most were rendered into oil as a highly valued condiment and sometimes food preservative, the definitive eulachon product for trade (see, also, McNeary, 1976: 13, 86-89). The rendering process was carried out at fish camps, on shore near where the fish were taken. Today's Greenville residents continue this tradition in the spring, travelling about 4 km down river to Fishery Bay *(Da'oots'ip)* (GgTj 2 on Fig. 1) where cabins and rendering facilities are maintained for an annual three or four weeks harvesting of eulachon and production of "grease," as the finished product is commonly known.

Osmeridae accounted for 38.25% of the non-intrusive identified bone in the Greenville faunal sample. The vast majority of the specimens (87.9%) were recorded in Layer B, particularly the middle to lower levels, suggesting an antiquity

---

[15] As reported in Table 4, Chapter III, the volume of the midden deposits excavated at the Boardwalk site was 1,041 m³, a figure over seven times the estimated volume of the Greenville deposits. Frances Stewart (1977) reported the recovery of only 1,409 more vertebrate faunal elements, thus lending further doubt to the representativeness of the Boardwalk sample for ecological interpretations.

on the order of 1,000 to 1,500 years (Chapter II). If that period mirrored the ethnographic pattern and the site represented a village deposit, the number of eulachon would appear extraordinarily high. Eulachon would undoubtedly have been underrepresented as a procured resource. Whatever eulachon were rendered into oil would not likely be reflected in the deposits of a permanent settlement. Traditionally, the solid matter remaining from the extraction process was discarded at the fishery (McNeary, 1976:90). Even at a fish camp, it is unlikely that this solid matter would be preserved; according to Stephen McNeary (ibid., p. 91), the cooking process used to render the oil was not completed until "the bones (would) squash easily when pressed with the finger."

Most probably, any eulachon bones found in the refuse of a village deposit would be from fish that had been smoked or dried and later transported to the site. Insofar as the Greenville midden itself is concerned, the eulachon bones found there may very well have been the remains of food offerings for the dead. As mentioned earlier, most of the bones (86.7%) were found in two adjacent clusters in one excavation unit. One cluster formed a discrete thin lens 70 cm long and up to 3 cm thick wherein some of the vertebrae were recorded as articulated, implying, at least in part, the deposition of intact fish. The two clusters were not associated with any human burials, but a third cluster of 491 elements (a minimum of six or seven fish) was found in the matrix "around" Burial 29, one of the earliest burials in the site. Unfortunately, this burial had been disturbed by a later interment, so the association could not be concluded as definite.

As food, eulachon proved vital to the Nisga'a at a time when winter reserves were almost exhausted, but apparently did not keep well and, therefore, contributed little to long-term provisions (McNeary, 1976:89). Rather, salmon were the mainstay of the traditional diet, with most of those taken during the various runs between spring and late fall dried, smoked, and stored for year-round consumption (ibid., p. 92). Given this ethnographic pattern and, again, a cautious projection into the past, the faunal sample might have been expected to show a significantly greater proportion of salmon than eulachon bones at a village site, particularly one with the time span of Greenville. The ratio of salmonids to Osmeridae at Greenville, however, was not vastly different, 1.2:1 on the basis of bone counts and 1.25:1 in MNI terms. It is not so much that there weren't enough salmon represented, but that there may have been too many eulachon. This is more to suggest that the Greenville eulachon were the remains of mortuary rather than everyday food. Perhaps they were deposited on the site only within a few weeks or days of the late winter or early spring deaths of some humans, possibly from starvation after an especially long winter, a recurrent theme in the Tsimshian and Nisga'a tales collected by Franz Boas (1916:399).

It remains to consider the predominance of salmon vertebrae and lack of cranial parts. Both taphonomic and cultural factors may have been at work. In their study of the Hoko River Rockshelter fauna, also within a shell midden environment, Rebecca Wigen and Barbara Stucki (1988) noted a paucity of salmon cranial bones as opposed to those of other fish and suggested differential decay as an explanation:

> . . . subjectively, we think that salmon cranial bones are particularly fragile, that flatfish crania are more durable, and that the crania of rockfish, red Irish lord and greenling are the toughest of these fishes' bones. (ibid., pp. 106-107).

The comparison in the present study has been between gadids and salmonids. Our own observations indicate that cranial bones of walleye pollock appear less fragile than those of salmon, perhaps accounting for the differences in element distributions shown on Figure 24.

Cultural factors could have related to the way fish were prepared and used as food. Traditionally, preparation of salmon for drying and smoking involved cleaning the fish, cutting off the head and tail, and cutting the flesh away from the backbone (McNeary, 1976:97-98). Tails and some heads, especially of the chinook salmon, were roasted and smoked for winter food, and salmon heads left to "ripen" in the river for several days were considered a delicacy among the Nisga'a, as they were among other northern Northwest Coast groups (Niblack, 1890).

Salmon backbones appear to have been discarded during the drying and smoking process. While backbone parts may have occasionally been recycled for later use in times of need, a circumstance that has been described for the Tlingit of Alaska (de Laguna, 1972:399), salmon backs were considered "poor food" by the Nisga'a (Boas, 1916:406) and may not have figured as a common dietary item. This raises an interesting possibility for the source of the Greenville site deposits. Although smokehouses are maintained in today's Nass River villages, most of the smoking in the old days apparently was done at the fish camps and the resultant meat transported to the village (McNeary, 1976:97-98). Perhaps the shell deposits reflected those of a fish camp or, possibly, a specialized activity area in a village where the backbones were discarded, while the heads, tails, and meat of the fish were taken to the village or main living area for storage and consumption. Unlike the eulachon remains, the salmon remains probably did not reflect mortuary food.

No clusters of these bones were apparent in the deposits.[16] Elsewhere in this book, it is noted that high status, "wealthy" people may have been buried at the site (see Chapters III and VII), hardly expected recipients for "poor food" in a mortuary context.

The presence of other fish bones in the Greenville site might also suggest a processing area, although few details are available in the ethnographies on how fish other than eulachon and salmon were prepared and used. The predominance of gadid vertebrae suggests processing similar to that for salmon, and, perhaps, gadid heads were not as relished as salmon heads. It is probably significant that most of the other identified fish, though marine, were not deep water types, given the location of Greenville. Their presence, however, does indicate that "other fish" were used. In a study of Northwest Coast paleoecology, Knut Fladmark (1975) reported the principal faunal resources of the Tsimshian as salmon, eulachon, herring, "other fish," and halibut, in that order of importance, followed by sea mammals, land mammals, and shellfish. While another broad brush portrait for all Tsimshian, the sequence involving the fish is closely simulated by the Greenville site findings except for the conspicuous absence of herring. Almost 400 herring bones were recovered at Hoko River Rockshelter (Wigen and Stucki, 1988), so midden preservation was probably not a factor. Their absence at Greenville is likely a more detailed reflection of ecological orientation in conjunction with timing factors. Herring spawn up the Nass only as far as Iceberg Bay, across from Kincolith, and almost simultaneously with the run of eulachon who travel upriver to and beyond Angidaa, above Greenville (locations on Fig. 1). Locals in the Greenville area could not be in both places at the same time, and eulachon were probably far more important to them than herring. Alternatively, absence of the bones may have been due to the fact that herring, like eulachon, did not keep well for storage purposes (McNeary, 1976:99), another point for the presence of eulachon bones at Greenville as a ritual rather than dietary element.

About the only other clear indication of food at the Greenville site was represented among the sea mammal bones. More than half the sample of seal bones

---

[16] There was no reason to conclude that the clustered eulachon bones might have been cache deposits unrelated to the mortuary significance of the site. This is a fair assumption for consideration since, prior to the use of wooden storage bins, today as in the late 19th century (Collison, 1981:41), freshly caught eulachon were stored in pits to await their processing into oil at the fish camp (McNeary, 1976:90). There was no suggestion of pits with the eulachon bones in the Greenville deposits and, as noted previously, one of the two large clusters was represented as an elongate lens, not as a pit-like grouping as might be expected in a cache.

and one-third of the sea lion bones were from flippers, "a special delicacy" for the Nisga'a (McNeary, 1976:107).

With relatively few exceptions, it can be concluded that almost all of the remaining elements in the faunal assemblage probably reflected cultural uses other than food. For example, over 80% of the bird bones were from the wings or legs, and wing bones were twice as abundant as leg bones. This suggests the use of feathers. Of related interest is the prevalence of gulls among the birds. According to William Collison (1981:40-42), gulls arrived by the hundreds and thousands during the 19th century Nass River eulachon runs, and while they sometimes served as a source of food, they also supplied the Indians with "comfortable featherbeds and pillows." The long hollow bones of wings and legs could also have served as raw material for awls, beads, and whistles, as described in Appendix B. As noted previously, most of the deer bones were those that might most usefully serve as tools and ceremonial items. The sea otter and beaver bones were those that might expectedly have been left in pelts, while the beaver teeth were those valued for wood-carving. Dogs may have been eaten, but the prevalence of cranial parts at the site may have indicated ritual significance related to its mortuary context, a subject treated in Chapter III.

Human Biology

This chapter and the following report information derived from the human skeletal remains during laboratory analysis. Exceptions include age at death and sex determinations, already reported in Chapter II, and tooth abrasion facets from labrets, reported in Chapter III. The purpose here is to detail continuous (metric) and discontinuous or discrete (non-metric) morphological skeletal features which might be used to reconstruct the biology of the Greenville population sample and ultimately ascertain its affinities with other Northwest Coast groups.

Stature and Limb Proportions

Measurements of limb bones are used to reconstruct the height of an individual during life and provide information on body proportions. Almost all measurements in this study were taken according to the techniques described by Georges Olivier (1969). Summary statistics for the adult male and female samples from Greenville are reported in Appendix G, Tables 16 and 17. In Table 16, I have also included a deltoid index introduced by Owen Beattie (1981:105) in his study of south coast British Columbia skeletons.

Table 17 reports limb proportions and stature. For males, stature was estimated from lower limb bone lengths using the regression equations developed by Mildred Trotter and Goldine C. Gleser (1958) for "Mongoloid" males. Stature in females was estimated from lower limb bone lengths using those authors' equations for modern white females (Trotter and Gleser, 1952), as none are available for "Mongoloid" females.[17] The two sets of equations have previously been applied to native coastal British Columbia skeletal populations and there is little reason to

---

[17] "Mongoloid" is a classical term used by anthropologists to differentiate "yellow-skinned" peoples from whites ("Caucasoid") and blacks ("Negroid"), the three so-called major human races. Although the names may be questioned, studies have shown skeletal variations of sufficient importance to maintain the categories in medico-legal investigations of unknown human remains for the purposes of identification (e.g., Krogman and Iscan, 1986). Stature estimation is frequently used in such cases, and limb bone lengths vary among whites, blacks, and "Mongoloid" peoples relative to total body height. Because of their presumed northeast Asiatic origins and some physical similarities, American Indians have traditionally been included with "Mongoloid" peoples in forensic anthropology.

suspect that they do not give acceptable estimates of living stature for these groups (Cybulski, 1978a; 1990).

In the 19th century, native peoples from different Northwest Coast cultural groups were measured by Franz Boas and co-workers. Group male means ranged from 160.66 cm (5'3") to 165.89 cm (5'5") (Cybulski, 1990:54). The estimated heights of the Greenville males, based on their skeletal remains, ranged from 159.60 cm (5'3") to 168.64 cm (5'6") with a mean of 163.54 cm (5'4"). The Greenville females varied individually from 147.08 cm (4'10") to 163.50 cm (5'4") with a mean of 152.95 cm (5'). A 10 to 12 cm mean sex difference is usual for most human populations.

The top part of Figure 26 compares the mean heights of the men of Greenville with those from Blue Jackets Creek, Prince Rupert Harbour, a historic Haida skeletal series, and a sample of Nisga'a living in the 19th century. The data for the Haida and Nisga'a are as previously reported in my overview of Northwest Coast human biology for the Smithsonian Institution's Handbook of North American Indians (ibid.). The data for Blue Jackets Creek and Prince Rupert Harbour differ slightly from that presentation due to the addition of three and four individuals respectively. In the earlier report, I included only the Blue Jackets Creek males identified by Jeffrey Murray (1981), while the data here incorporate my revised sex identifications for the series as explained in Chapter III. I have studied additional Prince Rupert Harbour remains since the manuscript for the 1990 article was prepared.

The men of Greenville appear to be just over 2 cm (close to 1") shorter on the average than their presumed 19th century Nisga'a descendants. Indeed, the chart suggests that a temporal trend toward increased stature might have existed among north coast British Columbia males from 4,000-5,000 years ago to the 19th century. However, the sample sizes for the Early Developmental Stage of prehistory, here represented by Blue Jackets Creek, and for the Late Developmental Stage, represented by Greenville, are small and, therefore, may not be representative. No similar temporal trend is evident for men of the British Columbia coast as a whole as may be seen in the bottom part of Figure 26. In this connection, it may be noted that the largely Early Developmental Stage Namu series of males present a mean stature similar to those of the historic period samples (Cybulski, 1990).

Table 8 provides some comparative skeletal data on limb proportions and other limb indices. The deltoid index is of interest because it provides a measure of the sinuousness of the humerus, the bone of the upper arm: the higher the index, the more strongly developed is the upper part of the shaft, the portion to which the large shoulder muscle (*Deltoideus*) and some back and chest muscles attach. The

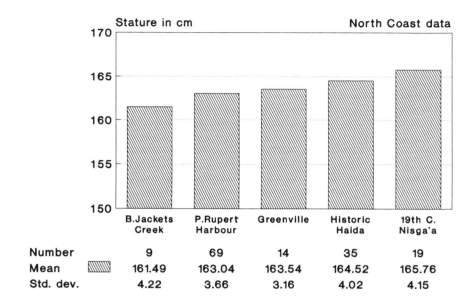

		B.Jackets Creek	P.Rupert Harbour	Greenville	Historic Haida	19th C. Nisga'a
Number		9	69	14	35	19
Mean		161.49	163.04	163.54	164.52	165.76
Std. dev.		4.22	3.66	3.16	4.02	4.15

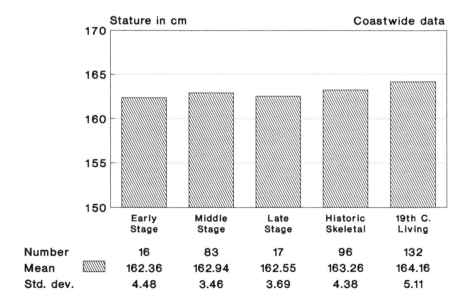

		Early Stage	Middle Stage	Late Stage	Historic Skeletal	19th C. Living
Number		16	83	17	96	132
Mean		162.36	162.94	162.55	163.26	164.16
Std. dev.		4.48	3.46	3.69	4.38	5.11

FIGURE 26. *Heights of men in British Columbia samples: north coast groups above; coastwide series arranged by time below.*

upper arm bones in the Prince Rupert Harbour skeletons are quite strongly developed, and they produce the highest deltoid index so far known for any group of coastal British Columbia skeletons including Greenville. The Greenville index is more comparable to that of Namu, though somewhat higher, and higher than that reported for prehistoric skeletons from the Strait of Georgia (Beattie, 1981). There does not appear to be an appreciable sex difference in these groups, suggesting that sinuousness of the humerus may be a group feature of long-standing adaptive significance rather than a functional consequence of an individual's lifetime activity. The female left deltoid index is 112.16 for Namu (Curtin, 1984), 119.73 for Prince Rupert Harbour, and 113.89 for Greenville. No data for either sex are available for Blue Jackets Creek.

All four groups in Table 8 are broad-shouldered in terms of the claviculo-humeral index which relates the length of the clavicle (collarbone) to the length of the humerus. By convention, a relatively long clavicle is identified by an index of 48 or higher (Olivier, 1969:214).

The radiohumeral index is alternately known as the brachial index, an expression of the relative length of the forearm to the upper arm. The indices for Namu, Prince Rupert Harbour, and Greenville denote forearms which are neither relatively short nor long, while that for Blue Jackets Creek identifies a relatively long forearm (Olivier, 1969:232). Numerically, however, there seems to be a dichotomy between Blue Jackets Creek and Namu on one side, and Greenville and Prince Rupert Harbour on the other, with the greatest difference shown between Blue Jackets Creek and Greenville.

The tibiofemoral index, alternately known as the crural index, relates the length of the lower leg to the thigh (femur). There is little variation among the four groups in this character, as there is in the humerofemoral and intermembral indices, both of which are expressions of relative upper to lower limb lengths. The humerofemoral index, however, grows progressively larger from Blue Jackets Creek, through Namu and Prince Rupert Harbour, to Greenville.

All four pilastric indices identify "weak" femoral pilasters according to conventional classifications (ibid., p. 263). However, Namu is numerically outstanding, suggesting a more prominent linea aspera than that of the other groups. The linea aspera is an architectural feature which forms the posterior (back) border of the thighbone, an elongate ridge for the attachment of rump, thigh, and leg muscles. The Namu value suggests a more strongly developed lower limb than in the other groups.

TABLE 8. *Mean male limb indices for four B.C. coast skeletal series* [1]

Index	Blue Jackets	Namu	Prince Rupert	Greenville
Deltoid (L)	--	113.21	120.28	115.93
Pilastric (L)	104.77	108.76	104.14	103.69
Platymeric (L)	83.52	73.86	72.10	69.71
Cnemial (L)	61.29	61.11	64.70	61.38
Claviculohumeral	49.75	50.10	49.71	49.83
Radiohumeral	80.71	79.48	77.89	77.05
Tibiofemoral	81.70	81.38	82.16	81.79
Humerofemoral	72.20	73.04	73.80	73.90
Intermembral	71.84	71.75	72.15	71.70

[1] The four left side (L) index values for Namu are from A.J. Curtin's (1984) descriptive report. The other Namu index values were calculated from original individual measurements kindly supplied to me by A.J. Curtin (cf. Cybulski, 1990, Table 2). As in the other series reported here, those indices were calculated from average right and left side length measurements, or only the right or left side, as available for each individual. For Blue Jackets Creek, I recalculated all indices from Jeffrey Murray's (1981) published individual measurements using my revised sex identifications as explained in Chapter III (p. 48).

The platymeric index for Blue Jackets Creek is clearly outstanding among the four, differing by almost ten units from its nearest neighbour, Namu, and most unlike Greenville. In conventional classifications (Olivier, 1969:264), the values for Namu, Prince Rupert Harbour, and Greenville identify hyperplatymeria. This means that the upper part of the shaft of the femur is extremely flat in its anterior-posterior (front-to-back) direction. The value for Blue Jackets Creek is in the upper range of platymeria, meaning that the upper shaft is nearly rounded in all directions. According to one author, hyperplatymeria appears characteristic of American Indians in contrast to such diverse groups as Inuit, Australian aborigines, and 17th century British (Brothwell, 1981:89) whose indices are closer to or greater than that of Blue Jackets Creek.

The nearly identical cnemial indices for Blue Jackets Creek, Namu, and Greenville indicate platycnemic upper tibia (shin bone) shafts, or shafts which are flat in their medial-lateral (side-to-side) directions. The Prince Rupert Harbour value is different and within the mesocnemic range (Olivier, 1969:271), indicating an upper tibia shaft which is neither flat nor rounded.

Giving equal weight to all of the features described here, the men of Greenville appear more like the men of Prince Rupert Harbour than those of either Namu or Blue Jackets Creek.

Skull Size and Shape

Where possible, twenty-one measurements were taken on the Greenville crania and mandibles, and from these measurements, the cranial module and 13 indices were calculated, all according to the techniques outlined by Georges Olivier (1969) and William Bass (1981). Summary statistics for the resultant male and female samples are reported in Appendix G, Table 18.

Some comparative data, including the same series used for comparing limb proportions and indices, are reported in Table 9. The cranial module is an approximate indicator of the overall size of the neurocranium or braincase, depending on measurements of maximum length (glabello-occipital), breadth (biparietal), and height (basion-bregma). As an indicator of size, sex differences may be expected; male skulls are generally larger than female skulls, as exemplified by the cranial modules for the Greenville male and female samples reported in Table 18. With respect to the male mean values in Table 9, the Prince Rupert Harbour skulls are largest and the Namu skulls smallest. The Greenville skulls are intermediate in size between Namu and Blue Jackets Creek.

TABLE 9. Mean male cranial modules and craniometric indices for four B.C. coast skeletal series [1]

Feature	Blue Jackets	Namu	Prince Rupert	Greenville
Cranial module	155.87	151.85	157.20	153.90
Cranial (cephalic) index	73.54	75.83	76.08	80.48
Mean basion-height index	89.57	85.57	82.97	81.81
Transverse craniofacial index	92.44	104.13	100.03	101.03
Upper facial height index	59.09	53.44	50.60	48.37
Orbital index	86.32	84.74	81.18	80.99
Nasal index	47.71	45.00	48.68	50.14
Gnathic index	95.03	102.79	98.75	96.45
Maxillo-alveolar index	119.32	117.76	119.23	122.67

[1] All means for Namu are from A.J. Curtin's (1984) descriptive report. I recalculated those for Blue Jackets Creek from Jeffrey Murray's (1981) published individual measurements using my revised sex identifications as explained in Chapter III (p. 48).

The cranial index is similar to the cephalic index in the living, a traditional anthropological measure of the shape of the head depending on length and breadth. By convention, a cranial index less than 75 identifies a skull which is dolichocranic, or longheaded, while an index of 80 or greater identifies a skull which is brachycranic, or roundheaded (Olivier, 1969:131). The terms dolichocephalic and brachycephalic are usually applied to living individuals. Using distributional data on individual skulls from Blue Jackets Creek, Prince Rupert Harbour, and historic Haida, I previously illustrated an apparent trend from longheadedness to roundhead-edness through time on the north coast of British Columbia, possibly mimicking a trend to brachycephalization in human groups observed in other parts of the world (Cybulski, 1990:56). The north coast trend based on the prehistoric series appears borne out by the addition of Greenville and its male mean in the range of brachycrany. Five of eight measurable Greenville male skulls were in this range (one hyperbrachycranic) and none were dolichocranic. According to individual measurements reported by Franz Boas, 11 of 19 Nisga'a men living in the 19th century were brachycephalic and none were dolichocephalic (ibid., p. 53).

Figure 27 illustrates the distributions for Blue Jackets Creek, Prince Rupert Harbour, Greenville, and Nisga'a. In Table 9, it may be seen that the mean for Namu is closer to that of Prince Rupert Harbour than it is to Blue Jackets Creek. When individual variation is considered in the manner of Figure 27, the Namu skulls present an image further removed from Blue Jackets Creek, placing the group between Prince Rupert Harbour and Greenville. A.J. Curtin (1984:74) reported two male skulls as dolichocranic, three as mesocranic, and two as brachycranic. Thus, Namu, largely contemporary with Blue Jackets Creek, raises questions about the cranial index trend from the Early to Late Developmental Stages of prehistory apparent among the north coast groups. It may also be seen on Figure 27 that Greenville is much more like Nisga'a than like Prince Rupert Harbour despite its intermediate temporal position.

In addition to having the longest skulls of the groups in Table 9, Blue Jackets Creek has the highest, relative to length and breadth. Alone among the four groups, its mean basion-height index identifies the "high" category of conventional classification (Bass, 1981:65). The value for Namu borders on "high," at the uppermost end of the "medium" category range, while those for Prince Rupert Harbour and Greenville are decidedly "medium," neither high nor low in relation to length and breadth.

Blue Jackets Creek also appears uniquely different in its transverse craniofacial index, a measure of the breadth of the face relative to the breadth of the brain-case. Its very low value, akin to that often described for "Caucasoid" skulls (Olivier, 1969:150), indicates a very narrow facial skeleton. The values for the other three series, similar to those reported for Inuit and Australian aborigines (ibid.), indicate very broad facial skeletons relative to skull breadth. Namu has the broadest facial skeletons in this context, while Greenville and Prince Rupert Harbour are more similar to each other.

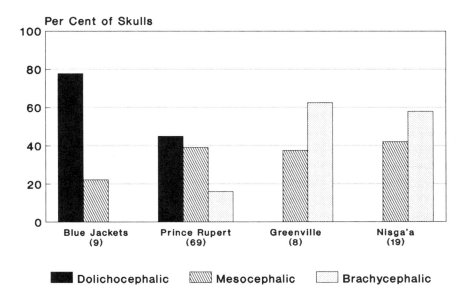

FIGURE 27. Distributions of male cranial (cephalic) indices in north coast British Columbia groups by descriptive category. (Sample sizes of individual skulls in parentheses).

The upper facial height index relates the breadth of the upper facial skeleton to its own height. Complementing the transverse craniofacial index, the upper facial index of Blue Jackets Creek alone defines a narrow or slender (leptene) face. Greenville has the lowest index, in the euryene classification which identifies a broad face relative to its height. The values for Namu and Prince Rupert Harbour are mesene, or medium, neither broad nor narrow in relation to height, but certainly broader than that of Blue Jackets Creek.

The orbital index appears to differentiate Blue Jackets Creek and Namu from Prince Rupert Harbour and Greenville. This index relates the height of the orbit, or eye socket, to its breadth. Blue Jackets Creek alone shows a value in the hypsiconch range of conventional classification (Olivier, 1969:152), identifying a high or narrow orbit. Namu is at the uppermost end of the mesoconch range, with a value that borders on being high or narrow. Prince Rupert Harbour and Greenville have decidedly mesoconch values; the orbits are neither high nor low in relation to their breadth.

The nasal index relates the breadth of the nasal opening to the height of the nasal area, measured from a point between the eye sockets, technically known as nasion, to the naso-spinal point at the base of the nasal opening. The values for

Greenville (highest), Prince Rupert Harbour, and Blue Jackets Creek identify mesorrhine noses, ones neither broad nor narrow in relation to height, while that for Namu identifies a leptorrhine nose, one with a narrow opening. The numerical range for the mesorrhine classification is only 3.9 units (ibid., p. 153). The Greenville index borders on platyrrhine (broad), and that for Blue Jackets Creek borders on leptorrhine.

The gnathic index measures the degree to which the facial skeleton projects anteriorly relative to the base of the skull. Namu and Prince Rupert Harbour have values conventionally classified as mesognathic (ibid., p. 158), meaning that the facial skeleton is mildly projecting. Their indices, however, are at opposite ends of this spectrum; Namu's borders on prognathism, a notably projecting face, while Prince Rupert Harbour's borders on orthognathism, a flat face. The values for Greenville and Blue Jackets Creek, the latter fully opposite from Namu, are decidedly orthognathic.

All four maxillo-alveolar indices identify brachyuranic, or broad, palates. The Greenville index is uniquely high, indicating a palate which is most broad of the four, while that for Namu is uniquely low (its palate is least broad).

Considering all of the skull indices reported in Table 9, a total of eight, Blue Jackets Creek is highest or lowest in six, and Greenville is highest or lowest in six. Speaking in relative terms, Greenville has the roundest (or broadest) and lowest skull vaults, the broadest facial skeletons in terms of their heights, the lowest (or broadest) orbits, the broadest nasal openings, and the broadest palates. There is an overall and particulate tendency to broadness in the Greenville skulls, though they are not far removed from Prince Rupert Harbour in some features. The Blue Jackets Creek skulls appear unique among the four groups in many shape features, and show an overall and particulate tendency to narrowness. Namu is highest or lowest in four indices, and seemingly unique in each of them. Prince Rupert Harbour does not appear distinctive among the four groups in any index. It features the highest cranial module, but its value is not far removed from that of Blue Jackets Creek.

Non-metric Skeletal Variants

Non-metric skeletal variants are structural elements of morphology observed for their presence or absence in skulls and other skeletal parts. They might include enamel pearls on the roots of molar teeth, congenitally missing third molars, or spina bifida occulta, features in the Greenville series which are described in the next chapter as developmental anomalies under the heading of paleopathology. There is, in fact, a fine line of interpretive perception between biology and paleopathology when it comes to the reporting of qualitative skeletal features. Many minor developmental anomalies which vary in their frequency of occurrence among different skeletal series may have a genetic basis for their expression and, therefore, be useful for study of the biological interrelatedness of earlier populations. In this report, I have taken a somewhat conventional approach by including in this chapter non-metric skeletal variants which have traditionally been reported for the purposes of measuring biological distance.

The frequencies of these variants are detailed for the adult segments of the Greenville burial population in Appendix H, Tables 19 and 20. Table 19 includes non-metric variants of the postcranial skeleton, many of which have been described and illustrated by Shelley R. Saunders (1978). Table 20 reports non-metric variants of the skull, some described and illustrated by A. Caroline Berry and R.J. Berry (1967) and others by Nancy S. Ossenberg (1976). Most of the variants listed in the tables can be studied for their occurrences on either side of the skull or skeleton. Following a theoretical argument for the comparative value of total side frequencies (Ossenberg, 1981), summed right and left side data have been reported here. Because of comparative data limitations I have restricted analytical discussion to the skull variants.

Table 10 compares the per cent frequencies of a subset of the variants for Blue Jackets Creek, Namu, Boardwalk, and Greenville. Rather than include the entire Prince Rupert Harbour series, I chose Boardwalk, the largest single site series, as representative in the present analysis to keep sample sizes more equitable among the four groups. As it is, the sample sizes of the individual variant observations for Boardwalk sometimes greatly exceeded those for Blue Jackets Creek, Namu, or Greenville.

In Table 10, the frequencies for each group are based on pooled sex data. Unlike metrical characters, few sex differences have been demonstrated in the occurrences of non-metric variants. Notable exceptions for the Northwest Coast include supraorbital grooves and tympanic dehiscence which tend to be more common in females than in males (Cybulski, 1975b). Supraorbital grooves are thin channels for the supraorbital nerve, which may be etched into either or both sides of the frontal bone. Their more frequent expression in females may have something to do with the more rounded prominence of the female frontal bone. Male frontal bones are generally sloping and less prominent. A tympanic dehiscence appears as an irregular perforation in the floor of the tympanic plate which forms the outside of the ear hole (external auditory meatus). It is a persistence in some adults of the Foramen of Huschke of infancy and early childhood, a normal feature

TABLE 10. Per cent adult frequencies of non-metric cranial variants for four B.C. coast skeletal series [1]

Variant	Blue Jackets	Namu	Boardwalk	Greenville
Os Inca	0.00	0.00	6.25	3.85
Coronal suture bones	9.52	5.71	0.00	0.00
Lambdic bone	6.67	10.00	3.85	0.00
Lambdoidal suture bones	7.14	56.41	49.30	38.10
Asterionic bone	7.69	20.59	10.47	14.89
Parietal notch bone	10.71	11.76	17.86	10.87
Supraorbital grooves	0.00	29.41	33.05	32.50
Sagittal sinus left	20.00	25.00	20.63	17.24
Parietal foramen absent	40.63	21.05	27.83	28.85
Posterior zygomatic fissure	33.33	13.33	2.08	7.14
Palatine torus	0.00	35.71	33.33	21.74
Spinobasal bridge	7.69	0.00	22.58	20.00
Divided hypoglossal canal	20.00	21.21	17.76	18.37
Tympanic dehiscence	3.33	37.14	29.13	41.67
Auditory exostoses	39.39	32.43	18.31	0.00
Mylohyoid arch	37.04	12.00	25.47	15.00
Multiple mental foramina	0.00	17.86	9.16	6.25

[1] Frequencies for Namu were calculated from data in A.J. Curtin's (1984) report. Sample sizes (number of observations) for each variant range from 15 to 33 for Blue Jackets Creek, 14 to 39 for Namu, 48 to 142 for Boardwalk, and 22 to 62 for Greenville.

of the growing temporal bone. Presumably, the foramen's failure to close in the adult has a genetic basis, though its expression may also depend on individual variation in the thinness of the tympanic plate. For reasons of size, females might be expected to have thinner plates than males, thus accounting for their higher frequency of tympanic dehiscence. However, the Greenville males and females showed almost equal frequencies of tympanic plates which were quite thick, reported in Appendix H as another non-metric cranial variant, though not necessarily in the same individuals.

It is, perhaps, also noteworthy that no Greenville females displayed mandibular torus or mylohyoid arch, both variants of which exceeded 30% in the male sample. Mandibular torus is indicated by single or multiple nodules of bone developed on the lingual (tongue) side of the body of the mandible. Development may be quite pronounced in some individuals and distinctly visible in living persons inside and just below the lower tooth rows. Mylohyoid arch is a bridge of bone across the mylohyoid groove, a channel for blood vessels and a nerve on the inside (medial surface) of the ascending ramus of the mandible. Both are variants of excess bone development which might expectedly be more common in men than in women for reasons of general sex differences in bone robustness. However, mylohyoid arch, compared in Table 10, was notably frequent in females from Blue Jackets Creek (44.4%) and Boardwalk (25.6%), and also represented in females from Namu (14.3%).

The variants listed in Table 10 were partly selected for their apparent discriminating properties among the four series studied here, but also for reasons of comparative data restrictions stemming from the inclusion of Namu. All of the data for Blue Jackets Creek, Boardwalk, and, of course, Greenville were drawn from my own studies of these series, while those for Namu were taken from A.J. Curtin's 1984 descriptive report.[18]   The frequencies of a few variants reported by A.J. Curtin appeared questionable from my perspective, possibly due to differences in the way we interpreted their manifestations. Included here were multiple expressions of supraorbital foramen/notch, clinoid bridging, pterygobasal bridge, paracondylar process, and mandibular torus, all frequencies of which appeared unusually high when measured against those reported in the literature for other skeletal series and my observations for Blue Jackets Creek, Boardwalk, and Greenville, as well as other Northwest Coast groups (Cybulski, 1975b). A.J. Curtin's observations may very well be valid, but rather than chance the possibility of interobserver error in deciphering manifestations of the variants, a not uncommon problem for comparative skeletal studies, I decided to exclude them from the present analysis. A.J. Curtin did not report frequencies for supraorbital foramen and tympanic plate thickening, and for the occurrence of epipteric bones by side.

Although the variants shown in Table 10 have often been used by other investigators to study biological affinities among earlier populations, they need not necessarily all be indicators of heredity. Auditory exostoses, tumour-like growths of bone in the external ear hole, have been proposed to be acquired developmental anomalies related to persistent diving for food resources in cold water (Kennedy, 1986; Frayer, 1988). It is difficult to accept this explanation for Northwest Coast occurrences unless one concludes, on the basis of the data in Table 10, that cold water diving was a favoured pursuit at Blue Jackets Creek and Namu, notably less

---

[18] The Blue Jackets Creek skeletal series, excavated by Patricia Sutherland (Severs, 1974) and initially studied by Jeffrey Murray (1981), was subsequently curated temporarily in the Canadian Museum of Civilization. During this time, I took the opportunity to study the collection for individual age at death and sex determinations (see Chapter III), cribra orbitalia (Cybulski, 1990:58), and cranial non-metric skeletal variants (reported here). On request, the collection has since been sent to the Royal British Columbia Museum in Victoria for return to the Queen Charlotte Islands.

favoured at Prince Rupert Harbour, and not practiced at all at Greenville. The fact that the other sites are more coastally oriented geographically than Greenville might suggest a greater dependency on deep sea resources possibly acquired through diving practices. Countering this thinking, however, is a striking contrast between Blue Jackets Creek and historic Haida skeletal series, the people of which might presumably have lived similar lifestyles on the Queen Charlotte Islands. Auditory exostoses have not been observed in a large sample of museum-collected historic Haida skulls (Finnegan, 1972), nor in the Gust Island Rockshelter skeletal sample (Cybulski, 1973). On the other hand, high frequencies, comparable to those of Blue Jackets Creek and Namu, have been observed in the skulls of riverine oriented Chinook peoples (Kennedy, 1986). Furthermore, it is difficult to reconcile the high frequencies for Blue Jackets Creek, Namu, Chinook, and, also, historic "Kwakiutl" as reported by Michael Finnegan (1972), in terms of the diving hypothesis. G.E. Kennedy (1986) predicted very low frequencies of auditory exostoses in peoples located north of 45° latitude due to the threat of lethal hypothermia from full body immersion in these cold waters. It would seem that Northwest Coast variation in the occurrence of auditory exostoses is not easily explained in terms of behaviour, but that a genetic interpretation may very well be valid.

Among the other variants shown in Table 10, Blue Jackets Creek has uniquely high frequencies of parietal foramen absent and posterior zygomatic fissure, and uniquely low frequencies of lambdoidal suture bones and tympanic dehiscence. The parietal foramen is a tiny opening for a vein through the skull on either side of the sagittal suture near the back-sloping top of the braincase. Posterior zygomatic fissure is sometimes identified as a trace of os japonicum, a minor division in the arch of the zygomatic (cheek) bone where it meets the temporal bone. In the living, the arch may be felt as a prominence just below the temples. Lambdoidal suture bones are small accessory bones, generally frequent in North American Indians, along the back of the braincase, between the occipital and parietal bones.

Blue Jackets Creek is also unusual for its absence of palatine torus, a bony prominence in the roof of the mouth, notably frequent in the other groups, and for its lack of multiple mental foramina which ranged from 17.86% in Namu to 6.25% in Greenville mandibles. The mental foramen is a normal finding on either side of the outside of the lower jaw, below the premolar teeth (bicuspids). Blue Jackets Creek may also be cited for its very high frequency of mylohyoid arch, reported to occur with high frequency in North American Indian remains in general (Ossenberg, 1974) but obviously variable in the series detailed here.

Though Greenville is the focus of this monograph, it is difficult not to draw attention to the uniqueness or difference of Blue Jackets Creek relative to Greenville and the other sites which also appears to be the case in certain of its metrical characteristics. In non-metrical characters, Greenville seems only outstanding in its absence of auditory exostoses, though it also has the highest frequency of tympanic dehiscence. In a number of other frequencies, it appears most closely tied to Boardwalk.

Biological Distance

While examinations of individual traits offer descriptive insight in studies of comparative skeletal biology, such univariate techniques of investigation favour particulate differences or similarities. Techniques of multivariate analysis, whereby a group of skeletal variants or measurements are considered in concert, allow for more comprehensive, evenhanded morphological portraits of individuals or populations. It is assumed on good theoretical grounds that the study of "total morphological pattern" provides more meaningful insight into the biological interrelationships of human populations. There is a practical advantage as well. Trait by trait comparisons can become unruly in overall interpretations, and suggest apparently contradictory findings. Multivariate assessments account for both similarities and differences between samples, and permit single estimates of biological distance based on these expressions.

Multivariate techniques of analysis usually demand complex statistical procedures to account for variations in sample size among compared skeletal series in the different traits used in the analysis, and to standardize or stabilize the basic numerical expressions of those traits. In this study, I focussed attention on the non-metric variants separately compared in Table 10 by using C.A.B. Smith's mean measure of divergence (MMD) as refined by Torstein Sjøvold (1977). The frequencies of the variants were stabilized using the Freeman-Tukey inverse sine transformation technique (ibid., p. 19).

The results of the analysis are shown in Table 11 and on Figure 28. Figure 28 is a tree diagram (dendrogram) constructed by a single linkage method (nearest neighbour) clustering technique (Wilkinson, 1990) from the mean measures in Table 11. The results are clear. Greenville is closest to Boardwalk in its overall non-metric morphological pattern, and these two sites form a first level cluster which is joined by Namu at approximately twice the distance between them. Blue Jackets Creek is so far removed that it appears independent of or unrelated to the other groups.

Figure 29 shows the results of similar multivariate assessments based on craniometric characters using the "size and shape" distance technique promoted by

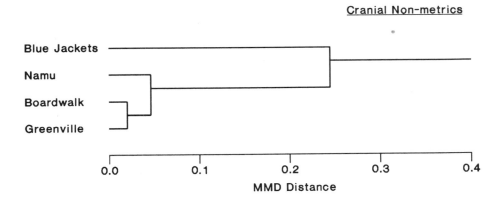

FIGURE 28. Relationships among four B.C. coast skeletal series
based on mean measures of divergence (MMD)
in non-metric cranial variants.

TABLE 11. Mean measures of divergence (MMD) among four B.C. coast
skeletal series based on 17 non-metric cranial variants

Comparison	MMD
Greenville vs. Boardwalk	0.020
Boardwalk vs. Namu	0.046
Greenville vs. Namu	0.090
Namu vs. Blue Jackets Creek	0.245
Boardwalk vs. Blue Jackets Creek	0.266
Greenville vs. Blue Jackets Creek	0.290

L.S. Penrose (1954).   Fourteen absolute cranial measurements in the four series
were used in this analysis to derive pairwise distances. Thirteen of them entered
into the calculations of the craniometric indices reported in Table 9; the fourteenth
measurement used in the distance statistic was minimum frontal breadth.

The "size" and "shape" components of the Penrose technique were separately
treated for the purposes of cluster analysis because they provide different kinds of
information. By definition, morphology is the form and structure of an organism

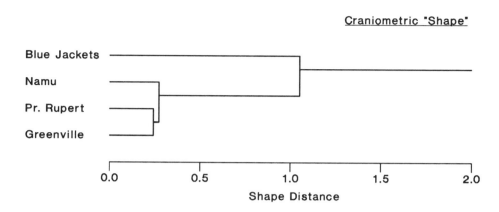

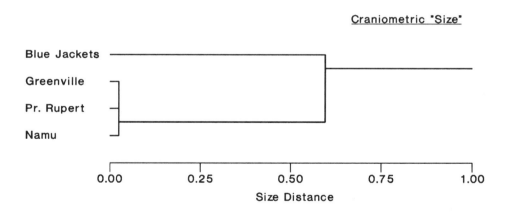

FIGURE 29. *Relationships among four B.C. coast skeletal series based on Penrose size and shape distances in cranial measurements.*

but not its size. Shape or form is preferable to size in classifying objects except when size differences are extreme (Penrose, 1954:338). As can be seen on Figure 29, the shape distances present a set of intergroup relationships very much like that shown by the non-metric variants. The latter are structural elements of morphology. Both representations discriminate Namu, Prince Rupert Harbour (or its Boardwalk representative), and Greenville in similar ways, suggesting meaningful relationships which might be explained in biological terms. Size is only of classificatory significance in the case of Blue Jackets Creek which indicates that its total skull pattern in size is extremely different from the other groups.

Blue Jackets Creek is clearly a distinct entity in the present fourfold investigation of known prehistoric populations from the north and central coasts of British Columbia. One could conclude that the sample is biologically unrelated to the others. It is clearly unrelated to Prince Rupert Harbour and Greenville. The three groups, therefore, do not present an image of a common north coast human biological complex which might have existed in British Columbia for 4,000 or 5,000 years, traceable to historic times. Interestingly in this connection, Jeffrey Murray (1981) noted more morphological differences than similarities between Blue Jackets Creek and historic Haida skeletal samples in his univariate comparative assessment of the site. Multivariate techniques of analysis may help to clarify these results, an assessment I plan to undertake in a separate study including some of the same Haida samples, the sample from Gust Island Rockshelter, and additional Prince Rupert Harbour site samples.

The relationships currently shown among Greenville, Prince Rupert Harbour, and Namu might be explained historically. Greenville is closest to Prince Rupert Harbour / Boardwalk, a relationship which might reflect their common candidacy for historic Tsimshian ancestry. Namu is further removed in time and space, and presumptively ancestral to Heiltsuk (Bella Bella), ethnolinguistically different from Tsimshian. Additional studies including historic skeletal samples from the central coast will help to clarify the historical biological position of Namu.

Chapter VI

Paleopathology

$\mathbf{P}$aleopathology offers a record of disease, injury, and congenital anomalies which may be registered in the physical remains of earlier human populations. This chapter summarizes laboratory findings for the Greenville burial population and draws comparisons with other Northwest Coast skeletal samples. Elements specific to each individual are reported in Appendix A.

Dental Disease

Signs of dental disease in the people buried at Greenville were mainly indicated by opened bone lesions around teeth (periapical abscesses), opened tooth pulp chambers from grinding wear on the chewing surfaces (occlusal attrition), and fully resorbed tooth sockets (ante mortem tooth loss). Evidence for tooth decay (caries) was negligible. There was only one carious tooth among 953 deciduous (milk) and permanent teeth (0.10%), a left second molar in the lower jaw of Burial 20. The cavity was minor, a tiny blackened (necrotic) pit in the occlusal surface.

A very low rate of caries is characteristic of coastal British Columbia populations, probably due to high rates of occlusal attrition and diets which were low in carbohydrates (sugars and starches) (Curtin, 1984). Prior to the Greenville analysis, I calculated caries rates of 0.34% for the prehistoric period and 0.82% for the historic period, each based on samples in excess of 6,000 teeth (Cybulski, 1990). The higher, statistically significant caries rate for the historic period might have reflected the introduction of European foodstuffs into the diets of the late 18th to late 19th century native populations. However, the people of that time likely still relied heavily on the traditional staples of fish and meat, foods high in protein and low in carbohydrates. Elsewhere in Canada, native agricultural diets high in carbohydrates have produced average caries rates of 26% in prehistoric and European-contact period populations (ibid.). Data on historic non-native North American skeletal samples are few. Caries rates from 11.9% to 21.7% have been reported for skeletal samples of military personnel from United States Revolutionary War through Civil War times (Sledzik and Moore-Jansen, 1991), and a rate of 27.1% has been documented for a mid-18th century Québec prisoner of war population of northeastern colonials and English and Scottish sailors (Cybulski, 1991c).

Clearly, tooth decay was an insignificant quantity in the dental pathology of early native populations of the British Columbia coast.

The high rates of occlusal attrition in these populations may be visualized from Figure 30 which details findings for the adult Greenville sample. Teeth were separately scored on a scale from 0 to 6 as follows: 0 = no wear; 1 = cusps or incisal edges blunted; 2 = cusps or incisal edges flattened and (or) spots of dentin evident; 3 = continuous dentin evident between two or more cusps or across the incisal edge of an anterior tooth; 4 = secondary dentin evident; 5 = crown almost worn away except for the presence of an enamel rim; 6 = roots functional. Mean degrees of wear were calculated for individual tooth types and individual dentitions per jaw.

Occlusal wear was generally advanced, more so in females than in males, and more so in the upper than in the lower jaw. It was not uncommon for individuals to show attrition with secondary dentin response, crowns almost completely worn, or functional roots. In 42 of 718 teeth (5.85%), rapid and severe wear had exposed the pulp chambers.

Consistent with other British Columbia findings (Hall and German, 1975; Beattie, 1981; Curtin, 1984), there was a greater degree of attrition in upper than in lower teeth. Individual male means for the upper and lower dentitions were 3.67 and 3.20 respectively, and the female means were 4.44 and 3.94. Of the 42 teeth with worn open pulp chambers, 40 were upper teeth (11.6% of 346; 0.5% of 372 lower teeth).

The sex difference was likely due in large measure to age differences between the samples. The female segment of the Greenville population presented an older age profile than the male segment (Chapter III), and tooth wear may be expected to increase with the increasing age of an individual, the basis for considering tooth wear in age at death estimations of skeletal remains.

There is little reason to suspect that other factors, such as different task-related activities, might have contributed to the sex differences. For three of the four jaw sets shown on Figure 30 -- the upper dentitions of both sexes and the lower dentition of males -- the differential pattern according to tooth type was similar. The earlier erupting teeth, notably the incisors and first molars, were more worn than the others, expected if the grinding wear from normal mastication was largely responsible. Substantiating this similarity between the sexes was the fact that in neither sex was there any obvious indication that teeth were differentially used as tools, as they were, for example, at Prince Rupert Harbour (Cybulski, 1974).

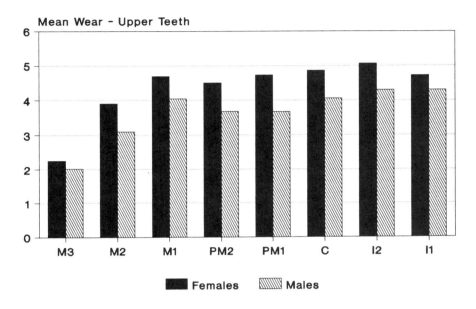

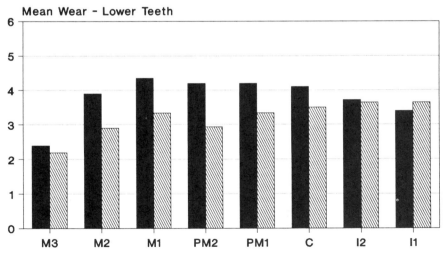

FIGURE 30. Occlusal wear patterns in upper and lower teeth of Greenville adults by sex. (M = molars; PM = premolars; C = canines; I = incisors; right and left teeth pooled).

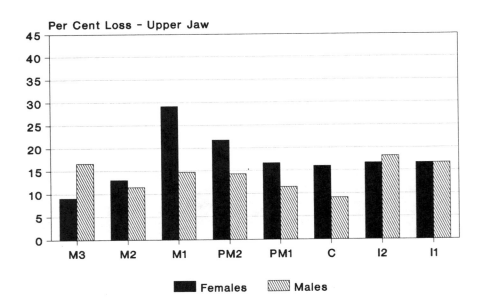

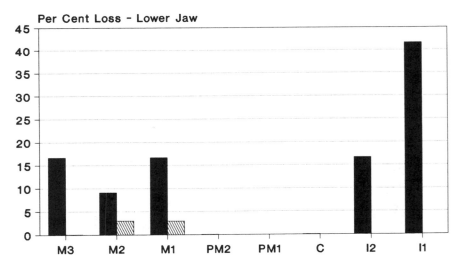

FIGURE 31. Distribution of ante mortem tooth loss in upper and lower jaws
of Greenville adults by sex. (Tooth type legend described in
Fig. 30; right and left tooth positions pooled.)

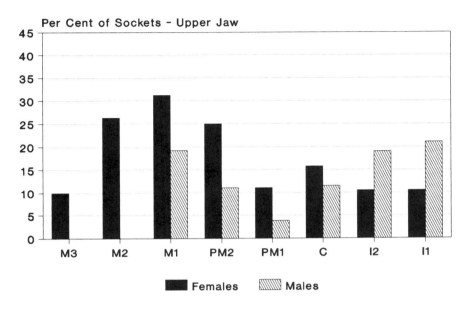

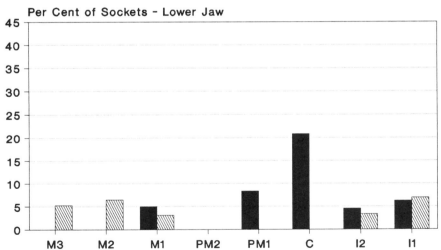

FIGURE 32. Distribution of periapical abscess lesions in upper and lower jaws of Greenville adults by sex. (Tooth type legend described in Fig. 30; right and left tooth positions pooled.)

The different pattern shown by the female lower dentition is probably illusory. Here, the anterior teeth, especially the incisors, appear to have been less worn than the cheek teeth. However, there were fewer incisors from older women which entered into the calculations for mean wear. As described in Chapter III, female incisors seem to have been lost as a function of labret use, a feature especially noticeable in older women (Table 5).

Overall, 99 of 900 tooth locations in the jaws (11.0%) exhibited ante mortem loss in the Greenville adults. Uppers were more frequently lost than lowers (15.3% of 457 upper teeth as opposed to 6.6% of 443 lower teeth), and females were more frequently affected than males (15.6% of 379 female teeth versus 7.7% of 521 male teeth). This pattern follows that of the occlusal attrition analysis, and it may be concluded that severe attrition likely resulted in opened pulp chambers which in turn led to infection resulting in periapical abscess lesions that eventually brought about tooth loss. Partly suporting this observation is the close correspondence between tooth loss and periapical abscess lesions according to tooth type in the upper jaws, shown on Figures 31 and 32. There is little correspondence in the lower jaws, likely due to two factors: first, there were far fewer abscesses and lost teeth in the lower jaws, producing sampling problems, and secondly, lower tooth loss in females was influenced as much or, perhaps, more so by labret use as it was by infected tooth sockets.

In total, 62 of 748 tooth locations, or 8.3%, were affected by periapical abscesses, a figure approaching that calculated for prehistoric alveolar sockets from throughout the British Columbia coast, 9.16% (Cybulski, 1990). Forty-five of 340 upper tooth sockets were affected (13.2%) and 17 of 408 lower sockets (4.2%). The total female frequency was 11.04% (35 of 317 tooth locations) as opposed to a frequency of 6.3% (27 of 431 locations) for males. Of interest is that males showed a somewhat different pattern of abscessing in the upper jaw than females, a distinct trend to increased abscesses in the anterior teeth. This is a male pattern also shown by the skeletal remains of Prince Rupert Harbour (Cybulski, 1990; n.d.a). In that series, comprised of a much larger number of individuals than Greenville, there was reason to suspect that frequent male abscessing resulted from chronic trauma to the anterior face and jaws, a situation often seen in modern dental practice. This may also have been the case at Greenville and is, in part, supported by a single occurrence in this smaller sample of a Class IV fractured male upper incisor (described later in this chapter). In the Prince Rupert Harbour group, there were more frequent occurrences of Class IV tooth fractures as well as other signs of injury to the face.

Chronic Sinus Infection

In two Greenville adults aged 40 years plus (Burials 3 and 32), periapical abscess lesions at a single tooth location had opened into the maxillary sinus. In each case, the opening in the floor of the sinus was surrounded by inflammatory growths of bone (osteitis) and, thus, probably precipitated a sinus-related infection.

There were at least four other persons in the Greenville burial ground who may have suffered chronic sinus infection. In these cases, there were spicules of bone adhering to the floor or walls of the maxillary sinus, occurrences which were unrelated to whether these individuals had dental abscesses. In one case (Burial 7) the condition was bilateral and in two cases (Burials 33 and 48) only one sinus was affected. In the fourth person (Burial 24), only one sinus was studiable, the other normally closed to visual inspection. The total frequency of these maxillary sinus inclusions was 18.2% (22 persons), much lower than frequencies of 47% to 68% reported for Prince Rupert Harbour and Namu (Curtin, 1984). The sample included 15 adults and seven immature persons.

Possible Middle Ear Disease

In the skull of Burial 44, a female aged 50-59 years, the right external auditory meatus (ear opening) was enlarged and the tympanic plate thinned in contrast to the normal left. In Burial 40, a female aged 22-28 years, the left tympanic plate was notably thinned and featured an unusually large dehiscence (persistent Foramen of Huschke; see Chapter V).

It is possible that both individuals had a cholesteatoma, a cyst-like deposit of inflammed tissue which may erode bone and enlarge the ear opening. This discharge has been related to chronic middle ear infections and perforated ear drums (Welin and Ratjen, 1969:490-492). While a dehiscence in the tympanic plate is a normal morphological variant in the skeleton, particularly frequent in women as reported in the preceding chapter, the very large opening in Burial 40, together with the abnormal thinness of the plate suggested that a destructive process contributed to its size. There was a very small dehiscence in the right tympanic plate, the thickness of which was normal.

In Burial 40, the outer shell of the mastoid process behind the ear opening with the thinned tympanic plate was damaged through soil erosion, exposing the internal structure. Here, one of the air cells appeared enlarged and its wall thickened or sclerotic, another sign of chronic middle ear disease in the form of mastoid infection (mastoiditis) (Juhl, 1981:1149-1150). In Burial 44, the mastoid processes were closed to gross inspection, as was the right mastoid process in Burial 40.

Otitis media, or middle ear disease, is much more frequent in modern American Indians than in whites (Sievers and Fisher, 1981:237-238) and has been clinically documented in at least one modern British Columbia Indian population (Cambon et al., 1965). While variable socioeconomic, hygienic, and climatic conditions have been suggested to account for the differences, good arguments have been advanced to suspect anatomical and genetic explanations (Sievers and Fisher, 1981:237-238). In addition to prehistoric Greenville, evidence for otitis media, in the form of ear cholesteatoma and mastoiditis, is apparent in the earlier Prince Rupert Harbour skeletal population where at least ten and as many as 14 individuals may have been affected (Cybulski, n.d.a).

Congenital Scoliosis

Burial 20, a male aged 22-28 years, had a severely twisted spine (Fig. 33), a developmentally based crippling condition that would clearly be noticeable to those around him, possibly from the time of birth. The curvature started at about the third thoracic vertebra and continued radically through the eighth thoracic to second lumbar units. The eighth thoracic through first lumbar units were incompletely developed "hemivertebrae" and fused to one another. The first lumbar unit appeared to be formed of two, right and left hemivertebrae, while the second lumbar was formed of a single additional half-vertebra. That bone was fused to the third lumbar which in turn was fused to the fourth lumbar congenitally and through subsequent calcification of the anterior longitudinal ligament. The fifth lumbar was fused to the sacrum through calcification of the ligament of the left side.

Other deformities were also apparent in this skeleton. Two sets of right and left ribs were congenitally fused to one another and the heads of four other ribs were distorted. There was a pronounced anterior curvature in the upper one-fourth of the left scapula (shoulder blade), concomitant with the likely hunched condition of the person due primarily to the scoliosis. The manubrium was prematurely fused to the body of the sternum (breastbone). The articular eminence of the left temporal, where the lower jaw joins the skull, was narrower anteroposteriorly than that of the right temporal. Probably related to this deformity was that the superior aspect of the left ascending ramus of the mandible was straighter and narrower than the right.

FIGURE 33. Scoliosis of the spine in Burial 20. Lower thoracic, lumbar, and sacral regions shown.

While Burial 20 was the only person in the Greenville burial population with such severe deformities, one other featured a relatively mild case of scoliosis. This was Burial 24, a woman aged 60+ years, in whom the lateral curvature of the spine was shown between the first and seventh thoracic vertebrae. From a comparative standpoint, it is worthwhile noting that one person in the Prince Rupert Harbour series, a female aged the same as Burial 20, exhibited marked congenital scoliosis of the spine with hemivertebrae (illustrated in MacDonald and Inglis, 1976:37), giving considerable antiquity to this condition on the northern British Columbia coast.   Owen Beattie (1981) reported severe scoliosis in a young adult male from Deep Bay on the south coast of British Columbia but attributed his finding to an acquired compression injury rather than a congenital anomaly.

Other Anomalies or Disturbances of Development

Burial 14, a female skeleton aged at 18-22 years, exhibited a crease-like defect in the mandibular fossa of the right temporal bone.   This anomaly likely was of little consequence to the individual during life, though it might have precipitated an early arthritic condition in the jaw joint if the woman had survived.

Congenital hip dysplasia

In Burial 40, another young adult female, the head of the right femur (thighbone) appeared mushroom-shaped, rather than normally ball-like, and positioned on a very short neck compared to the normal left.   The other part of the hip joint (acetabulum or pelvic socket) was normal.   The anomaly suggested an expression of congenital hip dysplasia which might have evolved into a severe arthritic problem had the woman lived to a later age.

Spina bifida occulta

Spina bifida occulta is a congenital midline separation in the neural arch of a vertebra.   It has been regarded as a commonly occurring normal variant in modern populations (Bennett, 1972).   In the Greenville series, two individuals, Burials 21 and 38, showed spina bifida occulta in the sacrum.   The minimum frequency among individuals in the total series was 5.6%, comparable to a frequency of 5.2% in the skeletal population of Prince Rupert Harbour (Cybulski, 1988a).   In that group, there were occurrences in upper vertebrae as well as in the sacrum.

Third molar agenesis

Congenital absence of third molars (wisdom teeth) was recorded in six of 31 Greenville individuals for a frequency of 19.4%.   Of interest is that all cases were limited to male dentitions (sample of 19 persons) although studies of larger samples, worldwide, have failed to establish sex differences (Brothwell et al., 1963).   The frequency per third molar for both sexes was 8.3% (9 of 109 tooth locations), slightly higher than Owen Beattie's (1981) frequency of 7.1% (9 of 127) for British Columbia south coast archaeological sites, much higher than A.J. Curtin's (1984) frequency of 3% for Namu (sample size not given), but notably lower than Marjory Gordon's (1974) frequency of 13.5% (13 of 96 tooth locations) for the south coast False Narrows site. Jeffrey Murray (1981) reported three affected individuals in a sample from Blue Jackets Creek on the Queen Charlotte Islands but did not give frequencies of occurrence. Marjory Gordon (1974) also reported congenitally missing lower incisors for False Narrows, not evident in the Greenville series.

One Greenville individual with a missing third molar (agenesis) in the left side of the lower jaw also had an impacted third molar in the right side. In Burial 15, both lower third molars were missing and the upper third molars were reduced in size or peg-like. Burial 11, a female, featured a partly impacted lower third molar.

Enamel pearls

An enamel pearl is a drop of enamel tissue, distinct from the crown enamel, on the root of a tooth. Some investigators have reported individual occurrences of enamel pearls as "enamelomata," a term which literally means enamel tumour (Koritzer, 1970), while others have described them in population contexts as discrete non-metric dental traits (Curtin, 1984). It is likely that enamel pearls do vary in their frequency of expression among different populations as minor developmental anomalies. I previously reported the occurrence of enamel pearls in 8 of 34 upper permanent molars (23.5%) and 9 of 152 lower permanent molars (5.9%) in a sample of historic period skeletal remains from Hesquiat Harbour, British Columbia (Cybulski, 1978a). A.J. Curtin (1984:101) reported their occurrence in 6 of 21 persons from Namu (28.6%) including 10 of 144 upper and lower teeth (6.9%). In the Greenville series, enamel pearls were present in 13 of 36 persons (36.1%) including 23 of 232 permanent molars (9.9%). Like Hesquiat Harbour, they were more common in the upper jaw (21 of 116 teeth, or 18.1%) than in the lower jaw (2 of 116 teeth, or 1.7%). For her sample, A.J. Curtin (ibid.) noted that enamel pearls were found only in the maxillary teeth.

Tooth crowding

Crowding of the dentition with irregularly spaced teeth was observed in ten of 31 Greenville individuals (32.3%) and restricted to lower jaws. Tooth crowding, when it occurs, is generally more visible in lower than in upper jaws of other British Columbia samples. The overall frequency at Greenville, however, was about twice that at Prince Rupert Harbour, 17% (Cybulski, 1988a), and Namu, 16% (Curtin, 1984). Owen Beattie (1981) reported five individuals with crowded teeth for the south coast but did not give a frequency of occurrence. Jeffrey Murray

(1981) reported four affected individuals at Blue Jackets Creek but also did not give a frequency of occurrence. Marjory Gordon (1974) reported that dental crowding was uncommon at False Narrows.

Brachydactyly

Brachydactyly, in the form of disproportionately short metacarpals in the hands or metatarsals in the feet, has previously been reported in prehistoric British Columbia skeletons from Prince Rupert Harbour (Cybulski, 1988a) and from Cache Creek in the interior of the province (Pokotylo et al., 1987). Based on the Prince Rupert Harbour findings which involved ten or, possibly, 11 affected individuals at four midden sites, brachydactyly was concluded to represent an inherited anomaly. Case reports of occurrences in other areas (Merbs and Vestergaard, 1985; Loveland and Gregg, 1988) suggest that brachydactyly was fairly widespread in North American Indians of the past.

At Greenville, two persons had unusually short first metatarsals. In Burial 11, an adult female, the left first metatarsal was 11 mm shorter than the right. The right first metatarsal of Burial 36, an adult male, was incomplete and thus not measurable but its shaft appeared stunted when compared with the normal left bone. These two occurrences suggested an overall frequency for brachydactyly of 6.1%, based on a sample of 33 individuals with either or both metacarpals and metatarsals present. While there were no affected metacarpals in the Greenville group, study of the Prince Rupert Harbour skeletons and modern clinical investigations suggest that either metacarpals or metatarsals may be shortened as part of a common genetic entity (Cybulski, 1988a). There were 46 studiable first metatarsals in the Greenville skeletal assemblage, providing a per bone frequency of 4.4%. This is notably higher than the frequency of affected first metatarsals at Prince Rupert Harbour (1.3%) where fourth metatarsals were most commonly affected. Based on all hand and foot components, however, the frequency of affected individuals at Greenville was comparable to that at Prince Rupert Harbour, differing by less than 1%.

Cribra Orbitalia and Anemia

Cribra orbitalia is a porous lesion in the roof of the eye socket, the possible cause of which has been tied to iron-deficiency anemia in British Columbia coastal populations (Cybulski, 1977b). At Greenville, eight of 38 individuals were affected for a frequency of 21.05%. The affected people included six of seven observable immature persons with the youngest at 9-12 months (Burial 51) and the oldest at 8-10 years (Burial 21), and two adult females, Burial 40, at 22-28 years, and Burial

24, at 60+ years. The concentration in the immature group may be expected since the condition has most frequently been observed in children (Stuart-Macadam, 1985).

Previous studies on human remains from the British Columbia coast have suggested regional, though no time-related variations in the frequencies of cribra orbitalia (Cybulski, 1990:58). The frequency at Greenville is comparable to that of historic Coast Salish, somewhat less than frequencies at prehistoric Blue Jackets Creek and Strait of Georgia sites, and two and one-half to three and one-half times higher than frequencies at Namu and Prince Rupert Harbour. A range of environmental conditions and, possibly, genetic factors may contribute to the presence of iron-deficiency anemia in any group of people. Variations in population density, leading to variably crowded living conditions, may have contributed to regional variations in the frequency of cribra orbitalia on the coast of British Columbia (ibid., p. 57).

Cranial Vault Porousness

One adult male skull and one adult female, Burials 52 and 46 respectively, displayed a fine porousness in the posterior part of the braincase including the parietals and occipital about lambda. The changes appeared superficial, possibly akin to the cranial osteoporosis described by Thomas W. McKern and T. Dale Stewart (1957) in American war dead from the 1950s Korean conflict. Those authors hypothesized that the porousness might have resulted from nutritional deficiencies but found equal frequencies of occurrence in the remains of prisoners of war likely to have suffered deficiencies and in the remains of non-prisoners, presumably healthy individuals.

Another kind of cranial lesion inconclusive as to cause, so-called porous periostosis (Ortner and Putschar, 1981:43), was observed in a second male skull, Burial 18. The change here, like a film of porous bone, covered the surface of the vault between the temporal lines. Both types of changes were previously reported in skeletons from Namu (Curtin 1984), and cranial osteoporosis has been reported in high frequency among remains from Strait of Georgia sites (Beattie, 1981). Neither study suggested possible etiologies. In the Greenville examples, there were no other skeletal changes which might have been related, although in Burial 52, a person of advanced age, there was general thinning of the bones, an indication of possible senile osteoporosis.

Fractures and Other Signs of Injury

Clear or suspected indicators of ante mortem trauma were recorded in 16 individuals in the Greenville site, three unassociated disturbed bones, and in one of the skeletons recovered from the 1984 water-line excavation. The changes are described in detail in Table 12 according to burial number, related sex and age at death identifications, and anatomical location or site of injury. There were 32 healed or, in one instance, unhealed traumatic bone fractures distributed among a minimum 13 or a maximum 15 individuals, four separate cases of ossified hematomas or so-called "button" osteomas, three separate cases of possible fatigue fractures in the spine, two cases of bony ankylosis (fusion) of joints probably due to injury, two possible cases of traumatic myositis ossificans (tendon calcification stimulated by injury to soft tissue), and one case of traumatic joint arthritis.

Based on the minimum Greenville sample of 59 individuals, the frequency of affected persons in all cases of trauma was 30.5% to 33.9%. This range allows the three disturbed bones the status of one person or three. Three different anatomical elements were involved and multiple injury sites in one person could not be ruled out as evidenced by just over one-half the sample of affected identified individuals. Since only adult bones were involved in all cases of trauma, the frequency range for the adult segment of the Greenville population would be 45.0% to 50.0%. At least 12 males and five females were involved, giving frequencies of 50.0% and 33.3% respectively. A thirteenth affected male was suggested by one of the disturbed bones. Inclusion of this statistic would raise the adult male frequency for the population to 54.2%.

Traumatic lesions may be attributed to three groups of causes, interpersonal violence, accident, or stress. The last occurs from intense physical activity, particularly in younger individuals, or from disease processes which may weaken bone, thus making them more susceptible than healthy bone to trauma (e.g., osteoporosis in aged persons). Traumatic fractures due to interpersonal violence (as in warfare) or accident generally hold the most meaning for social and cultural interpretations (Ortner and Putschar, 1981), while fractures due to stress are more likely to reflect individual physiological influences. For any skeletal population where there are no medical records, there is a measure of uncertainty to the cause of any form of trauma. Consideration must be given to the anatomical location of the lesion and detectable patterns of regional or segmental exclusiveness, the mechanics and definitions of trauma known from modern clinical study, and patterns of distribution by side of the body, by age, and by sex. For the interpretations of trauma in the Greenville series, many of which are detailed below, I also relied on patterns of frequent trauma shown by the prehistoric Prince Rupert Harbour skeletal series (Cybulski, 1990; n.d.a).

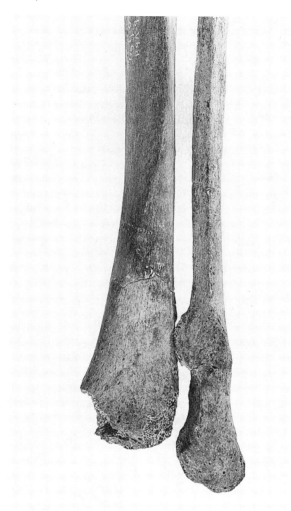

FIGURE 34. *Fractured distal left fibula and developed articulation with the the tibia (shin bone) in the lower leg of Burial 9.*

Included in Table 12 are three cases of possible fatigue fractures in lumbar vertebrae. They might be regarded as fractures due to stress, but whether they ought to be included with other forms of environmental trauma in comparative population studies is doubtful. These spinal fractures are more commonly known as "spondylolysis," a condition in a vertebra that involves separation of the neural arch (the part that covers the spinal cord) between the superior and inferior articu-

TABLE 12. *Trauma or suspected trauma in Greenville human remains by burial, sex, age, anatomical location, and description*

Burial	Sex	Age	Location	Description
5	M	48-54	L. tibia	Ossified subperiosteal hematoma, ca. 5 mm long, on anteromedial shaft.
			R. foot	Traumatic arthritis in joint formed by cuboid and 4th and 5th metatarsals; surfaces compressed and extensively eroded
			R. foot	Tendon calcification (possible traumatic myositis ossificans) suggested by bone spur on 4th metatarsal shaft.
9	M	40-44	L. fibula	Healed distal shaft fracture above metaphysis with developed articular facet and complementary facet on tibia shaft (Fig. 34).
			R. hand	Healed shaft fracture in 2nd proximal phalange.
			R. hand	Ossified subperiosteal hematoma on shaft of 4th proximal phalange.
10	F	45-54	R. tibia	Healed spiral shaft fracture with secondary infection (Fig. 35).
			R. foot	Bony ankylosis of fibula, talus, calcaneus, 2nd and 3rd cuneiforms, cuboid, and navicular; bony ankylosis at proximal ends of 4th and 5th metatarsals; complete breakdown of joint cartilage between tibia and talus shown by nearly perfect fit of distorted and pitted articular surfaces (Fig. 35).
16	M	50-59	Sk. vault	Healed depressed fracture in anterior right parietal at and medial to superior temporal line, the line deflected laterally; inner table protuberance; overall lesion measures 19 x 22 mm with central porous indentation of 9 x 10 mm.
			Sk. vault	Healed depressed fracture in centre right frontal; 5 x 12 mm; lesion is porous; no inner table protuberance.
			R. radius	Healed fracture of styloid process with fracture line through lateral half of distal articular surface (Fig. 36a).
			Spine	Possible fatigue fracture (spondylolysis) in 5th lumbar vertebra.

(TABLE 12 continued)

Burial	Sex	Age	Location	Description
19	M	20-24	L. radius	Healed neck fracture; proximal segment, including head, bent posteriorly; bone spur projects anteromedially at site of fracture (Fig. 37).
20	M	22-28	Sk. vault	Large, unhealed comminuted depressed fracture in left side to left occipital squama; step-fractures visible externally and inner table edges torn internally; all broken pieces recovered on site in correct anatomical position; fracture lines visible on planum nuchae, extending to foramen magnum (Fig. 38).
			Sk. vault	Healed or healing depressed fracture, 29 x 34 mm, in posteromedial quadrant of left parietal (Fig. 38).
			Face	Healed fracture of nasal bones.
22	F	40-49	Spine	Possible fatigue fracture (partial spondylolysis) in 5th lumbar vertebra.
23	M	55-64	Sk. vault	Ossified subperiosteal hematoma (button osteoma), 4 x 4 mm, in right frontal, lateral to temporal line.
			L. femur	Elongate bony exostosis (possible traumatic myositis ossificans) on linea aspera above midshaft.
24	F	60+	R. rib	Healed fracture in costal end of an upper (3rd or 4th) rib.
			R. rib	Healed fracture, with dislocation, in vertebral end of a floating rib.
			L. hand	Healed Bennett's fracture in 1st metacarpal.
			Spine	Compression fractures of 12th thoracic and 1st lumbar vertebrae; bony ankylosis at apophyseal joints (Fig. 39).
26	M	17-20	Spine	Possible fatigue fracture (spondylolysis) in 5th lumbar vertebra.
29	F	55-64	R. foot	Healed distal shaft fracture in 5th metatarsal.
			Spine	Compression fractures of 11th thoracic and 1st lumbar vertebrae; 12th thoracic appears missing congenitally.

(Table 12 continued)

Burial	Sex	Age	Location	Description
32	M	40-44	R. hand	Healed shaft fracture in 5th metacarpal.
			R. hand	Bony ankylosis between middle and distal phalanges of 2nd digit.
			Spine	Compression fractures of 11th and 12th thoracic and 1st lumbar vertebrae.
33	M	22-26	Face	Class IV (root) fracture of upper left lateral incisor; crown and adjacent root portion present.
40	F	22-28	R. radius	Healed Colles' fracture; slight "dinner fork" deformity and slight swelling in anterior aspect.
45	M	30-39	Sk. vault	Healed depressed fracture in centre right frontal; 9 x 17 mm.
52	M	60+	Spine	Compression fractures in 11th and 12th, and 1st and 2nd lumbar vertebrae.
56	M	40-49	Sk. vault	Large ossified subperiosteal hematoma, 25 x 34 mm, spanning both parietals at obelion (Fig. 40).
Disturbed	?	Adult	L. clavicle	Healed shaft fracture near lateral end; only lateral half of bone present.
Disturbed	?	Adult	R. radius	Healed Colles' fracture; gross "dinner fork" deformity; only distal third of bone present (Fig. 36b).
Disturbed	M?	Adult	R. foot	Healed shaft fracture in 3rd metatarsal.

lar processes (pars interarticularis), the pedicle, or the lamina (Merbs, 1983:35-42). Some studies have shown a familial predisposition for this form of fracture which apparently results from heavy loading stresses on the lower back (Wiltse, 1962). Because of the possible genetic component, I have excluded spondylolysis from the comparative population assessments of trauma described below. By itself, spondylolysis is known to vary in its frequency of occurrence among different skeletal series, perhaps due, in part, to relative differences in the extent to which family members may be represented in burial samples (e.g., Lundy, 1981).

All three cases in the Greenville series involved the fifth lumbar vertebra, the most commonly affected bone in any skeletal series. Based on 24 adult fifth lumbar vertebrae, the frequency of spondylolysis in the Greenville population was 12.5%. There were no occurrences in four immature bones which, if included in the sample, would reduce the population frequency to 10.7%. In two of the affected individuals, the separation of the arch from the body involved both sides of the bone (bilateral), while in the third case, a unilateral separation was indicated at the right pars interarticularis.

For all other cases of trauma in the Greenville series, there were 34 locations or sites of injury involving 52 bones and one tooth. This might suggest 34 separate events of injury but, in reality, multiple site involvement might plausibly have been due to single episodes of trauma in some persons. For example, in Burial 5, a possible case of traumatic arthritis in the right foot and tendon calcification at another site in the same foot could have resulted from a single episode of trauma. The latter, a possible indicator of traumatic myositis ossificans, was represented by a bony spur on the fourth metatarsal, a bone whose joint surface was also involved in the arthritis. In Burial 10, a shaft fracture of the right tibia (shin bone) and bony fusion in joints of the associated foot could have resulted from a single episode of trauma (Fig. 35). Fusion of the talus (anklebone) and calcaneus (heel bone), which were involved in Burial 10, may result after falling from a height and landing on the feet (Zimmerman and Kelley, 1982:48). Other foot bones were also involved in Burial 10, as was the distal end of the fibula (the outer bone of the lower leg). Additionally, the articular surfaces between the tibia and talus were distorted in complementary fashion, suggesting a complete breakdown of the joint cartilage that normally separates these bones. The healed configuration of the tibia shaft suggested a spiral fracture due to sudden rotational forces that could have occurred during the same fall (cf., Kaplan et al., 1977:316-319). Likewise, multiple right hand injuries, separately indicated for Burials 9 and 32, might have occurred at the same time, though not necessarily for reasons of accident.

Multiple fractures in Burial 24, an aged female, including two broken ribs, a so-called Bennett's fracture in the left hand, and two spinal compression fractures with bony ankylosis (Fig. 39), could also have resulted at the same time during a fall, though not necessarily from a height in this case. A Bennett's fracture involves shearing and distal displacement of the ventral articular segment or "volar beak" of the bone (that part at the base of the thumb side of the palm) and usually results from a protective response to a fall, with the thumb absorbing most of the impact on an outstretched hand (Sandzén, 1979:202-211). The same fall could explain the compression fractures in the spine of this person because of a related sudden twisting movement of the body, again, as a possible protective balancing response (Brocher, 1969:77-78).

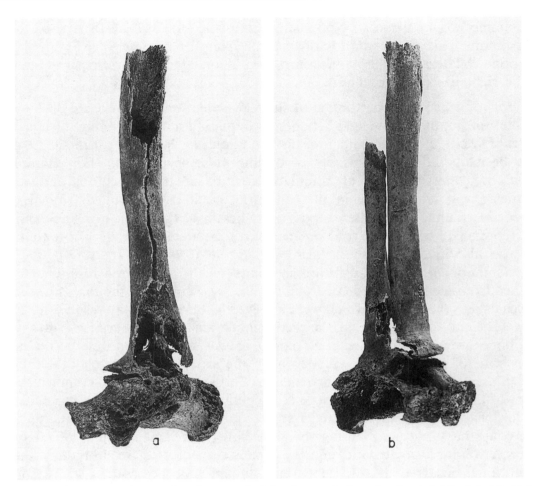

FIGURE 35. Two views of a fractured right leg and foot in Burial 10. (a) Medial view including tibia (the long crack and missing portions reflect post-mortem damage). (b) Anterolateral view including fibula.

Because of the advanced age of Burial 24, and that of Burial 52 who also exhibited spinal compression fractures but without other signs of accidental trauma, osteoporosis could have been a contributing factor or solely responsible. In this study, including the comparative data to follow, I have treated all spinal compression fractures as indicators of stress-related injuries. In aged persons, especially females who are more susceptible than males, osteoporosis and, therefore, physiological weakening of bone, may be primarily responsible for spinal compression fractures. In younger persons, such fractures may result from intense physical activity alone (non-specific in paleopathological cases) or in concert with accident or interpersonal violence. Young men engaged in hand-to-hand combat may per-

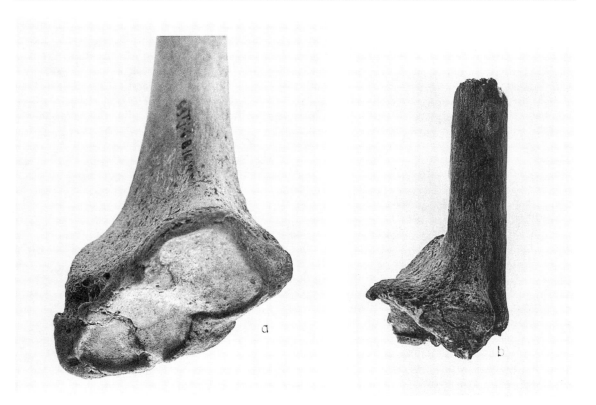

*FIGURE 36. (a) Intraarticular fracture through distal end of right radius
(thumb-side forearm bone) of Burial 16. (b) Colles' fracture
in disturbed fragment of a distal radius.*

form sudden twisting movements of the body, either as offensive or defensive maneuvers. Thus, there is too much uncertainty to attributing spinal compression fractures, as a group or separately, solely to accident.

There were four fractured thumb-side forearm bones (radius) in the Greenville series, all of which probably resulted accidentally. Two cases, Burial 40 and a disturbed bone (Fig. 36b), were represented as Colles' fractures of the distal or wrist end of the shaft, and a third, Burial 16, as an intraarticular fracture affecting dislocation of the styloid process at the wrist end (Fig. 36a). In modern clinical experience, both types of fracture are characteristic of a fall on an outstretched hand (Sandzén, 1979:71-94; Kaplan et al., 1977:283).

The fourth radius, in Burial 19, was fractured through the neck, at the elbow end of the bone, affecting a backward bending of the head (Fig. 37). This type of fracture is associated with strains of the medial (ulnar) collateral ligament (Kaplan et al., 1977:275), also sometimes imparted through an accidental fall.

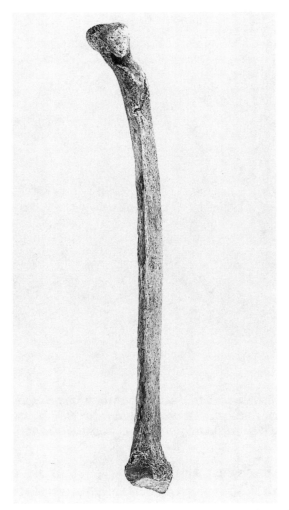

FIGURE 37. Healed neck fracture in proximal end of left radius of Burial 19.

There was one fractured clavicle (collarbone) in the Greenville series, found as a disturbed bone in the site, in which the break occurred near the lateral or shoulder end of the bone, lateral to the conoid tubercle. Today, fractures here are less common than those further along the shaft (Juhl, 1981:162). Shaft fractures result from direct blows or from falls on the shoulder.

In addition to the possible case of traumatic myositis ossificans in a fourth metatarsal, there was a possible case in a thighbone belonging to Burial 23. In that instance, a flat bony spur was attached to the linea aspera on the back of the bone just above midshaft. This would suggest deep trauma to the muscles of the thigh, probably precipitated by a direct blow.

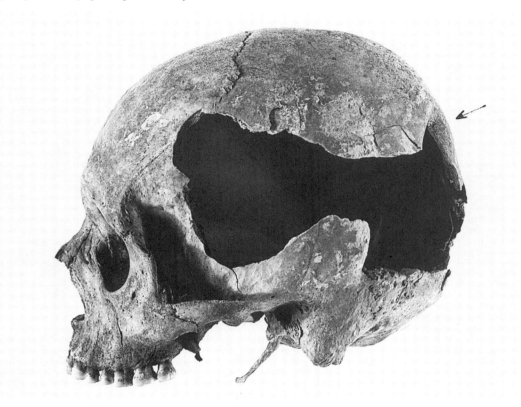

FIGURE 38. *Comminuted depressed fracture (large unhealed opening) in skull of Burial 20. Arrow points to earlier, partly healed depressed fracture.*

Aside from Bennett's fractures, there are few clinically known distinctive hand fractures which may be attributed to either accident or violence. In the Prince Rupert Harbour series, there were 21 fractured metacarpals, 20 of which were identified as to sex of the individual and showed patterned differences in that respect according to affected digits (Cybulski, n.d.a). The first and second metacarpals, those most likely to be fractured accidentally in a balancing response to a fall, were exclusively involved in females, while in males, the fourth and fifth metacarpals were more often affected. This sex-related pattern, together with other information on fractures in the series, suggested that interpersonal violence in hand-to-hand combat was responsible for the male injuries, a factor which might also explain the fifth metacarpal fracture in Burial 32 of the Greenville site. Outer hand fractures, much like "parrying" shaft fractures of the forearm (Ortner and Putschar, 1981:57), might be incurred through defensive maneuvers taken to protect the head and face from an opponent's blows.

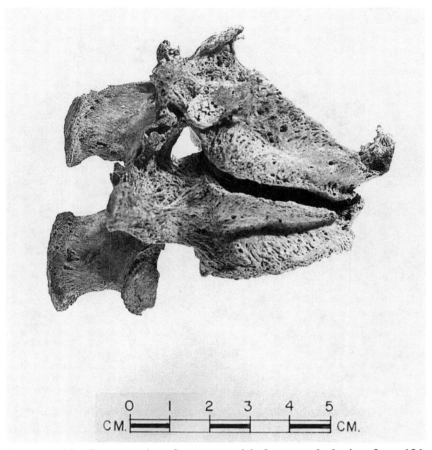

FIGURE 39. Compression fractures with bony ankylosis of twelfth thoracic and first lumbar vertebrae of Burial 24.

More certain evidence of interpersonal violence at Greenville was shown by five depressed fractures in the skull vaults of three males. The most spectacular example was in the skull of Burial 20 (Fig. 38), an individual also crippled with spinal scoliosis as reported earlier in this chapter. The left side of the braincase and adjacent posterior portion were opened by what was almost certainly a death-dealing comminuted depressed fracture. There were no signs of healing at the broken edges, some of which showed step fractures on the outer surfaces and torn inner table segments. These features are characteristic of breaks in living, or so-called "green" bone. Also, the edges appeared "old" (discolored) rather than "new," the latter more characteristic of freshly broken dry bone, a circumstance which

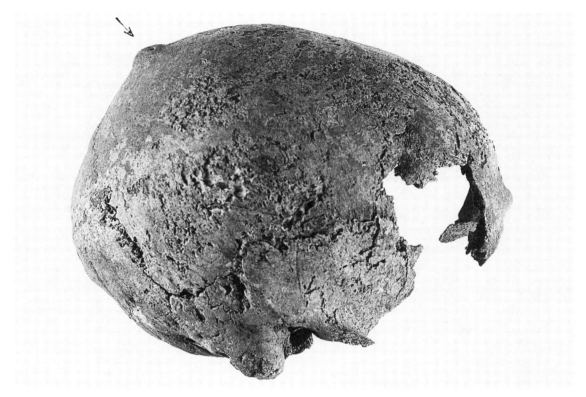

FIGURE 40. Ossified subperiosteal hematoma (arrow) in skull of Burial 56.

might result from soil pressure in burial or damage during recovery of a skeleton. Of further importance for the identification is that all of the broken pieces from this opening were recovered *in situ;* they lay in expected anatomical position beneath the left side of the skull, indicating that pieces of scalp and, probably, periosteum, the thin skin of living bone, held the fragments in place when the man was buried.

Signs of an earlier depressed skull fracture, a focal lesion, were also present in Burial 20, in the posteromedial quadrant of the left parietal bone (also visible on Fig. 38). This fracture, from a blow to the head from behind the individual, appeared still to have been healing at the time of death, indicating it occurred not long before the blow that probably killed the man.

Two healed depressed fractures were visible in the skull of Burial 16, and one in Burial 45. Two of the three fractures, one in each person, involved the frontal bone, indicating blows incurred from the front.

Other indicators of interpersonal violence were suggested by a button osteoma in the skull of Burial 23 (frontal bone) and by a large ossified subperiosteal hematoma on the posterior parietals of the skull of Burial 56 (Fig. 40). Burial 20 also suffered fractured nasal bones, and in Burial 33, there was a complete fracture of an upper incisor through the root above the crown, known as a "Class IV" tooth fracture in modern dental practice (Matteson and Tyndall, 1983, Fig. 1). The fractured crown was still in its tooth socket, suggesting the blow which produced the damage did not occur long before the death of the man.

All head and facial injuries were incurred by males, possibly suggesting episodes of warfare involving the Greenville burial population. Given the crippled condition of Burial 20, there can be some doubt that this man was a "warrior," but, because of his condition, he might more easily have been killed than other inhabitants during a surprise attack on his village. At the Lachane site in Prince Rupert Harbour, there were four known or suspected cases of decapitation, the bodies very closely situated in the site, suggesting the result of a one-time warfare-related raid.

Broadly speaking, the anatomical distribution of trauma in the Greenville series was similar to that of Prince Rupert Harbour as may be seen on Figure 41. This suggests broadly similar environmental and, perhaps, social and cultural conditions, albeit with some variation. In both groups, injuries to the head (vault, face, teeth, and lower jaw) and spinal compression fractures were most common, followed by injuries to the hand, forearm, and lower leg. An initially obvious difference on the chart is suggested by trauma to the feet. Foot injuries were more than twice as common in the Greenville series as in the Prince Rupert Harbour series. Offsetting this difference, there were relatively fewer head injuries in the Greenville group, no traumatic fractures in the spine other than body compression, and no injuries to the humerus or upper arm. These variations might suggest culturally or socially interpretable factors related to cause. To examine this possibility, the anatomical data were further reduced to investigate population distributions based on the causes of trauma. For example, forearm fractures, lumped on Figure 41, were examined according to those most likely due to accident (wrist or elbow ends) and those likely due to interpersonal violence (shaft fractures). Also, the data were reorganized to consider the numbers of affected individuals rather than bones.

Figure 42 compares five coastal British Columbia skeletal series according to the percentage of individuals with trauma most likely due to interpersonal violence, accident, or physiological stress. Included are Namu, Prince Rupert Harbour, Strait of Georgia, Greenville, and historic period remains. The last includes individuals from Gust Island Rockshelter, Owikeno Lake, Hesquiat Harbour, and museum-collected remains from throughout the Queen Charlotte Islands. The number of

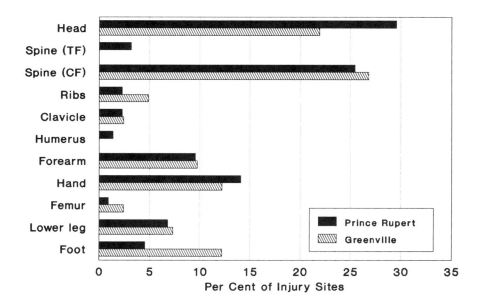

FIGURE 41. Relative distribution of injured anatomical sites in Prince Rupert Harbour and Greenville skeletal series. (TF = non-compression fracture; CF = compression fracture).

individuals considered in the Strait of Georgia portrait is 31 less than that reported in Appendix C as data on trauma were not specifically available for those remains. In this respect, I relied on the reports of the various investigators cited in Appendix C except for my own studies of Duke Point, Maple Bay, some of the Crescent Beach remains, and a few skulls from False Narrows. The latter were reported by Marjory Gordon (1974) as having "cranial lesions" assigned as non-metric skeletal variants, but possibly signifying depressed fractures. The lesions were, indeed, those of healed depressed skull fractures.

A great deal of care was taken in the causal interpretation of the traumatic injuries, and those injuries which might be interpreted in different ways were relegated to a fourth category, "undecided." For example, most of the "violence" component for each series includes head injuries. It may be noted, however, that not all head injuries may automatically be attributed to interpersonal violence as is often the case in studies of prehistoric skeletal series. While this is almost certainly true for Greenville and for the Namu fractures described by A.J. Curtin (1984), including depressed vault fractures, fractured upper facial bones, and Class IV tooth fractures, one Prince Rupert Harbour male skeleton exhibited a horizontal

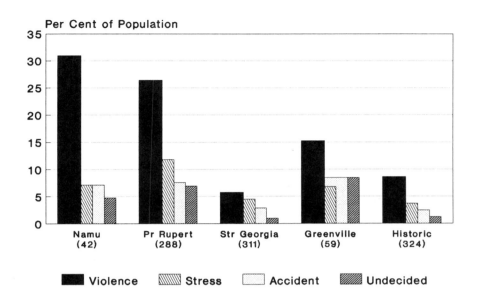

FIGURE 42. Population distribution of trauma due to interpersonal violence, accident, and physiological stress in five coastal British Columbia skeletal series. (Sample sizes in parentheses).

chin fracture plausibly attributable to an accidental fall.   For one individual from a Strait of Georgia site, Owen Beattie (1981) described a possible linear fracture in the skull vault.   Modern clinical studies indicate that stand-alone linear skull fractures are more often associated with accidents than with assaults, typically falls from high places or vehicle crashes.   They result when a moving head strikes a stationary object, usually at a point on the skull distant from the impact, in contrast to a depressed fracture which results when a head is stationary and struck by a moving object as, for example, in the case of a club blow (Gurdjian et al., 1950; Gurdjian and Webster, 1958; Gurdjian et al., 1970; Tedeschi, 1977).

For each series on the chart, the individuals represented in each component of trauma are not necessarily mutually exclusive.   For example, Burial 16 at Greenville exhibited two depressed skull fractures (violence) and a distal intraarticular radius fracture (accident).   The idea here is to show and compare the actual percentage of individuals with each component type.   The total percentages of known injured individuals in each series, regardless of cause, were 35.7% at Namu, 39.6% at Prince Rupert Harbour, 12.5% in the Strait of Georgia sites, 27.1% at Greenville, and 14.5% in the historic series.   For the reasons cited earlier in this section, spondylolysis was excluded from the comparisons.

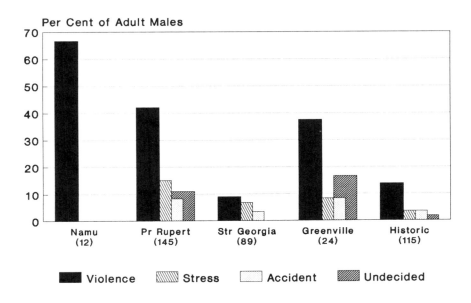

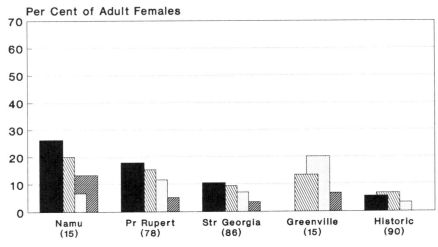

FIGURE 43. Adult distribution by sex of trauma due to interpersonal violence, accident, and physiological stress in five coastal British Columbia series. (Sample sizes in parentheses).

In the section on vital statistics in Chapter III, I reported marked differences between the Prince Rupert Harbour and Strait of Georgia regions in the frequency of trauma plausibly attributable to intertribal warfare. This is clearly evident on the chart for these two large prehistoric population samples mainly attributable to the Middle Developmental Stage. Indeed, the overall frequency of any type of trauma is much lower in the Strait of Georgia group than it is in any of the other prehistoric series.

The other groups on the chart suggest a possible time-related trend toward reduced intertribal warfare from the Early Developmental through Late Developmental stages of coastal British Columbia prehistory, on through the historic period. However, the trend would obviously not apply to the entire coast if, indeed, it existed. Aside from the substantially low frequency of trauma in the Strait of Georgia series, virtually no trauma was reported for the Early Developmental Stage Blue Jackets Creek series. I did not include it in the chart because Jeffrey Murray (1981) reported only one vertebral compression fracture.

The possible trend is also compromised in the other groups when consideration is given to the distribution of component-type trauma by sex, illustrated on Figure 43. Here, Prince Rupert Harbour and Greenville present a more equitable portrait with respect to males with trauma plausibly attributable to hand-to-hand combat. The chart also demonstrates a marked sex difference in violence-related injuries in these groups, Namu, and, to some extent, the historic series, expected if warfare were at issue. Interestingly, as well, none of the Greenville females showed trauma due to interpersonal violence. The skeletal injuries they manifested were more likely due to accidental falls.

The predominance of young males in the late component of Greenville as opposed to the more demographically equitable shell component, reported in Chapter III, suggested to me that the late component burial group might have reflected a restrictive sample of warfare-related deaths. However, this is not demonstrated by the available skeletal data. Only two of the nine males in the late component showed fractures plausibly attributable to interpersonal violence, while five did so among the same number of males in the shell component. Other reasons would have to be examined to explain the demographic difference and 200 or so years gap between the two components of the site.

Degenerative Joint Disease

Almost all of the adult skeletons in the Greenville series for which the observation was possible, 89.2%, exhibited some degree of degenerative joint disease in the form of osteoarthritis of diarthrodial joints (86.5%) or osteophytosis of vertebral bodies (56.7%). In some cases, only a single joint was involved, but most individual expressions involved two or more joints. For the most part, expressions varied according to increasing age at death, supporting the widely accepted contention that degenerative joint disease results from "normal" wear and tear on joints.

During observation, the degree of osteoarthritis was scaled according to four expressions, severe, advanced, moderate, and slight. Severe expressions were identified by eburnation of joint surfaces, indicating bone-on-bone contact following complete breakdown of the joint cartilage. Advanced expressions were identified by heavy lipping or marginal hypertrophy of joint surfaces and (or) advanced erosion short of eburnation. Moderate and slight changes were identified by moderate or slight degrees of lipping and (or) surface pitting.

Seven individuals, including four males and three females, exhibited severe manifestations of osteoarthritis, five (one male and four females) exhibited advanced changes, nine (six males and three females) showed moderate manifestations, and 11 individuals (nine males and two females) exhibited slight changes. Overall, females showed a greater degree of osteoathritis than males with 58.3% of the affected females having severe or advanced changes as opposed to 25.0% of the affected males.

This sex difference was also evident in individual joint complex involvements shown on Figure 44. Sixteen major joint complexes were examined and the chart includes all degrees of expression. With three exceptions, females were more frequently affected than males. Males greatly exceeded females in the frequency of temporomandibular (jaw) joint arthritis, and the sexes were about equally affected in frequencies involving the sternoclavicular joint (breastbone - collarbone connection) and wrist complex. In both sexes, the sacroiliac joint, which connects the pelvis to the spine, was most commonly involved. The overall sex difference in the frequency and degree of osteoarthritis can probably be attributed to age differences. As noted earlier in this book, there was a relatively higher proportion of older females than males in the Greenville series. Also, there were seven females over the age of about 45 years, probably post-menopausal. Robert Jurmain (1977) noted that post-menopausal women show an increase in the frequency of osteoarthritis because of hormonal changes.

Lesions simulating arthritic pitting or erosion were apparent in the vertebrae of three immature persons. All lesions were in the articular facets of the apophyseal joints, the interconnecting parts of the neural arches which surround the spinal cord. In Burial 4, 12-16 years of age, the affected vertebrae included the second and third cervicals (neck), and the fourth, seventh, tenth and eleventh thoracics

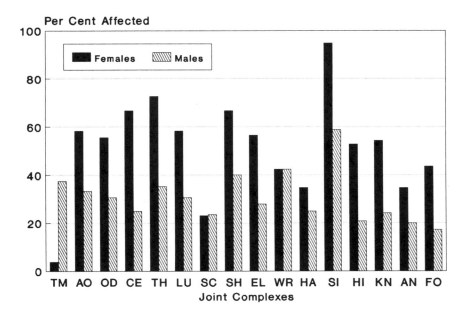

TM = temporomandibular   EL = elbow
AO = atlanto-occipital   WR = wrist
OD = odontoid   HA = hand
CE = cervical   SI = sacroiliac
TH = thoracic   HI = hip
LU = lumbar   KN = knee
SC = sternoclavicular   AN = ankle
SH = shoulder   FO = foot

FIGURE 44. Frequency of osteoarthritis in the Greenville skeletal
series by major joint complex and sex.

(middle to lower back). In Burial 13, 9-11 years old, the second cervical, third through tenth thoracic, twelfth thoracic, and first lumbar vertebrae were affected. In Burial 21, 8-10 years old, the second and fourth cervical, and the fourth, fifth, eighth, and ninth thoracic vertebrae were involved. The cause of these lesions is unknown. While they might have represented remodeling features of the growing vertebrae, they were not observed in all of the vertebrae of these persons or in the vertebrae of other youngsters. Burial 21 also exhibited cribra orbitalia but its association with the vertebral changes is doubtful. Burial 13 displayed no other pathological changes. In Burial 4, there were definite signs of slight or moderate vertebral body wedging in the fourth through twelfth thoracic units.   However, it is uncertain that these changes were associated with the articular facet lesions.

Schmorl's Nodes

Schmorl's nodes are herniations of intervertebral disc tissue into the vertebral bodies (Saluja et al., 1986).   While the cause is not wholly understood, disc herniations have been associated with trauma, growth disorders, advanced arthritis, and other diseases that involve weakening of the bone or disruption of the cartilage endplate in the developing vertebral body.   In skeletal remains, they are represented as depressions or elongate channels of varying depth in the superior and (or) inferior surfaces of the bodies.

Ten of 28 individuals (35.7%) for which observations were possible featured Schmorl's node scars, including five of 17 men (29.4%) and five of 11 women (45.45%).   Six of those people were of advanced age and also showed severe or advanced arthritic changes.   Four also exhibited spinal compression fractures.

In two people, the presence of Schmorl's node scars could not be explained by advanced age, advanced or severe arthritis, or associated instances of acute trauma. They were Burial 34, aged 28-34 years, and Burial 38, 16-18 years old.   In Burial 34, the spine was poorly preserved and, therefore, not amenable to investigating a possible cause for a Schmorl's node scar in the fourth lumbar.

Burial 38 featured a Schmorl's node scar in the eighth thoracic vertebra.   There were no degenerative changes in the generally well-preserved spine of this person, and the vertebra itself was otherwise normal.   However, the fourth and fifth lumbar vertebrae showed extensive destruction of the bodies, perhaps due to pyogenic osteomyelitis secondary to an infection of the intervertebral disc.   While this was a significant finding on its own terms, it is uncertain that the Schmorl's node in the higher vertebra was related, though consequences of the infection might have added undue stresses to the upper spine.   Elsewhere, three individuals of advanced years with Schmorl's node scars also featured erosions in the lower lumbar region which suggested inflammation or destruction from adjacent intervertebral disc infection.

Soft Tissue Calcifications

The remains of two elderly females, Burials 24 and 29, were recovered with unusual bony elements which may represent calcified soft tissue.   All of the pieces resembled half-cylinders.   Burial 24 had a segment 32 mm long by 6 mm in diameter, the configuration of which, with an angular branching at one end, suggested a part of the tertiary bronchi (Cybulski, 1991c, Fig. 15).   There were ten fragments

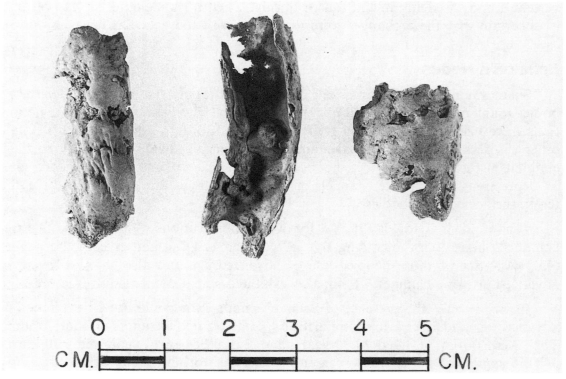

FIGURE 45.   Atheromatous half-casts with Burial 29.

with Burial 29, the largest a gently curving structure 36 mm long by 9 mm in diameter (Fig. 45). A second, shorter piece had a diameter of 14 mm. Conceivably,
the ten pieces could have represented atheromatous arterial half-casts. Atheroma
are the lesions of a form of arteriosclerosis or hardening of the arteries. The
ossified elements may indicate an advanced stage of the disease which is not uncommon today among the late middle-aged and elderly.

Chapter VII

Summary and Discussion

This book has given an account of the excavation and analysis of a Northwest Coast burial ground in the Nass River valley of west-central British Columbia. The site at Greenville has also provided a focus for a broader investigation of native coastal British Columbia history with respect to mortuary practices, burial chronology, vital statistics, human biology, and paleopathology. Related interpretive elements have been considered and discussed in the preceding chapters. In this chapter, I summarize certain findings and elaborate on issues concerning ethnographic connections with the prehistoric past, biological relationships on the north coast of British Columbia, Northwest Coast shell middens as cemetery areas, a possibility of separate burial areas in the prehistoric past for people of different social classes and (or) lineages, and aspects of diet, disease, injury and death. The focus is on Greenville. Not to be ignored is the bi-component nature of the site and the apparent 200-year gap between the earlier shell and later soil components.

Nisga'a Ethnographic Connections

One question this study cannot answer with finality is whether the burial ground at Greenville provides evidence for the existence of *Laxgalts'ap*, the "ancient" principal Nisga'a village recognized through oral history to have been at the location of the modern village (see Chapter I). While the presence of shell, animal bones, and artifacts suggested habitation refuse, the burial site provided no specific habitation features. No systematic archaeological excavations had been conducted in the general area prior to this excavation. Although residents of the modern village have on occasion recovered stone tools suggesting a prehistoric occupation at Greenville (Carlson, 1977), our agreement with the Lakalzap Band to excavate the burial site precluded other field explorations which might have helped to place those tools within a definable archaeological context or relate the burial ground to a contemporary village site.

Just how ancient *Laxgalts'ap* might have been is unknown. Radiocarbon and related stratigraphic evidence indicates that the burial ground existed for about 700 years and ended in this capacity in the interval A.D. 1200-1300, about 500 years before initial Indian and European contact on the Northwest Coast in 1774. The modern village of Greenville was not established until about 100 years after contact (see Chapters I and II). Thus, 600 years separate the burial site and modern Greenville, and 500 years separate knowledge from the burial site and "historic" Nisga'a culture.

The artifacts recovered from the Greenville site indicate little in the way of material culture which might be considered specifically Nisga'a. Patricia Sutherland, responsible for the artifact analysis, reported to me that the largely utilitarian assemblage is "fairly typical" of those recovered from other prehistoric sites on the northern Northwest Coast. Detailed counts of artifacts, by type, form, and function, which have been recovered from sites in the Prince Rupert Harbour region, Queen Charlotte Islands, and neighbouring Tlingit areas are not yet available for statistical treatments which might otherwise discriminate among the sites or temporal components within them.

Other elements in the Greenville burial ground, however, may reflect Nisga'a oral traditions. They include the single hearth in the site which may have been used to burn food and clothing for the dead, a reported Nisga'a burial ritual (Chapter II), and the presence of elderberry seeds with 16 individuals (heavily concentrated in eight cases), a finding possibly connected with a deeply rooted Tsimshian origin myth set in the Nass River valley (Chapter III).

Dental evidence from the Greenville site indicates that most or, possibly, all of the women whose remains were buried there wore labrets through a hole pierced through the skin below the lower lip. In ethnographic times, "the labret was symbolic of the importance of the matriarch in Nisgha Society (sic)" (Nisga'a School District 92, Bilingual-Bicultural Department, 1981:46). While this suggests a Nisga'a connection with the Greenville burial ground, labrets were also worn by women in other northern Northwest Coast societies. Hence, the finding, and the interpretations I have offered concerning possible Late Developmental Stage origins for north coast social organization based on matrilineal descent, need not be ethnically specific. Similarly, the findings reported in Chapter III concerning the remains of dogs in the Greenville site and their possible ethnographic ritual connotations may have broader implications for Tsimshian cultural practices. They might reflect a framework for the origin and cultural transmission through time of a "secret society" known to the Tsimshian at large. Studies of earlier burial sites in the Nass River valley and other than Middle Developmental Stage burial sites elsewhere in traditional Tsimshian areas (e.g., Prince Rupert Harbour) might help to clarify or, better, test the speculations put forth in Chapter III concerning both labret use on the north coast and dog remains in human burial grounds.

As reported in Chapter IV, the predominant fish content of the vertebrate faunal remains recovered from the Greenville site mirrors dietary practices known historically among Nisga'a. Noteworthy is the prevalence of salmon and eulachon remains, though the latter may have represented food for the dead rather than the living. The faunal distribution pattern, however, also reflects an expected ecological orientation for the location of the Greenville site when compared with outer coast and inland archaeological sites for which representative faunal data are available. This latter finding does not necessarily compromise Nisga'a ethnographic connections. It simply means that any people who built the site used the available resources. The presence of other faunal remains in the site might also be explained by traditional Nisga'a cultural practices or ecological orientation.

What is not easily explained in terms of the ethnographic present is the obvious difference between reported Nisga'a mortuary customs involving above ground disposal of the dead and the evidence of the Greenville site pointing to below ground midden burial. This difference between the known prehistoric and historic periods is not unique to the Greenville area but widespread on the British Columbia coast as discussed in Chapter III. Below ground burial, evident on the coast for 4,000-5,000 years, seems to have ended by A.D. 1300, at which time above ground corpse disposal may have been initiated. Why such a major change should have occurred in a long-standing socially important custom, especially over a wide area of the coast, is unknown, but it may have implications for broader interpretations of Northwest Coast prehistory in the last 500 to 800 years before European contact.

Another coastwide mortuary pattern detected in this study may have involved selective burial of infants. As presented in Chapter III, infant remains are consistently more frequent in historic than in prehistoric sites, Greenville included. Greater intersite variability in the prehistoric period may indicate that infants were relegated to special burial areas, a cultural practice which may no longer have been possible in the historic period due to generally high and rapid mortality resulting from newly introduced, European-borne diseases. On the other hand, a postulated end to the practice may have been related to the shift from below ground burial to above ground corpse disposal methods.

Biological Relationships

As detailed in Chapter V, multivariate assessments of metric and non-metric cranial characteristics in the skeletons from Greenville, Prince Rupert Harbour, Namu, and Blue Jackets Creek indicate that Greenville is most closely related to Prince Rupert Harbour, possibly denoting a common ancestral connection to later Tsimshian peoples. However, the relationships among the four groups that emerge from the analyses might also be expected on geographic and physiographic grounds.

Greenville and Prince Rupert Harbour are geographically more accessible to one another than to Namu or Blue Jackets Creek, and Blue Jackets Creek, in its island enclave, is physiographically remote among the four. This might explain the presumed biological uniqueness of Blue Jackets Creek. Studies of skeletal remains from the same areas but at different time levels are needed to further explore questions of biological ancestry and descent on the north coast of British Columbia. Data on historic Tsimshian and Nisga'a skeletal remains would be particularly valuable to test the apparent ancestral commonality suggested for Greenville and Prince Rupert Harbour.

While the present lack of Nisga'a skeletal data indicates that we as yet have no clear basis to assume biological continuity between Greenville and Nisga'a, a hint of that kind of continuity may be indicated by the graphical comparisons in head shape shown in Chapter V. The categorical distributions of the cranial index in Greenville males and the cephalic index in 19th century Nisga'a men are very similar and appear set apart from the male cranial index distributions for Prince Rupert Harbour. If a general north coast temporal trend to brachycephalization were the only variable effecting the relationships shown on Figure 27, a less abrupt change might be expected between Prince Rupert Harbour and Greenville.

Shell Middens as Cemeteries

The lack of any concrete evidence for habitation at the Greenville site appears to indicate that it was solely used as a burial ground. This is further suggested by a low density of artifacts at the site. At prehistoric Hoko River Rockshelter on the Olympic Peninsula, a known habitation site in use for about the same length of time as the Greenville burial ground, 1,657 artifacts were reported by Rebecca Wigen and Barbara Stucki (1988), seven times the number recovered from Greenville. Based on other figures reported by those authors, I calculated the excavated volume of the Hoko River Rockshelter deposits at 142 m^3, almost identical to that of Greenville (Table 4, Chapter III). This indicates a density of 11.7 artifacts per cubic metre at Hoko River Rockshelter but only 1.6 artifacts per cubic metre at Greenville. Similarly, the density of vertebrate faunal elements reported for Hoko River Rockshelter exceeded that for the Greenville burial ground by more than 2.6 to 1.

Northwest Coast archaeologists have generally viewed shell middens, including burial areas within them, as habitation sites. Large middens have commonly been interpreted as "semipermanent" settlement grounds, or "winter villages" in the context of ethnographic Northwest Coast culture, continuously occupied for long periods of time, while smaller middens have been assigned the status of temporary settlements such as seasonal camps used for fishing or hunting activities (e.g., MacDonald and Inglis, 1981). Greenville and Fishery Bay might serve as analogous modern examples of such historically known Northwest Coast settlement patterns (see discussion in Chapter IV).

In a discussion of the importance of sampling strategy in the excavation of shell middens, viewed in this orthodox fashion, David Burley (1980:11-12) noted that any one area of a particularly large midden need not necessarily reflect all aspects of the culture the midden is presumed to represent. Some portions of a site may have been used for specialized activities for a certain period of time, but then changed with ongoing occupation. House locations, for example, may have been abandoned for considerable periods of time when the occupants moved to areas further along the beach. In other words, prehistoric village sites may be seen as changing structural entities, possibly dependent on variations in population size over time, changes in defense strategies, natural environmental influences, or other cultural influences. Modern Greenville might, again, here serve as an analogous example owing to the very circumstances which led to excavation of the burial ground. In 1981, a new housing development was initiated in a previously unbuilt section of the village to accomodate a growing population.

Historically for the Tsimshian area, village cemeteries were designated on land contiguous with the villages or nearby on offshore islands (Boas, 1916; Garfield, 1939). Today, there is a village cemetery at the back of Greenville in which deceased members of the community are interred, following one of the two possible historical traditions. It may be that the ancient burial ground reflected a similar situation long before European contact.

We know that today's cemetery at Greenville is coeval with the occupation of the village. There is little hard data, however, to conclude that past, prehistoric midden cemeteries on the British Columbia coast were contiguous and coeval with village occupations, although that is generally assumed by most archaeologists. Contemporaneity has yet to be tested at large middens such as Boardwalk and Lachane in the Prince Rupert Harbour region where both cemetery and habitation areas are apparent (see discussion of disturbed skeletal elements in Chapter III). It is conceivable that whole village sites were periodically abandoned, during which time the accumulated shell refuse was used as a repository for the dead from neighbouring occupied areas. Some of these sites may have subsequently been resettled either by descendants of the same population or by different local or neighbouring regional populations. Resettlement after a period of abandonment may account for the finding, as in the case of Boardwalk, of occasional human burials in parts of a site identified as habitation areas. Resettlement by a different population after a particularly long period of abandonment may account in part for disturbed human remains in cemetery areas unknown to the new population.

The possibility of periodic village abandonment on a major scale might be illustrated by the Greenville site itself. Two time-related burial components were identified, separated by an apparent 200-year gap. Initially, human remains seem to have been deposited continuously at the site over a period of 400 years or so. Subsequently, a number of individuals were buried between A.D. 1200 and 1300. Unfortunately, there is little in the cultural or skeletal data which might identify a reason for the abandonment of the cemetery and its subsequent reuse. Apparent demographic differences between the two components may reflect differences in the compositions of the source populations, by age, sex, or, possibly, size. The original population who contributed their dead to the site may have been driven out by another group through warfare, or simply abandoned the area because of a change in resource availability perhaps instigated by a fluctuation in climatic conditions. The fact that the same location was used may indicate that it was known as a burial ground to the population who later buried their dead there. It may have been descendants of the original contributing population who returned to the site, but on a much smaller scale than previously.

One finding that seems almost constant in British Columbia shell midden sites is the presence of human remains. While cultural features suggesting habitation are occasionally reported, they are comparatively rare. James J. Hester (1978:7), who directed the University of Colorado excavations at Namu, interpreted as a habitation site, reported that "in general the major cultural features in the middens were burials." Because of the almost ubiquitous presence of human remains, one might wonder whether shell deposits were specifically sought out as cemeteries in the prehistoric past; whether, in some cases, shell mounds may have specifically been built for the interment of deceased individuals; or, whether the construction of shell middens was, in some cases, a by-product of a corpse disposal ritual.

The shell deposit excavated at Greenville was discrete (see Chapter II). The senior technician with the engineering and planning firm partly responsible for the discovery of the site, was of the opinion that the depositional materials were foreign, that, in fact, the shell had been brought to the site's location from somewhere else. Perhaps the shell midden was a secondary deposition from village refuse elsewhere in the area of Greenville, specifically brought to the site for mortuary purposes. One might further speculate that a long-standing coastal ritual of shell-related burial then persisted at the site for about 400 years. This ritual ended at the time of abandonment, perhaps for the same reason(s) that the site itself was abandoned. Village midden material was no longer used by the later source population, reflected in the fact that statistically fewer bone than stone artifacts, but not humans, were represented in the soil layer (A2). The artifact content in the shell layer was different from that in the soil layer, more representative of a range of utilitarian items which might expectedly be found in village refuse. Perhaps the later use of the burial site was by seasonal hunters or fishers, an observation which might account for the predominance of adult male deceased.

Burial by Social Class and (or) Lineage

As noted in Chapter III, prehistorians on the Northwest Coast have traditionally looked for the associations of "grave goods" with human burials as potential indicators of the relative social rank or status of the deceased. Cultural artifacts which might be interpreted as wealth or ritual objects were not associated with any of the Greenville burials. Indeed, only one burial was accompanied by an artifact, this an apparently utilitarian item, possibly a favoured chopping or scraping tool used by the woman in question to prepare animal skins for clothing.

Other features of the Greenville burial ground, however, suggest that it might have been limited to high ranking individuals as a group. Most notably, 75% of the females in the site exhibited abrasion facets on their teeth from the use of labrets. Because of missing jaws or relevant lower teeth, the remaining 25% (4 individuals) could not adequately be studied for labret abrasion facets. It is quite possible, therefore, that all of the women buried in the site may have worn labrets. Labrets were indicators of high rank among the Nisga'a (Nisga'a School District 92, Bilingual-Bicultural Department, 1981:46) and appear to have been a hallmark of status in other northern Northwest Coast groups (Collison, 1981:175-176).

Wealth and high rank were associated in Northwest Coast culture. In addition to its mythological significance, elderberry was regarded as "rich food" by the Nisga'a and other Tsimshian (see "food for the dead" section in Chapter III). The presence of seeds with one-half the sample of intact burials, therefore, could also be an indication that the Greenville site was a mortuary enclave for high ranking people. If my speculations concerning the presence of dog remains in the Greenville site are palatable, this may indicate further evidence for the presence of high ranking individuals. According to Viola Garfield (Garfield and Wingert, 1951:45), membership in the Dog Eaters society "was open to any Tsimshian who had the wealth necessary for an initiatory ceremony."

Other possible indicators of "wealth" were recovered from the site, including two small samples of red ochre, an ochre-stained human big toe phalange in an isolated disturbed context, and three pieces of mica. While these examples could hardly be considered frequent, their potential significance is of interest. Among

Nisga'a, red ochre was used for self-decoration and for painting wood. It was considered a luxury good, extremely difficult of access in the mountains and, therefore, highly valued (McNeary, 1976:68). Mica might have held similar significance for the group who buried their dead there. It is known to have been used for self-decoration among other Northwest Coast Indians (McMillan, 1988:196).

Alfred Niblack reported the occasional occurrence of square burial boxes at Tlingit gravesites, citing 18th century observers' conclusions "that only 'certain persons' were thus entombed" (see Chapter III). There was a prevalence of square burial boxes in the Greenville site. Though they could plausibly have represented a secondary use of food storage boxes, they might also have served to contain "certain persons" of rank and nobility.

If the site at Greenville was a common village burial ground, it is difficult to account for the recovery of only 57 individuals from a period of 700 years. Even the more demographically equitable shell component, used for 400 years, would not be representative of a cemetery used by all the inhabitants of a village unless the "village" were exceedingly small. Extrapolating from the proportions of individuals which could be assigned to either the shell or soil component, figures for the shell component would yield a local population death rate of only 0.10 persons per year. Perhaps, only upper class individuals were buried there and, perhaps, only those members of a single lineage that persisted over many generations. Rather than only one midden burying ground, several burying grounds may have existed in the Greenville area and been used contemporaneously by different segments of a community. The two individuals recovered during a 1984 water-line excavation 35-40 m from the limits of the site we excavated in 1981-1983 may be indicative.

It may also be noted that Greenville is not a unique midden cemetery site in terms of small burial yield relative to the length of time it was used. As shown in Table 4, Chapter III, the "shell-dumps" at Boardwalk, the most completely excavated of the Prince Rupert Harbour middens, yielded 108 people, 90% of the site's deceased. Radiocarbon dates suggest that Areas A and C were used as cemeteries for about 900 years, indicating a contributing population death rate of 0.12 persons per year. As argued elsewhere, lineage burial could have accounted for hereditary brachydactyly at Boardwalk and other Prince Rupert Harbour middens (Cybulski, 1988a).

Diet, Disease, Injury, and Death

The Greenville skeletal series featured a very low rate of dental caries and a high rate of occlusal attrition as in prehistoric coastal British Columbia populations in general. Such findings are common in human "hunter-gatherer" populations where diets are low in carbohydrates (sugars, starches, and cellulose), important contributors to the formation of dental caries in agricultural groups. Food preparation techniques probably contributed abrasives to the daily food intake, encouraging high rates of occlusal attrition due to a reliance on fish (e.g., dried salmon) and meats, the staples of the traditional Northwest Coast diet.

There were no bone changes in the population which might point to poor nutrition. Cribra orbitalia, evident in 8 of 38 individuals (21%), has in past theory been suggested to reflect nutritional problems stemming from an iron-poor diet or the presence of iron-chelating agents in an otherwise adequate diet. Current academic thinking, however, minimizes the role of diet in the production of cribra orbitalia (porotic hyperostosis) as an indicator of iron-deficiency anemia. Rather, the variable occurrence of this skeletal lesion may reflect a group's successful adaptation to the "pathogen load" of its local environment (Stuart-Macadam, 1992). Included in the pathogen load are all fungi, viruses, bacteria, and parasites to which a local population is subjected. The extent of the load is dependent on many local factors such as "climate, geography, topography, population size and density, hygiene, food resources, seasonality, customs, and subsistence patterns" (ibid., p. 42). It is difficult to identify any one factor to account for the occurrence of porotic hyperostosis in any one population. Most of the cited factors, including climate, geography, topography, and, probably, resources, seasonality, customs, and subsistence patterns, would have been similar in most coastal British Columbia groups, leaving variations in population size and density, and sanitation, perhaps, to account for observed local or regional variations in the frequency of cribra orbitalia.

Early in the analysis of the Greenville skeletons, I submitted bones from Burials 2 and 3 for stable carbon isotope studies carried out by Brian Chisholm at Simon Fraser University. Delta ^{13}C values of -13.50 and -13.96 were returned, similar to values for human bones sampled from other coastal British Columbia prehistoric sites (Chisholm et al., 1983). As indicators of diet, the values for the two Greenville deceased suggest marine-based protein intakes (including anadromous fish species) of 93% and 86% respectively, compared to a range of 85% to 100% for five individuals from three Prince Rupert Harbour sites (ibid., p. 397). In all cases, there is a 10% uncertainty in the proportions, measured against protein intakes based on terrestrial resources.

Signs of disease in the Greenville skeletal remains included abscessed tooth sockets, probable chronic sinus infections, possible otitis media or middle ear infections, and frequent expressions of degenerative joint disease. At least one person, an old woman, may have suffered from arteriosclerosis or hardening of the arteries. There were no indications of specific or non-specific system-wide infections in any individuals which might be represented by gross morphological changes in the skull, spine, or long bones. Changes like this, possibly or probably due to treponemal infection, have been noted in Middle Developmental Stage skeletons from Prince Rupert Harbour and Duke Point (Cybulski, 1990) and in bones from Crescent Beach (Conaty and Curtin, 1984).

Major congenital disturbances in the Greenville series appeared limited to vertebral scoliosis and related anomalies in a young adult male and hip dysplasia in a young woman.

Next to degenerative joint disease, the most common form of pathological change in the Greenville deceased involved trauma. Excluding spondylolysis, a form of fatigue fracture in the spine which may be influenced by heredity, 27.1% of the Greenville burial population were affected by some form of skeletal or dental trauma. The proportion is less than reported for either Namu or Prince Rupert Harbour but greater than proportions for Strait of Georgia prehistoric sites and a coastwide historic British Columbia skeletal sample. Unlike the other series, trauma in the adult female segment of the population was most likely due to accident and this group showed no obvious indicators for interpersonal violence. The male segment, on the other hand, exhibited a frequency of trauma plausibly attributable to interpersonal violence on the order of 40%, similar to that of the male population of Prince Rupert Harbour. Warfare was probably an issue during both the Middle and Late Developmental stages of prehistory on the north coast of British Columbia.

Only rarely is it possible to determine the cause of death from unknown skeletal remains. Burial 20, a young adult male with crippling scoliosis of the spine, may have met his fate through a warfare-related raid on his village. The skull revealed a large, unhealed comminuted depressed fracture, a type of injury readily effected by a blow with a stone club. Some speculation was offered in Chapter III on a possible cause of death for the old woman represented in Burial 29. A cluster of eulachon may have been associated as food for the dead. Eulachon ran the Nass River at a time when winter village reserves were almost exhausted. Possibly, the old woman died at the end of the winter from starvation, though her apparent arterial condition may have been a contributing factor.

References Cited

Adams, J.W. (1973): *The Gitksan Potlatch: Population Flux, Resource Ownership and Reciprocity.* Holt, Rinehart and Winston, Toronto.

Allen, G.M. (1920): Dogs of the American aborigines. *Bulletin of the Museum of Comparative Zoology, Harvard* 63:431-517.

Allen, M.J., and G.B. Smith (1988): Atlas and zoogeography of common fishes in the Bering Sea and the northeastern Pacific. *National Oceanic and Atmospheric Administration Technical Report, National Marine Fisheries Service* 66:1-151.

Aro, K.V., and M.P. Shepard (1967): Pacific salmon in Canada. Salmon of the north Pacific Ocean Part IV. *International North Pacific Fisheries Commission Bulletin* 23:225-327.

Banfield, A.W.F. (1974): *The Mammals of Canada.* University of Toronto Press, Toronto.

Bass, W.M. (1981): *Human Osteology: A Laboratory and Field Manual of the Human Skeleton.* 2nd edition. Missouri Archaeological Society, Columbia.

Beattie, O.B. (1976): Skeletal pathology of prehistoric human remains from Crescent Beach. *In* Current Research Reports, edited by R.L. Carlson, *Simon Fraser University Department of Archaeology Publication* 3, Burnaby, pp. 155-164.

Beattie, O.B. (1981): An analysis of prehistoric human skeletal material from the Gulf of Georgia region of British Columbia. Unpublished Ph.D. Dissertation, Department of Archaeology, Simon Fraser University, Burnaby.

Beattie, O.B. (1985): A note on early cranial studies from the Gulf of Georgia region: long-heads, broad-heads, and the myth of migration. *BC Studies* 66:28-36.

Bennett, K.A. (1972): Lumbo-sacral malformations and spina bifida occulta in a group of proto-historic Modoc Indians. *American Journal of Physical Anthropology* 36:435-440.

Bent, A.C. (1922): Life histories of North American petrels and pelicans and their allies. *U.S. National Museum Bulletin* 121. Washington, D.C.

Bernick, K. (1983): A site catchment analysis of the Little Qualicum River site, DiSc 1: a wet site on the east coast of Vancouver Island, B.C. *National*

Museum of Man Mercury Series, Archaeological Survey of Canada Paper 118. National Museums of Canada, Ottawa.

Berry, A.C., and R.J. Berry (1967): Epigenetic variation in the human cranium. *Journal of Anatomy* 101:361-379.

Boas, F. (1890): First general report on the Indians of British Columbia. *Report of the Meeting of the British Association for the Advancement of Science,* 1889, pp. 801-893.

Boas, F. (1895): Fifth report on the Indians of British Columbia. *Report of the Meeting of the British Association for the Advancement of Science,* 1895, pp. 523-592.

Boas, F. (1902): Tsimshian texts. *Bureau of American Ethnology Bulletin* 27:1-244.

Boas, F. (1916): Tsimshian mythology. *Thirty-first Annual Report of the Bureau of American Ethnology,* 1909-1910, pp. 29-1037.

Borden, C.E. (1976): A water-saturated site on the southern mainland coast of British Columbia. *In* The excavation of water-saturated archaeological sites (wet sites) on the Northwest Coast of North America, edited by D.R. Croes, *National Museum of Man Mercury Series, Archaeological Survey of Canada Paper* 50, National Museums of Canada, Ottawa, pp. 233-260.

Bork-Feltkamp, A.J. van (1960): *Some Remarks on Skulls and Skull Fragments of the Fraser Middens (British Columbia).* Nederlandsch Museum voor Anthropologie.

Boyd, R.T. (1990): Demographic history, 1774-1874. In *Handbook of North American Indians, Vol. 7, Northwest Coast,* edited by W. Suttles, Smithsonian Institution, Washington, pp. 135-148.

Brocher, J.E.W. (1969): Spine. In *Roentgen Diagnosis, Vol. 3: Spine, Skull, Nerves, Eye, Sinuses, Teeth,* 2nd American edition, edited by L.G. Rigler, Grune and Stratton, New York and London, pp. 1-116.

Brothwell, D.R. (1981): *Digging up Bones; the Excavation, Treatment and Study of Human Skeletal Remains.* 3rd edition. Cornell University Press, Ithaca.

Brothwell, D.R., V.M. Carbonell, and D.H. Goose (1963): Congenital absence of teeth in human populations. *In* Dental Anthropology, edited by D.R. Brothwell, *Symposia of the Society for the Study of Human Biology* 5, Pergamon Press, Oxford, pp. 179-190.

Burley, D.V. (1980): Marpole: anthropological reconstructions of a prehistoric Northwest Coast culture type. *Simon Fraser University Department of Archaeology Publication* 8. Burnaby.

Burley, D.V. (1989): Senewelets: culture history of the Nanaimo Coast Salish and the False Narrows midden. *Royal British Columbia Museum Memoir* 2. Victoria.

Calvert, G. (1968): The Co-op site: a prehistoric midden site on the northern northwest coast of British Columbia. Manuscript on file (No. 175), Scientific Records Section, Archaeological Survey of Canada, Canadian Museum of Civilization, Hull.

Calvert, G. (1970): The St. Mungo Cannery site: a preliminary report. *BC Studies* 6&7:54-76.

Cambon, K., J.D. Galbraith, and G. Kong (1965): Middle-ear disease in Indians of the Mount Currie reservation, British Columbia. *Canadian Medical Association Journal* 93:1301-1305.

Capes, K.H. (1977): Archaeological investigations of the Millard Creek site, Vancouver Island, British Columbia. *Syesis* 10:57-84.

Carlson, R.L. (1977): Archaeological survey of the lower Nass, Observatory Inlet, and Portland Canal. Manuscript on file (No. 2112), Scientific Records Section, Archaeological Survey of Canada, Canadian Museum of Civilization, Hull.

Carlson, R.L. (1985): The 1984 excavations at the Canal site (DeRt 1 and DeRt 2). Manuscript on file (Permit 1984-13), Ministry Library, Ministry of Municipal Affairs, Recreation and Culture, Province of British Columbia, Victoria.

Carlson, R.L. (1986): The 1985 excavations at the Canal site (DeRt 1 and DeRt 2). Manuscript on file (Permit 1985-10), Ministry Library, Ministry of Municipal Affairs, Recreation and Culture, Province of British Columbia, Victoria.

Carlson, R.L., and P.M. Hobler (1976): Archaeological survey of Seymour Inlet, Quatsino Sound, and adjacent localities. *In* Current Research Reports, edited by R.L. Carlson, *Simon Fraser University Department of Archaeology Publication* 3, Burnaby, pp. 115-141.

Chisholm, B.S., D.E. Nelson, and H.P. Schwarz (1983): Marine and terrestrial protein in prehistoric diets on the British Columbia coast. *Current Anthropology* 24:396-398.

Cole, D., and D. Darling (1990): History of the early period. In *Handbook of North American Indians, Vol. 7, Northwest Coast,* edited by W. Suttles, Smithsonian Institution, Washington, pp. 119-134.

Collison, W.H. (1981): *In the Wake of the War Canoe.* Based on the edition originally published 1915. Sono Nis Press, Victoria.

Colton, H.S. (1970): The aboriginal southwestern Indian dog. *American Antiquity* 35:153-159.

Conaty, G.T., and A.J. Curtin (1984): Crescent Beach monitoring programme: final report. Manuscript on file (Permit 1983-45), Ministry Library, Ministry of Municipal Affairs, Recreation and Culture, Province of British Columbia, Victoria.

Conover, K. (1978): Matrix analysis. *In* Studies in Bella Bella prehistory, edited by J.J. Hester and S.M. Nelson, *Simon Fraser University Department of Archaeology Publication* 5, Burnaby, pp. 67-99.

Connolly, G.E. (1981): Assessing populations. In *Mule and Black-tailed Deer of North America; A Wildlife Management Book,* edited by O.C. Wallmo, University of Nebraska Press, Lincoln, pp. 287-345.

Cook, F.R. (1984): *Introduction to Canadian Amphibians and Reptiles.* National Museum of Natural Sciences, Ottawa.

Cowan, I.M.T., and C.J. Guiguet (1978): The mammals of British Columbia. *British Columbia Provincial Museum Handbook* 11. Victoria.

Cox, S.L., and A. Spiess (1980): Dorset settlement and subsistence in northern Labrador. *Arctic* 33:659-669.

Curtin, A.J. (1984): Human skeletal remains from Namu (ElSx 1): a descriptive analysis. Unpublished M.A. Thesis, Department of Archaeology, Simon Fraser University, Burnaby.

Curtin, A.J. (1990): Supra-inion depressions and artificial cranial deformation: the evidence from Tsawwassen, B.C. (DgRs 2). Paper read at 18th annual meeting of the Canadian Association for Physical Anthropology, Banff, Alberta.

Curtin, A.J. (n.d.): Analysis of Burial 2 from the Beach Grove site DgRs 1. Manuscript on file, Department of Archaeology, Simon Fraser University, Burnaby.

Cybulski, J.S. (1973): The Gust Island burial shelter: physical anthropology. *National Museum of Man Mercury Series, Archaeological Survey of Canada Paper* 9, National Museums of Canada, Ottawa, pp. 60-113.

Cybulski, J.S. (1974): Tooth wear and material culture: precontact patterns in the Tsimshian area, British Columbia. *Syesis* 7:31-35.

Cybulski, J.S. (1975a): Physical anthropology at Owikeno Lake, 1975. *Canadian Archaeological Association Bulletin* 7:201-210.

Cybulski, J.S. (1975b): Skeletal variability in British Columbia coastal populations: a descriptive and comparative assessment of cranial morphology. *National Museum of Man Mercury Series, Archaeological Survey of Canada Paper* 30. National Museums of Canada, Ottawa.

Cybulski, J.S. (1977a): Physical Anthropology Programme. *In* Archaeological Survey of Canada Annual Review 1975 and 1976, edited by G.F. MacDonald, *National Museum of Man Mercury Series, Archaeological Survey of Canada Paper* 66, National Museums of Canada, Ottawa, pp. 50-54.

Cybulski, J.S. (1977b): Cribra orbitalia, a possible sign of anemia in early historic native populations of the British Columbia coast. *American Journal of Physical Anthropology* 47:31-40.

Cybulski, J.S. (1978a): An earlier population of Hesquiat Harbour, British Columbia: a contribution to Nootkan osteology and physical anthropology. *British Columbia Provincial Museum, Cultural Recovery Papers* 1. Victoria.

Cybulski, J.S. (1978b): Modified human bones and skulls from Prince Rupert Harbour, British Columbia. *Canadian Journal of Archaeology* 2:15-32.

Cybulski, J.S. (1980): Osteology of the human remains from Yuquot, British Columbia. *History and Archaeology* 43:175-194.

Cybulski, J.S. (1985): Elcho Harbour human remains in National Museums of Canada collections. Manuscript on file (No. 2588), Scientific Records Section, Archaeological Survey of Canada, Canadian Museum of Civilization, Hull.

Cybulski, J.S. (1986): Human remains from Lucy Island, British Columbia, site GbTp 1, 1984/85. Manuscript on file (No. 2630), Scientific Records Section, Archaeological Survey of Canada, Canadian Museum of Civilization, Hull.

Cybulski, J.S. (1988a): Brachydactyly, a possible inherited anomaly at prehistoric Prince Rupert Harbour. *American Journal of Physical Anthropology* 76:363-376.

Cybulski, J.S. (1988b): Human skeletal remains from site DeRu 12, Maple Bay, British Columbia (April, 1988). Appendix I in: Report on the results of an archaeological impact assessment and mitigation project at the Maple Bay site (DeRu 12) Vancouver Island, by B. Simonsen, Manuscript on file (Permit 1988-20), Ministry Library, Ministry of Municipal Affairs, Recreation and Culture, Province of British Columbia, Victoria.

Cybulski, J.S. (1990): Human biology. In *Handbook of North American Indians, Vol. 7, Northwest Coast,* edited by W. Suttles, Smithsonian Institution, Washington, pp. 52-59.

Cybulski, J.S. (1991a): Human remains from Duke Point, British Columbia, and probable evidence for pre-Columbian treponematosis. Manuscript on file, Ministry Library, Ministry of Municipal Affairs, Recreation and Culture, Province of British Columbia, Victoria.

Cybulski, J.S. (1991b): Observations on dental labret wear at Crescent Beach, Pender Canal, and other Northwest Coast prehistoric sites. Manuscript on file (No. 3409), Scientific Records Section, Archaeological Survey of Canada, Canadian Museum of Civilization, Hull.

Cybulski, J.S. (1991c): Skeletons in the walls of Old Québec. *Northeast Historical Archaeology* 17(1988):61-84.

Cybulski, J.S. (n.d.a): Skeletal remains and mortuary elements at prehistoric Prince Rupert Harbour. Manuscript in preparation.

Cybulski, J.S. (n.d.b): Owikeno Lake skeletal remains, 1975-1977. Unpublished laboratory data and notes.

Damon, P.E., C.W. Ferguson, A. Long, and E.I. Wallick (1974): Dendrochronologic calibration of the radiocarbon time scale. *American Antiquity* 39:350-366.

Deetz, J. (1977): *In Small Things Forgotten; The Archaeology of Early American Life*. Anchor Press/Doubleday, Garden City.

Dewhirst, J. (1980): The indigenous archaeology of Yuquot, a Nootkan outside village. *History and Archaeology* 39:1-362.

Digance, A.M. (1988): Canid remains from the [Pender] Canal sites. (Abstract). *Northwest Anthropological Research Notes* 22:186.

Drucker, P. (1951): The northern and central Nootkan tribes. *Bureau of American Ethnology Bulletin* 144.

Drucker, P. (1955): *Indians of the Northwest Coast*. The Natural History Press, Garden City, New York.

Finnegan, M.J. (1972): Population definition on the Northwest Coast by analysis of discrete character variation. Unpublished Ph.D. Dissertation, Department of Anthropology, University of Colorado, Boulder.

Fisher, H.I. (1972): Sympatry of Laysan and black-footed albatrosses. *Auk* 89:381-402.

Fladmark, K.R. (1975): A paleoecological model for Northwest Coast prehistory. *National Museum of Man Mercury Series, Archaeological Survey of Canada Paper* 43. National Museums of Canada, Ottawa.

Fladmark, K.R. (1986): *British Columbia Prehistory.* National Museums of Canada, Ottawa.

Frayer, D.W. (1988): Auditory exostoses and evidence for fishing at Vlasac. *Current Anthropology* 29:346-349.

Garfield, V.E. (1939): Tsimshian clan and society. *University of Washington Publications in Anthropology* 7(3):167-340.

Garfield, V.E., and P.S. Wingert (1951): *The Tsimshian Indians and Their Arts.* Douglas and McIntyre, Vancouver.

Gilbert, B.M., and T.W. McKern (1973): A method for aging the female os pubis. *American Journal of Physical Anthropology* 38:31-38.

Godfrey, W.E. (1986): *The Birds of Canada.* Revised edition. National Museum of Natural Sciences, Ottawa.

Gordon, M.E. (1974): A qualitative analysis of human skeletal remains from DgRw-4, Gabriola Island, British Columbia. Unpublished M.A. Thesis, Department of Archaeology, University of Calgary, Calgary.

Greenway, J.C., Jr. (1958): Extinct and vanishing birds of the world. *American Committee for International Wild Life Protection, Special Publication* 13. New York.

Guiguet, C.J. (1978): The birds of British Columbia. *British Columbia Provincial Museum Handbook.* Victoria.

Gurdjian, E.S., D. Gonzales, R.T. Hodgson, L.M. Thomas, and S.W. Greenberg (1970): Comparisons of research in inanimate and biologic material: artifacts and pitfalls. In *Impact Injury and Crash Protection,* edited by E.S. Gurdjian, L.M. Patrick, and L.M. Thomas, Charles C. Thomas, Springfield, pp. 234-255.

Gurdjian, E.S., and J.E. Webster (1958): *Head Injuries: Mechanisms, Diagnosis and Management.* Little, Brown and Company, Boston and Toronto.

Gurdjian, E.S., J.E. Webster, and H.R. Lissner (1950): The mechanism of skull fracture. *Radiology* 54:313-339.

Haggarty, J.C., and J.H.W. Sendey (1976): Test excavation at the Georgeson Bay site, Gulf of Georgia region, British Columbia. *Occasional Papers of the British Columbia Provincial Museum* 19. Victoria.

Hall, E.R., and K.R. Kelson (1959): *The Mammals of North America.* 2 volumes. Ronald Press, New York.

Hall, R.L., and T. German (1975): Dental pathology, attrition, and occlusal surface form in a prehistoric sample from British Columbia. *Syesis* 8:275-289.

Hall, R.L., and J.C. Haggarty (1981): Human skeletal remains and associated cultural material from the Hill site, DfRu 4, Saltspring Island, British Columbia. *In* Contributions to physical anthropology, 1978-1980, edited by J.S. Cybulski, *National Museum of Man Mercury Series, Archaeological Survey of Canada Paper* 106, National Museums of Canada, Ottawa, pp. 64-105.

Halpin, M.M., and M. Seguin (1990): Tsimshian peoples: Southern Tsimshian, Coast Tsimshian, Nishga, and Gitksan. In *Handbook of North American Indians, Vol. 7, Northwest Coast,* edited by W. Suttles, Smithsonian Institution, Washington, pp. 267-284.

Hart, J.L. (1973): Pacific fishes of Canada. *Fisheries Research Board of Canada Bulletin* 180:1-740.

Heglar, R. (1958): Indian skeletal remains from the Whalen site, Pt. Roberts, Washington. Manuscript on file, Museum of Anthropology, University of British Columbia, Vancouver.

Hester, J.J. (1978): The Bella Bella prehistory project. *In* Studies in Bella Bella prehistory, edited by J.J. Hester and S.M. Nelson, *Simon Fraser University Department of Archaeology Publication* 5, Burnaby, pp. 1-9.

Inglis, Richard I. (1974): Contract salvage 1973: a preliminary report on the salvage excavations of two shell middens in the Prince Rupert Harbour, B.C. GbTo-33 /36. *In* Archaeological Salvage Projects 1973, edited by W.J. Byrne, *National Museum of Man Mercury Series, Archaeological Survey of Canada Paper* 26, National Museums of Canada, Ottawa, pp. 64-73.

Inglis, R.I. (1976): Wet site distribution--the northern case GbTo 33 - the Lachane site. *In* The excavation of water-saturated archaeological sites (wet sites) on the Northwest Coast of North America, edited by D.R. Croes, *National Museum of Man Mercury Series, Archaeological Survey of Canada Paper* 50, National Museums of Canada, Ottawa, pp. 158-185.

Johnstone, D. (1989): Long Harbour interim report: 1988 excavations. Manuscript on file (Permit 1988-42), Ministry Library, Ministry of Municipal Affairs, Recreation and Culture, Province of British Columbia, Victoria.

Juhl, J.H. (1981): *Paul and Juhl's Essentials of Roentgen Interpretation.* 4th edition. Harper and Row, Hagerstown.

Jurmain, R.D. (1977): Stress and the etiology of osteoarthritis. *American Journal of Physical Anthropology* 46:353-366.

Kaplan, R.F., B.C. Dorn, J.S. Hood, and P.D. McGann (1977): Musculoskeletal system. In *Forensic Medicine: A Study in Trauma and Environmental Hazards, Vol. 1. Mechanical Trauma,* edited by C.G. Tedeschi, W.G. Eckert and L.G. Tedeschi, W.B. Saunders, Philadelphia, pp. 259-361.

Keddie, G.R. (1981): The use and distribution of labrets on the North Pacific rim. *Syesis* 14:59-80.

Kennedy, G.E. (1986): The relationship between auditory exostoses and cold water: a latitudinal analysis. *American Journal of Physical Anthropology* 71:401-415.

Klein, J., J.C. Lerman, P.E. Damon, and E.K. Ralph (1982): Calibration of radiocarbon dates: tables based on the concensus data of the workshop on calibrating the radiocarbon time scale. *Radiocarbon* 24:103-150.

Koritzer, R. (1970): Enameloma in a prehistoric Indian skull. *American Journal of Physical Anthropology* 33:439-442.

Kozloff, E.N. (1987): *Marine Invertebrates of the Pacific Northwest.* University of Washington Press, Seattle.

Krogman, W.M., and M.Y. Iscan (1986): *The Human Skeleton in Forensic Medicine.* 2nd edition. Charles C. Thomas, Springfield.

Laguna, F. de (1972): Under Mount Saint Elias: the history and culture of the Yakutat Tlingit. *Smithsonian Contributions to Anthropology* 7 (Parts 1-3). Washington.

Lamb, A., and P. Edgell (1986): *Coastal Fishes of the Pacific Northwest.* Harbour Publishing, Madeira Park.

Larsen, C.S. (1990): The archaeology of Mission Santa Catalina de Guale: 2. Biocultural interpretations of a population in transition. *Anthropological Papers of the American Museum of Natural History* 68:1-150.

Lazenby, R.A. (1986): Case 85-25: an aboriginal skeleton from White Rock, B.C. (DgRq 18). Manuscript on file (Permit 1985-4), Ministry Library, Ministry of Municipal Affairs, Recreation and Culture, Province of British Columbia, Victoria.

Lovejoy, C.O., R.S. Meindl, T.R. Pryzbeck, and R.P. Mensforth (1985): Chronological metamorphosis of the auricular surface of the ilium: a new method for the determination of adult skeletal age at death. *American Journal of Physical Anthropology* 68:15-28.

Loveland, C.J., and J.B. Gregg (1988): Brachydactyly in a prehistoric Texas skeleton. *Plains Anthropologist* 33:399-404.

Luebbers, R. (1978): Excavations: stratigraphy and artifacts. *In* Studies in Bella Bella prehistory, edited by J.J. Hester and S.M. Nelson, *Simon Fraser University Department of Archaeology Publication* 5, Burnaby, pp. 11-66.

Lundy, J.K. (1981): Spondylolysis of the lumbar vertebrae in a group of prehistoric Upper Puget Sound Indians at Birch Bay, Washington. *In* Contributions to physical anthropology, 1978-1980, edited by J.S. Cybulski, *National Museum of Man Mercury Series, Archaeological Survey of Canada Paper* 106, National Museums of Canada, Ottawa, pp. 107-114.

MacDonald, G.F. (1969): Preliminary culture sequence from the Coast Tsimshian area, British Columbia. *Northwest Anthropological Research Notes* 3:240-254.

MacDonald, G.F. (1973): Haida burial practices: three archaeological examples. *National Museum of Man Mercury Series, Archaeological Survey of Canada Paper* 9, National Museums of Canada, Ottawa, pp. 1-59.

MacDonald, G.F., D.W. Clark, and K.R. Fladmark (1967): Field notes - Ishkeenickh River cave site - GfTj-1. Manuscript on file (No. 5, Vol. 27), Scientific Records Section, Archaeological Survey of Canada, Canadian Museum of Civilization, Hull.

MacDonald, G.F., and R.I. Inglis (1976): *The Dig; An Archaeological Reconstruction of a West Coast Village.* National Museums of Canada, Ottawa.

MacDonald, G.F., and R.I. Inglis (1981): An overview of the north coast prehistory project (1966-1980). *BC Studies* 48:37-63.

MacFarlane, R. (1891): Notes on and list of birds collected in Arctic America, 1861-1866. *Proceedings of the U.S. National Museum* 14:413-446.

Matteson, S.R., and D.A. Tyndall (1983): Pantomographic radiology, Part II. Pantomography of trauma and inflammation of the jaws. *Dental Radiography and Photography* 56:21-48.

Matson, R.G. (1976): The Glenrose Cannery site. *National Museum of Man Mercury Series, Archaeological Survey of Canada Paper* 52. National Museums of Canada, Ottawa.

Matson, R.G. (1989): The Locarno Beach phase and the origins of the Northwest Coast ethnographic pattern. *Reprint Proceedings of the Circum-Pacific Prehistory Conference,* Seattle, 44 pp.

Matson, R.G., H. Pratt, and L. Rankin (1991): 1989 and 1990 Crescent Beach excavations, final report; the origins of the Northwest Coast ethnographic pattern: the place of the Locarno Beach phase. Manuscript on file, Laboratory of Archaeology, University of British Columbia.

May, J. (1979): Archaeological investigations at GbTn 19, Ridley Island: a shell midden in the Prince Rupert area, British Columbia. Manuscript on file (No. 1530), Scientific Records Section, Archaeological Survey of Canada, Canadian Museum of Civilization, Hull.

McKern, T.W., and T.D. Stewart (1957): Skeletal age changes in young American males; analyzed from the standpoint of age identification. *Technical Report EP-45*. U.S. Quartermaster Research and Development Center, Natick.

McMillan, A.D. (1988): *Native Peoples and Cultures of Canada.* Douglas & McIntyre, Vancouver and Toronto.

McNeary, S.A. (1976): Where fire came down: social and economic life of the Niska. Unpublished Ph.D. Dissertation, Department of Anthropology, Bryn Mawr College, Bryn Mawr.

Meindl, R.S., and C.O. Lovejoy (1985): Ectocranial suture closure: a revised method for the determination of skeletal age at death based on the lateral-anterior sutures. *American Journal of Physical Anthropology* 68:57-66.

Merbs, C.F. (1983): Patterns of activity-induced pathology in a Canadian Inuit population. *National Museum of Man Mercury Series, Archaeological Survey of Canada Paper* 119. National Museums of Canada, Ottawa.

Merbs, C.F., and E.M. Vestergaard (1985): The paleopathology of Sundown, a prehistoric site near Prescott, Arizona. *In* Health and Disease in the Prehistoric Southwest, edited by C.F. Merbs and R.J. Miller, *Arizona State University Anthropological Research Papers* 34, Tempe, pp. 85-103.

Miller, L. (1940): Observations on the black-footed albatross. *Condor* 42:229-238.

Mitchell, D.H. (1971): Archaeology of the Gulf of Georgia area, a natural region and its culture types. *Syesis* 4 (Supplement 1):1-228.

Mitchell, D.H. (1988): The J. Puddleduck site: a northern Strait of Georgia Locarno Beach component and its predecessor. *Contributions to Human History (Royal British Columbia Museum)* 2:1-20.

Mitchell, D.H. (1990): Prehistory of the coasts of southern British Columbia and northern Washington. In *Handbook of North American Indians, Vol. 7, Northwest Coast,* edited by W. Suttles, Smithsonian Institution, Washington, pp. 340-358.

Montagu, M.F.A. (1960): *An Introduction to Physical Anthropology.* 3rd edition. Charles C. Thomas, Springfield.

Moser, C. (1926): *Reminiscences of the West Coast of Vancouver Island.* Acme Press Ltd., Victoria.

Murray, J.S. (1981): Prehistoric skeletons from Blue Jackets Creek (FlUa 4), Queen Charlotte Islands, British Columbia. *In* Contributions to physical anthropology, 1978-1980, edited by J.S. Cybulski, *National Museum of Man Mercury Series, Archaeological Survey of Canada Paper* 106, National Museums of Canada, Ottawa, pp. 127-168.

Murray, R.A. (1982): Analysis of artifacts from four Duke Point area sites, near Nanaimo, B.C.: an example of cultural continuity in the southern Gulf of Georgia region. *National Museum of Man Mercury Series, Archaeological Survey of Canada Paper* 113. National Museums of Canada, Ottawa.

Niblack, A.P. (1890): The coast Indians of southern Alaska and northern British Columbia. *Report of the U.S. National Museum* 1888:225-386.

Nisga'a School District 92, Bilingual-Bicultural Department (1981): *Am'ugithl Nisga'a; Nisgha Clothing.* Totem Press Terrace Ltd., Terrace, B.C.

Olivier, G. (1969): *Practical Anthropology.* Translated by M.A. MacConaill. Charles C. Thomas, Springfield.

Ortner, D.J., and W.G.J. Putschar (1981): Identification of pathological conditions in human skeletal remains. *Smithsonian Contributions to Anthropology* 28. Smithsonian Institution Press, Washington.

Ossenberg, N.S. (1974): The mylohyoid bridge: an anomalous derivative of Meckel's cartilage. *Journal of Dental Research* 53:77-82.

Ossenberg, N.S. (1976): Within and between race distances in population studies based on discrete traits of the human skull. *American Journal of Physical Anthropology* 45:701-716.

Ossenberg, N.S. (1981): An argument for the use of total side frequencies of bilateral nonmetric skeletal traits in population distance analysis: the regression of symmetry on incidence. *American Journal of Physical Anthropology* 54:471-479.

Ossenberg, N.S. (n.d.): Origins and affinities of the native peoples of northwestern North America: the evidence of cranial nonmetric traits. Revised version of a paper read at the Circum-Pacific Prehistory Conference, Seattle, 1989.

Parmalee, P.W., A.A. Paloumpis, and N. Wilson (1972): Animals utilized by Woodland peoples occupying the Apple Creek site, Illinois. *Illinois State Museum Reports of Investigations* 23. Springfield.

Penrose, L.S. (1954): Distance, size and shape. *Annals of Eugenics* 18:337-343.

Percy, R.C.W. (1974): The prehistoric cultural sequence at Crescent Beach, British Columbia. Unpublished M.A. Thesis, Department of Archaeology, Simon Fraser University, Burnaby.

Pike, G.C., and I.B. MacAskie (1969): Marine mammals of British Columbia. *Fisheries Research Board of Canada Bulletin* 171:1-54.

Pokotylo, D.L., M.E. Binkley, and A.J. Curtin (1987): The Cache Creek burial site (EeRh 1), British Columbia. *Contributions to Human History (Royal British Columbia Museum)* 1:1-14.

Purdue, J.R. (1983): Epiphyseal closure in white-tailed deer. *Journal of Wildlife Management* 47:1207-1213.

Rick, A.M. (1989): Appendix II: Preliminary report on animal remains from the Kitwanga Fort National Historic Site. In *Kitwanga Fort Report*, by G.F. MacDonald, Canadian Museum of Civilization, Hull, pp. A5-A9.

Robinson, W. (1962): *Men of Medeek*. Northern Sentinel Press Ltd., Kitimat.

Saluja, G., K. Fitzpatrick, M. Bruce, and J. Cross (1986): Schmorl's nodes (intravertebral herniations of intervertebral disc tissue) in two historic British populations. *Journal of Anatomy* 145:87-96.

Sandzén, S.C., Jr. (1979): *Atlas of Wrist and Hand Fractures*. PSG Publishing Company, Littleton.

Sanger, G.A. (1974): Pelagic studies of seabirds in the central and eastern Pacific Ocean. 4. Laysan albatross *Diomedea immutabilis. Smithsonian Contributions to Zoology* 158:129-153.

Sapir, E. (1915): A sketch of the social organization of the Nass River Indians. *Canada Geological Survey Museum Bulletin* 19 (Anthropological Series 7):1-30.

Sapir, E. (1920): Nass River terms of relationship. *American Anthropologist* 22:261-271.

Saunders, S.R. (1978): The development and distribution of discontinuous morphological variation of the human infracranial skeleton. *National Museum of Man Mercury Series, Archaeological Survey of Canada Paper* 81. National Museums of Canada, Ottawa.

Scammon, C.M. (1968): *The Marine Mammals of the Northwestern Coast of North America, Together with an Account of the American Whale-fishery.* Reprint of 1874 edition. Dover, New York.

Schmid, E. (1972): *Atlas of Animal Bones for Prehistorians, Archaeologists and Quaternary Geologists.* Elsevier, Amsterdam.

Schulting R., and J. Ostapkowicz (1990): Cultural modification, depressed fractures, and sorcery: a cranium from the Bella Coola Valley, British Columbia. Paper read at 18th annual meeting of the Canadian Association for Physical Anthropology, Banff, Alberta.

Severs, P.D.S. (1974): Archaeological investigations at Blue Jackets Creek, FlUa-4, Queen Charlotte Islands, British Columbia, 1973. *Canadian Archaeological Association Bulletin* 6:165-205.

Seymour, B.D. (1976): 1972 Salvage excavations at DfRs3, the Whalen Farm site. *In* Current Research Reports, edited by R.L. Carlson, *Simon Fraser University Department of Archaeology Publication* 3, Burnaby, pp. 83-98.

Seymour, B.D. (1977): Archaeological investigation at Owikeno Lake, British Columbia, 1975. Manuscript on file (Permit 1975-8), Ministry Library, Ministry of Municipal Affairs, Recreation and Culture, Province of British Columbia, Victoria.

Seymour, B.D. (1979): Further archaeological investigation at Owikeno Lake, British Columbia: a preliminary report on excavations at EkSp 13 in 1977. Manuscript on file (Permit 1977-14), Ministry Library, Ministry of Municipal Affairs, Recreation and Culture, Province of British Columbia, Victoria.

Shane, A.P.M. (1984): Power in their hands: the gitsontk. In *The Tsimshian; Images of the Past: Views for the Present,* edited by M. Seguin, University of British Columbia Press, Vancouver, pp. 160-173.

Sievers, M.L., and J.R. Fisher (1981): Diseases of North American Indians. In *Biocultural Aspects of Disease,* edited by H. Rothschild, Academic Press, Inc., Orlando, pp. 191-252.

Simonsen, B.O. (1988a): Final report on archaeological salvage excavations and construction monitoring at the Lachane site (GbTo-33) Prince Rupert, B.C. Manuscript on file (No. 3033), Scientific Records Section, Archaeological Survey of Canada, Canadian Museum of Civilization, Hull.

Simonsen, B.O. (1988b): Report on the results of an archaeological impact assessment and mitigation project at the Maple Bay site (DeRu 12) Vancouver Island. Manuscript on file (Permit 1988-20), Ministry Library, Ministry of

Municipal Affairs, Recreation and Culture, Province of British Columbia, Victoria.

Sjøvold, T. (1977): Non-metrical divergence between skeletal populations; the theoretical foundation and biological importance of C.A.B. Smith's mean measure of divergence. *OSSA* 4 (Supplement 1):1-133.

Skinner, M.F. (1989): Salvage recovery from an ossuary cave and rock crevice burial complex on Gabriola Island, (DgRw 199). *Canadian Association for Physical Anthropology Newsletter,* Spring 1989, p. 19. (Abstract).

Sledzik, P.S., and P.H. Moore-Jansen (1991): Dental pathology. In *Snake Hill: An Investigation of a Military Cemetery from the War of 1812,* edited by S. Pfeiffer and R.F. Williamson, Dundurn Press, Toronto and Oxford, pp. 227-246.

Smith, G.R., and R.F. Stearley (1989): The classification and scientific names of rainbow and cutthroat trouts. *Fisheries* 14:4-10.

Stewart, F.L. (1974): Fish remains from the Boardwalk site (GbTo-31) of northern British Columbia. Manuscript on file (No. 983), Scientific Records Section, Archaeological Survey of Canada, Canadian Museum of Civilization, Hull.

Stewart, F.L. (1977): Vertebrate faunal remains from the Boardwalk site (GbTo 31) of northern British Columbia. Manuscript on file (No. 1263), Scientific Records Section, Archaeological Survey of Canada, Canadian Museum of Civilization, Hull.

Stuart-Macadam, P. (1985): Porotic hyperostosis: representative of a childhood condition. *American Journal of Physical Anthropology* 66:391-398.

Stuart-Macadam, P. (1992): Porotic hyperostosis: a new perspective. *American Journal of Physical Anthropology* 87:39-47.

Stuiver, M., and G.W. Pearson (1986): High-precision calibration of the radiocarbon time scale, AD 1950-500 BC. *Radiocarbon* 28:805-838.

Stuiver, M., and P.J. Reimer (1986): A computer program for radiocarbon age calibration. *Radiocarbon* 28:1022-1030.

Sutherland, P.D. (1978): Dodge Island: a prehistoric Coast Tsimshian settlement site in Prince Rupert Harbour, British Columbia. Manuscript on file (No. 1345), Scientific Records Section, Archaeological Survey of Canada, Canadian Museum of Civilization, Hull.

Suttles, W. (1990): Central Coast Salish. In *Handbook of North American Indians, Vol. 7, Northwest Coast,* edited by W. Suttles, Smithsonian Institution, Washington, pp. 453-475.

Taylor, R.E. (1987): *Radiocarbon Dating; An Archaeological Perspective.* Academic Press, Orlando.

Tedeschi, C.G. (1977): Head and spine. In *Forensic Medicine: A Study in Trauma and Environmental Hazards, Vol. 1. Mechanical Trauma,* edited by C.G. Tedeschi, W.G. Eckert, and L.G. Tedeschi, W.B. Saunders, Philadelphia, pp. 29-75.

Todd, T.W. (1920): Age changes in the pubic bone. Part I. The male white pubis. *American Journal of Physical Anthropology* 3:285-334.

Trace, A.A. (1981): An examination of the Locarno Beach phase as represented at the Crescent Beach site, DgRr 1, British Columbia. Unpublished M.A. thesis, Department of Archaeology, Simon Fraser University, Burnaby.

Trotter, M., and G.C. Gleser (1952): Estimation of stature from long bones of American whites and negroes. *American Journal of Physical Anthropology* 10:463-514.

Trotter, M., and G.C. Gleser (1958): A re-evaluation of estimation of stature based on measurements of stature taken during life and of long bones after death. *American Journal of Physical Anthropology* 16:79-123.

Ubelaker, D.H. (1978): *Human Skeletal Remains: Excavation, Analysis, Interpretation.* Aldine, Chicago.

Wallmo, O.C. (1981): Mule and black-tailed deer distribution and habitats. In *Mule and Black-tailed Deer of North America; A Wildlife Management Book,* edited by O.C. Wallmo, University of Nebraska Press, Lincoln, pp. 1-26.

Watson, L. (1981): *Sea Guide to Whales of the World.* Nelson Canada Ltd., Scarborough.

Weeks, S.M. (1985): Skeletal remains from DeRt 2. In: The 1984 excavations at the Canal site (DeRt 1 and DeRt 2), by R.L. Carlson, Manuscript on file (Permit 1984-13), Ministry Library, Ministry of Municipal Affairs, Recreation and Culture, Province of British Columbia, Victoria, pp. 78-118.

Weeks, S.M. (1986): Skeletal remains from DeRt 1 and DeRt 2. In: The 1985 excavations at the Canal site (DeRt 1 and DeRt 2), by R.L. Carlson, Manuscript on file (Permit 1985-10), Ministry Library, Ministry of Municipal Affairs, Recreation and Culture, Province of British Columbia, Victoria, pp. 94-116.

Welin, C.S.H., and E. Ratjen (1969): Temporal bone. In *Roentgen Diagnosis, Vol. 3: Spine, Skull, Nerves, Eye, Sinuses, Teeth,* 2nd American edition, edited by L.G. Rigler, Grune and Stratton, New York and London, pp. 471-514.

Wigen, R.J., and B.R. Stucki (1988): Taphonomy and stratigraphy in the interpretation of economic patterns at Hoko River rockshelter. In *Prehistoric Economies of the Pacific Northwest Coast,* edited by B.L. Isaac, JAI Press, Greenwich, pp. 87-146.

Wilkinson, L. (1990): *SYSTAT: The System for Statistics.* SYSTAT, Inc., Evanston.

Willis, Cunliffe, Tait/DeLCan (1982): Completion report, Lakalzap Lot Preparation Project. Manuscript on file, Department of Indian Affairs and Northern Development, Terrace.

Wilmeth, R. (1978): Canadian archaeological radiocarbon dates (revised version). *National Museum of Man Mercury Series, Archaeological Survey of Canada Paper* 77. National Museums of Canada, Ottawa.

Wiltse, L.L. (1962): The etiology of spondylolisthesis. *Journal of Bone and Joint Surgery* 44a:539-560.

Wing, E.S. (1978): Use of dogs for food: an adaptation to the coastal environment. In *Prehistoric Coastal Adaptations: the Economy and Ecology of Maritime Middle America,* edited by B.L. Stark and B. Voorhies, Academic Press, New York, pp. 29-41.

Yesner, D.R. (1976): Aleutian Island albatrosses: a population history. *Auk* 93:263-280.

Zimmerman, M.R., and M.A. Kelley (1982): *Atlas of Human Paleopathology.* Praeger, New York.

Individual Greenville Human Remains

Burial 1 (Female, 30-34 years)

Remains: incomplete postcranial skeleton including a sternum, left upper and lower limbs, right lower limb less patella and fibula, two right carpals and hand phalanges, partial tenth and eleventh thoracic vertebrae, fifth lumbar vertebra, and sacrum.

Context: all but right lower limb and fifth lumbar vertebra partly articulated in Unit 6, Layer B; apparently tightly flexed on left, heading northwest, body facing northeast; greatly disturbed during construction contractor's excavation of minor drainage ditch; four right lower limb bones and fifth lumbar added in laboratory from group of disturbed bones 3 m to the northeast in overburden of Unit 19 (field burial 30).

Paleopathology: slight or moderate arthritic changes in left elbow, hips, right foot, and lower thoracic apophyseal joints.

Burial 2 (Male, 30-34 years)

Remains: partial postcranial skeleton including a distal left humerus fragment, incomplete left ulna, fragmentary innominate bones and sacrum, incomplete right femur and proximal fragments of a left, incomplete tibiae and fibulae, most right and left foot bones, and partial twelfth thoracic and first lumbar vertebrae.

Context: partly articulated in Unit 6, Layer B; apparently tightly flexed on front, heading southwest; greatly disturbed during construction contractor's excavation of minor drainage ditch.

Paleopathology: slight arthritic changes in left elbow and in rib facet of twelfth thoracic vertebra.

Burial 3 (Female, 45-49 years)

Remains: variably preserved skeleton missing a left patella, some hand and foot bones, and a sacrum.

Context: articulated in Unit 9, Layer B, in a shallow pit that greatly disturbed Burial 9; torso on right, heading north, body facing west, thighs irregularly flexed to right with lower legs tightly flexed, head vertical facing west.

Paleopathology: labret wear facet on a lower central incisor; general osteoporosis; slight or moderate arthritic changes in most limb joint surfaces and in right temporomandibular joint; advanced or severe arthritic changes in thoracic apophyseal joints; slight vertebral osteophytosis; ante mortem tooth loss at four upper sites (including partial loss of a molar) and one lower site; abscess lesions at eight upper tooth sites, one opened through maxillary sinus.

Burial 4 (Male, 12-16 years)

Remains: virtually complete skeleton; several hand and foot bones, and first and third thoracic vertebrae missing.

Context: articulated in Unit 5, Layer B, in a pit that truncated Burial 5; torso on left, heading southwest, body facing northwest, thighs irregularly half-flexed to left with lower legs tightly flexed, head on left facing west; dog skull against upper chest, partly under proximal right humerus; concentration of elderberry seeds by humerus and dog skull.

Paleopathology: deep, irregular, erosive pits in superior articular facets of second and third cervical vertebrae; less pronounced pits in articular facets of four thoracic vertebrae; moderate anterior wedging of fourth through twelfth thoracic vertebral bodies.

Burial 5 (Male, 48-54 years)

Remains: partial postcranial skeleton with ossified laryngeal cartilages; bones present include claviculae, partial sternum, six ribs or fragments, left forearm bones, a few right and left hand bones, innominata and sacrum, left femur and patella, tibiae and fibulae, most right and left foot bones, fourth cervical vertebra, and second through fifth lumbars.

Context: articulated in Unit 5, Layer B, on Layer C; apparently tightly flexed on left (though pelvis on front), heading southwest, body facing northwest; small concentration of friable wood associated with left calcaneus; large quantity of associated elderberry seeds; much of upper body truncated by pit dug for Burial 4.

Paleopathology: apparent osteoporosis; ossified subperiosteal haematoma on left tibia shaft; apparent traumatic arthritis in right foot; possible traumatic myositis ossificans on right fourth metatarsal shaft; arthritic right and left wrist bones; severe arthritis in lumbosacral apophyseal joint; moderate lumbar osteophytosis.

Burial 6 (Sex unknown, 2-4 years)

Remains: variably preserved skeleton; all hand and most foot bones missing; other parts show advanced soil erosion.

Context: articulated in Unit 7, in distinctly ovoid Layer A2 pit dug into Layer B; tightly flexed in circular configuration with skull on top facing northwest; possible basket burial.

Paleopathology: cribra orbitalia in left orbit (right not observable).

Burial 7 (Female, 60+ years)

Remains: virtually complete, variably preserved skeleton; left first metacarpal, trapezium and pisiform, left first through fourth metatarsals, and sixth cervical vertebra missing.

Context: articulated in Units 7 and 7b, Layer B, on Layer C in a shallow pit and probable box that slightly disturbed Burial 20; tightly flexed on right, heading southeast, body facing northeast, head vertical facing northeast; thin concentration of elderberry seeds in surrounding burial matrix.

Paleopathology: general osteoporosis; slight or moderate arthritic changes in many limb joint surfaces; advanced arthritic changes in cervical apophyseal joints, and slight changes in lower thoracic and lumbar regions; prominent osteophytes on lumbar vertebrae; Schmorl's node scars in first and second lumbar vertebral bodies; arthritic lipping on left occipital condyle; bilateral maxillary sinus inclusions; edentulous upper jaw (right first molar to left first premolar sites observable); ante mortem loss of at least eight lower teeth; abscess lesions in at least two lower tooth sites; vascular grooves in tibiae and right femur.

Burial 8 (Sex unknown, 9-11 years)

Remains: incomplete postcranial skeleton; includes claviculae, right forearm and hand bones, left proximal ulna and some hand bones, innominata, right femur, patella, tibia and fibula, most right and left foot bones, two cervical, a thoracic, and four lumbar vertebrae, and ten ribs or fragments.

Context: several bones articulated but most scattered in Unit 9, Layer B; likely disturbed by growth of large tree root along which the articulated parts were found.

Paleopathology: no apparent changes.

Burial 9 (Male, 40-44 years)

Remains: partial postcranial skeleton; includes claviculae, proximal right ulna and 11 hand bones, left radius and two hand bones; left pubis, femur, tibia and fibula, right patella, several right and left foot bones and ribs, partial sixth cervical vertebra, first and two other fragmentary thoracic vertebrae, and third through fifth lumbar vertebrae.

Context: left lower limb articulated (tightly flexed) in Unit 9, Layer B, next to skull of Burial 3; other bones scattered in unit; likely disturbed by pit dug for Burial 3.

Paleopathology: healed fracture of distal left fibula shaft with developed articular facet and complementary facet on tibia shaft; healed fracture of right second proximal phalange shaft and ossified subperiosteal haematoma on fourth proximal phalange shaft in right hand; slight arthritic changes in left knee and first thoracic vertebra; moderate osteophyte development on lumbar vertebrae.

Burial 10 (Female, 45-54 years)

Remains: incomplete, poorly preserved postcranial skeleton; includes partial right forearm and hand bones, left ulna and hand bones, incomplete innominata, femora, tibiae and fibulae, right patella, right and left foot bones and ribs, and vertebrae from the tenth thoracic through the sacrum.

Context: articulated in Unit 10, Layer B, on Layer C; apparently tightly flexed on right, heading southeast, body facing northeast, in a configuration similar to that of Burials 3 and 7; elderberry seeds surrounding and beneath most bones; possibly disturbed by the interment of Burial 15.

Paleopathology: general osteoporosis; healed fracture of right tibia shaft with secondary infection; bony ankylosis of right ankle and foot bones with near fusion of distal tibia; slight arthritic changes in left elbow, left hip, and right knee; moderate arthritic changes in left hand and in lower thoracic apophyseal joints and rib facets; advanced arthritis in lumbar apophyseal joints; moderate development of lower thoracic and lumbar osteophytes; Schmorl's node scars in second through fifth lumbar vertebral bodies.

Burial 11 (Female, 28-34 years)

Remains: incomplete, poorly preserved skeleton; missing parts include claviculae, sternum, left innominate, femur and patella, a few hand and foot bones, vertebrae from the atlas through the eighth thoracic, fifth lumbar, and sacrum.

Context: articulated in Unit 10, Layer B, on Layer C; very tightly flexed on back with legs over to right, heading east, arms crossed on top of skull, head slightly raised, facing southwest; small piece of wood on pelvis; large cobble tool on lower spine; skeletal parts probably lost through *in situ* decay.

Paleopathology: labret wear facet on a lower central incisor; slight arthritic lipping on occipital condyles; arthritic rib facet in eleventh thoracic vertebra; slight anterior wedging of first lumbar vertebral body; abscess lesion at lower right central incisor site; slight crowding of lower dentition and partly impacted right third molar; disproportionately short left first metatarsal (brachydactyly).

Burial 12 (Female, 30-39 years)

Remains: almost complete, well preserved skeleton; pubic bones and some hand and foot bones missing.

Context: articulated in Units 13 and 13b, in Layer A2 pit into Layer B; partly disturbed by intrusive pit containing modern cultural debris; tightly flexed on left heading southeast, body facing southwest, head on left facing northwest.

Paleopathology: labret wear facets on lower central incisors; incipient osteoporosis; arthritic pitting in both shoulder joints; slight arthritic changes in right hip; advanced degenerative changes in sacroiliac joints; slight or moderate arthritic changes in vertebral rib facets; crowded lower anterior teeth and premolars; enamel pearls on left lower molars.

Burial 13 (Sex unknown, 9-11 years)

Remains: mandible, three loose upper teeth, and incomplete postcranial skeleton; most postcranial bones represented but incomplete; right tibia diaphysis, some hand and foot bones, third and fourth lumbars, and most of sacrum missing.

Context: partly articulated in Unit 13, Layer B; apparently flexed on left, heading southwest, body facing northwest; disturbance probably of modern origin.

Paleopathology: erosive pits in many vertebral articular facets.

Burial 14 (Female, 18-22 years)

Remains: incomplete skeleton; right scapula, left ulna, many right hand bones, right femur, patella, tibia, and fibula, and all right metatarsals and foot phalanges missing.

Context: articulated in Unit 12, Layer B, on Layer C; very tightly flexed on right, heading east, body facing north, head bent over on top of skeleton, on left, crown pointing to pelvis, facing north; small concentration of elderberry seeds on west side of skeleton; parts disturbed and possibly lost during construction activity.

Paleopathology: arthritic rib facet in seventh thoracic vertebra; vascular groove in left tibia shaft; developmental crease in right mandibular fossa.

Burial 15 (Male, 22-28 years)

Remains: poorly preserved partial skeleton; includes skull and mandible, right clavicle and part of left, part of right humerus shaft, incomplete left innominate and right and left femora, small fragment of right tibia, 13 rib fragments, two left metacarpals and a carpal, nine hand phalanges, and fragmented vertebrae from the atlas through the fourth thoracic.

Context: articulated in Unit 10, Layer B, on Layer C; very tightly flexed, heading northwest, head face down; large section of wood plank at south edge (foot) of skeleton, forming south side of an apparent box; rocks around skeleton may have been associated; some skeletal parts disturbed by root growth, and loss of many a function of *in situ* decay.

Paleopathology: slight arthritic changes in rib facets of first thoracic vertebra; dental abscess lesion in upper jaw; congenitally missing lower third molars; upper third molars reduced in size with right almost peg-like.

Burial 16 (Male, 50-59 years)

Remains: almost complete, well preserved skeleton; right innominate missing.

Context: articulated in Unit 13, Layer B; slightly disturbed by rodent activity; very tightly flexed on left, heading southwest, body facing northwest, head on left, almost face down, looking northeast; square box outline formed by small rocks along southwest and northwest edges of skeleton, the corner in which the head was situated; several small rocks on top of skeleton.

Paleopathology: two healed depressed fractures in cranial vault; intraarticular fracture in distal right radius; spondylolysis of fifth lumbar; severe arthritic changes (eburnation) on occipital condyles; moderate to advanced bilateral temporomandibular joint arthritis; arthritic changes in most limb and vertebral joint surfaces (including severe changes in atlas surfaces for articulation with occipital condyles); osteophytes on most vertebrae; Schmorl's node scars in eight vertebral bodies; slight anterior wedging of seventh thoracic vertebral body; anterolateral wedging of twelfth thoracic body; ante mortem loss of upper right first molar and partial loss of left; abscess lesions at eight upper tooth sites, almost all associated with worn-open pulp chambers; enamel pearl on two upper molars.

Burial 17 (Male, 35-44 years)

Remains: poorly preserved skull, mandible, and five long bone fragments.

Context: clustered remains in Unit 15, Layer C, under Layer A (no shell in immediate area), though possibly in a Layer A2 pit that might have been responsible for partial disturbance of Burial 21; most parts evidently lost through *in situ* decay.

Paleopathology: no apparent changes.

Burial 18 (Male, 35-44 years)

Remains: complete skeleton, extremely wet *in situ;* most parts crumbled on removal so that few intact pieces were available for analysis.

Context: articulated in Unit 11, suspected Layer A2 pit with pronounced Layer B fill, on Layer C; distinct square box outline (60 cm x 61 cm) formed by thick concentration of elderberry seeds encasing skeleton; very tightly flexed on front, heading west, head face down in west corner of box and pelvis in opposite, east corner; small rocks on central part of skeleton and along perimeter of box outline; thin layer of preserved wood at bottom of burial.

Paleopathology: considerable surface porousness and fine periostitis on skull vault between temporal lines; ante mortem loss of an upper premolar; abscess lesions at four upper tooth sites; enamel pearls on three upper molars; crowded lower right cheek teeth.

Burial 19 (Male, 20-24 years)

Remains: virtually complete, variably preserved skeleton with many vertebrae fragmented and not repairable.

Context: articulated in Unit 8, in mixed Layer A/B depositional materials, (probably pit fill), on Layer C; square box outline (65 cm x 63 cm) formed by small rocks around base of skeleton and thick concentration of elderberry seeds in northeast corner; very tightly flexed on front with legs to left, heading southeast, head face down in southeast corner of box and pelvis in opposite, northwest corner; many rocks on top of skeleton; thick concentration of seeds also recorded in centre of box; thin layer of wood apparent in southwest corner.

Paleopathology: healed fracture of left radius neck; slight arthritic changes in left temporomandibular joint; congenitally missing upper third molars; crowding and displacement of lower anterior teeth; bony union of middle and distal phalanges in fifth digit of both feet.

Burial 20 (Male, 22-28 years)

Remains: almost complete skeleton; four right metatarsals, one left metatarsal, and most foot phalanges missing.

Context: articulated in Unit 7b, Layer B, on Layer C, probably in a pit that disturbed Burial 29, and slightly disturbed by the interment of Burial 7; very tightly flexed on back, legs to right, heading northeast, head facing up; some associated elderberry seeds.

Paleopathology: large, unhealed comminuted depressed fracture in left side of skull vault; healed or healing focal depressed fracture in posterior skull vault; healed fracture of nasal bones; pit-type occlusal caries in lower left second molar; roots of both upper central incisors unusually short; distorted development of left mandibular ramus compared to normal right, and articular eminence of mandibular fossa narrower anteroposteriorly than right; marked anterior curvature of superior one-fourth of left scapula; premature fusion of manubrium to sternal body; marked scoliosis and spinal fusion with development of hemi-vertebrae in lower thoracic and upper lumbar regions; two sets of right and left ribs fused.

Burial 21 (Sex unknown, 8-10 years)

Remains: incomplete skeleton; innominata, femoral diaphyses, right fibula, left tibia diaphysis, many hand and foot bones, and eleventh thoracic vertebra missing.

Context: partly articulated in Unit 15, Layer B, possibly disturbed by interment of Burial 17; apparently very tightly flexed on left, heading southwest, body facing northeast, head partly face down; concentration of elderberry seeds surrounding skeleton.

Paleopathology: bilateral cribra orbitalia; erosive pits in many vertebral articular facets; sacral spina bifida (only second segment present).

Burial 22 (Female, 40-49 years)

Remains: virtually complete skeleton with most vertebrae fragmented and first, second, and fourth lumbars missing.

Context: articulated in Unit 14, Layer B, in a pit that may have been responsible for the disturbance of Burial 31a; tightly flexed on front and right, heading south, body facing east, head vertical, facing southeast; several rocks on top of skeleton; small number of elderberry seeds associated with skull.

Paleopathology: labret wear facets on lower lateral incisors and probable labret-related ante mortem loss of central incisors; partial spondylolysis (right pars) of fifth lumbar; slight arthritic lipping on occipital condyles; small flat arthritic exostosis at distal end of left fibula; slight arthritic changes in some limb and vertebral joints; advanced arthritis in right wrist; anterior body wedging of eleventh and twelfth thoracic vertebrae; abscess lesions at two upper tooth sites; enamel pearl on an upper molar; manubrium fused to sternal body but xiphoid process separate.

Burial 23 (Male, 55-64 years)

Remains: almost complete skeleton; sternum, left patella, some hand, and many foot bones missing.

Context: articulated in Unit 7b, Layer B; very tightly flexed on front and left, heading southwest, body facing northwest, legs flexed up behind back, head bent forward on left, facing pelvis and knees, northeast; heavy concentration of elderberry seeds.

Paleopathology: general osteoporosis; button osteoma on right frontal; possible traumatic myositis ossificans on left femur shaft; arthritic changes on occipital condyles; advanced arthritic changes in temporomandibular joints, more so in right than left; arthritic changes in most limb and many vertebral joint surfaces; osteophytes on most vertebrae; edentulous upper jaw; ante mortem loss of three left lower molars; abscess lesions at six lower tooth sites.

Burial 24 (Female, 60+ years)

Remains: virtually complete skeleton; sternum and a few of the smaller foot bones missing.

Context: articulated in Unit 13a, Layer B; very tightly flexed on front, spine curved to right, heading southwest, head face down; two rocks on left shoulder blade.

Paleopathology: labret wear facets on two lower anterior teeth; general osteoporosis; Bennett's fracture of left first metacarpal; two fractured right ribs; compression fractures and bony ankylosis of twelfth thoracic and first lumbar vertebrae; arthritis in occipital condyles and in most limb joint surfaces including advanced changes in shoulder joints and severe changes in knee joints and left wrist; degenerative changes in most vertebral bodies, including anterior wedging of tenth thoracic and Schmorl's node scars in tenth thoracic through second lumbars; arthritic changes in many vertebral apophyseal joints and rib facets; cribra orbitalia (unilateral left); maxillary sinus inclusions; edentulous upper jaw; ante mortem loss of nine lower teeth; abscess lesions at three lower tooth sites; evident "mild" scoliosis in upper and middle thoracic regions; small cyst-like cavity in ventral surface of spinous process of sixth thoracic vertebra; suspected bronchial half-cast; vascular grooves in tibia shafts; six lumbar vertebrae.

Burial 25a (Sex unknown, 3-5 years)

Remains: incomplete skull, loose lower tooth, and partial postcranial skeleton; the latter includes a left clavicle and fragmentary scapula, right radius and proximal left ulna, two metacarpals and two distal hand phalanges, right femur diaphysis, right and left tibia diaphyses and distal epiphyses, several right and left foot bones, a few rib fragments, and a partial second cervical vertebra.

Context: partly articulated in Unit 12, Layer B, on Layer C; very tightly flexed on left, heading south; disturbed and parts lost possibly during construction activity.

Paleopathology: cribra orbitalia in left orbit (right not studiable).

Burial 25b (Sex unknown, 3-5 years)

Remains: lower limb bones including right innominate and femur diaphysis, incomplete tibia and fibula diaphyses, and proximal left femur diaphysis.

Context: unarticulated remains clustered immediately to the north of Burial 25a, Layer B, on Layer C; possibly the remnants of a formerly intact burial disturbed during construction activity and (or) by the interment of Burial 32.

Paleopathology: no apparent changes.

Burial 26 (Male, 17-20 years)

Remains: almost complete, variably damaged skeleton; most hand and foot bones missing.

Context: articulated in Unit 12 in a Layer A2 pit dug deeply through Layer B, on Layer C; distinct square box outline, 58 cm x 60 cm, with wood along sides and bottom; very tightly flexed on left and front, heading southeast, body facing southwest, head face down in southeast corner of box, pelvis in opposite, northwest corner, and feet in southwest corner; concentrations of elderberry seeds, particularly in southwest corner.

Paleopathology: spondylolysis of fifth lumbar vertebra; slight degeneration in body surfaces of third cervical vertebra; slight crowding of lower anterior teeth.

Burial 27 (Male, 20-24 years)

Remains: fragmentary skull, mandible, left humerus and scapula, and second thoracic vertebra.

Context: grouped remains in Unit 14, Layer B; probable primary interment with most parts lost through *in situ* decay.

Paleopathology: enamel pearl on an upper molar.

Burial 29 (Female, 55-64 years)

Remains: mandible, three loose upper teeth, and incomplete postcranial skeleton; besides the skull, the left humerus, proximal two-thirds of left ulna, left innominate, femur and tibia, right patella, tibia and fibula, and most of the left fibula are missing.

Context: partly articulated in Unit 13, Layer B; greatly disturbed, probably by the interment of Burial 20; apparently very tightly flexed; large concentration of elderberry seeds, 6 cm deep, including a straight edge likely formed by the northwest side of a box containing Burial 20.

Paleopathology: labret abrasion on canines; fractured right fifth metatarsal; compression fractures of eleventh thoracic and first lumbar vertebrae; arthritic changes in most limb joint surfaces, severe in ankle bones; severe arthritic changes in occipito-atlanto-axial joints; advanced changes in sacrolumbar articulation; Schmorl's node scar in third lumbar; degenerative changes and osteophytes in most vertebral bodies; ante mortem loss of four incisors and one molar, the former possibly due to labret use; abscess lesions at four tooth sites; suspected atheromatous half-casts; suspected gall or kidney stones; calcified costal cartilage; spine contains 11 rather than the usual 12 thoracic units.

Burial 31a (Male, 20-34 years)

Remains: right and left tibiae, incomplete right fibula, six right and four left ankle bones, a metacarpal, six metatarsals, two foot phalanges, four ribs, atlas, and seventh thoracic vertebra.

Context: clustered remains in Unit 17, Layer B; probable primary interment possibly disturbed by the interment of Burial 22.

Paleopathology: no apparent changes.

Burial 31b (Female, 12-16 years)

Remains: skull, mandible, fragmentary left humerus and scapula, two rib fragments, one metacarpal, one hand phalange, seventh cervical, and first and second thoracic vertebrae.

Context: clustered remains in Unit 17, Layer B, ca. 50 cm north of Burial 31a; source of disturbance unknown.

Paleopathology: no apparent changes.

Burial 32 (Male, 40-44 years)

Remains: virtually complete, variably preserved skeleton.

Context: articulated in Unit 12a, in a Layer A2 pit dug into Layer B; tightly flexed on right, heading south, body facing east, head vertical facing east.

Paleopathology: fractured right fifth metacarpal; probable traumatic fusion of middle and distal phalanges of second digit of right hand; compression fractures of eleventh and twelfth thoracic and first lumbar vertebrae; slight arthritic changes in some limb joints; slight to prominent osteophytes on most vertebral bodies, and Schmorl's node scars in 11 units; abscess lesion at an upper molar site, opened into maxillary sinus; enamel pearls on two upper molars.

Burial 33 (Male, 22-26 years)

Remains: incomplete, poorly preserved skeleton; sternal body, left clavicle, patellae, most hand and some foot bones, and ten upper vertebrae missing.

Context: articulated in Units 21 and 21a, in a Layer A2 pit into Layer B, crosscut by a pit dug for Burial 34 and slightly disturbed by that interment; very tightly flexed on back and left, heading southwest, body facing northwest, head slightly raised, facing northeast.

Paleopathology: fractured upper incisor (Class IV); inclusions in left maxillary sinus (right normal); congenitally missing lower left third molar; impacted lower right third molar; sacralized fifth lumbar vertebra; localized depressions in some vertebral articular facets.

Burial 34 (Male, 28-34 years)

Remains: incomplete, variably preserved skeleton; sternum, distal ends of forearm bones, all hand bones, and several vertebrae missing.

Context: articulated in Units 21 and 21a, in a Layer A2 pit dug into Layer B; torso on right and front, heading southwest, body facing southeast, thighs irregularly flexed to right, lower legs tightly flexed, head raised and turned back, facing partly up and partly northeast.

Paleopathology: arthritic pitting in right shoulder; slight degenerative changes in a few vertebral surfaces; congenitally missing lower left third molar; lumbarized first sacral vertebra.

Burial 35a (Sex unknown, 8-10 years)

Remains: poorly preserved skeleton; sternum, right scapula, forearm bones and fibula, left patella, some hand and foot bones, and many vertebrae missing.

Context: articulated in Unit 21, in a Layer A2 pit dug into Layer B; partly disturbed and parts lost possibly by the interment of Burial 42; very tightly flexed on front, right arm and lower leg to right, heading northeast, head face down.

Paleopathology: no apparent changes.

Burial 35b (Sex unknown, 9-11 years)

Remains: partial mandible, fragmentary right scapula, left humerus diaphysis, proximal left femur diaphysis, a third metacarpal, and a distal hand phalange.

Context: disturbed remains near Burial 35a; possibly a formerly intact burial disturbed by the interment of Burial 42.

Paleopathology: no apparent changes.

Burial 35c (Sex unknown, 12-16 years)

Remains: fragments of five lower limb long bones, a right navicular, and four ribs.

Context: unarticulated remains near Burial 35a; possibly a formerly intact burial disturbed by the interment of Burial 42.

Paleopathology: no apparent changes.

Burial 36 (Male, 40-49 years)

Remains: very poorly preserved incomplete skeleton including a fragmentary skull, loose upper and lower teeth, incomplete left scapula, humerus and forearm bones, incomplete femora, tibiae, and fibulae, some hand and many foot bones, and nine pieces of vertebrae.

Context: articulated in Unit 19, in a Layer A2 pit partly intrusive through Burial 37 (no Layer B in immediate area); apparently tightly flexed on left, heading northeast, body facing southeast, head apparently on left and partly face down; thick triangular concentration of elderberry seeds with initial exposure of femur, likely forming the southeast corner of a box in which the body was placed; loss of many skeletal parts probably a function of *in situ* decay.

Paleopathology: slight arthritic changes in left elbow; disproportionately short right first metatarsal (brachydactyly).

Burial 37 (Male, 35-44 years)

Remains: very poorly preserved skeleton including skull, mandible, several rib fragments, claviculae, humeri, ulnae, right radius, right hand, incomplete right innominate, femora, tibiae, fibulae, two right ankle bones, and eight vertebrae.

Context: articulated in Unit 12, in a Layer A2 pit on Layer C/D (no Layer B in immediate area); slightly disturbed on discovery and by Burial 36; tightly flexed on left, heading southwest, body facing northeast, head on left, facing north; 10 cm x 15 cm patch of wood underlying chest cavity.

Paleopathology: slight arthritic changes in sternoclavicular joints; dental abscess lesions at three upper tooth sites; slight crowding of lower anterior teeth.

Burial 38 (Male, 16-18 years)

Remains: virtually complete skeleton; a few hand and foot bones missing.

Context: articulated in Unit 22, in a Layer A2 pit (no shell in this area); very tightly flexed on front and left, heading southeast, head on left, bent back on spine, facing southeast; highly compressed skeletal outline in distinct square configuration, 65 cm x 70 cm, head in south corner, pelvis in north corner, legs forming northwest side of "box;" elderberry seeds distributed throughout matrix, increasing in concentration through lower levels of skeleton.

Paleopathology: destructive signs of pyogenic osteomyelitis in fourth and fifth lumbar vertebrae; apparent Schmorl's node scar in eighth thoracic vertebra; sacral spina bifida (first and second segments); enamel pearls on upper molars; congenitally missing lower left third molar.

Burial 39 (Sex unknown, adult, ca. 20+ years)

Remains: fragments of arm and leg bones.

Context: very poorly preserved postcranial skeleton articulated in Unit 17, in Layer C, clearly below Layer B; only a few fragments recoverable; tightly flexed on left, heading northeast, body facing southeast; under a layer of large rocks.

Paleopathology: no apparent changes.

Burial 40 (Female, 22-28 years)

Remains: almost complete, variably damaged skeleton; some hand and foot bones missing.

Context: articulated in Units 21 and 21c, Layer B; in square wooden box, 59 cm x 64 cm, with well preserved sides and bottom; very tightly flexed on front and left, heading west, body facing north, head partly on left and partly face down in west corner of box, pelvis in opposite, east corner, and legs aligned with northeast side; four or five small rocks within box; sparse distribution of elderberry seeds in box fill; east corner of box cut by intrusion of Burial 34.

Paleopathology: labret wear facets on all four lower incisors and left canine; Colles' fracture in right radius; slight or moderate arthritic changes in sacroiliac joints, left navicular, and some vertebral apophyseal joints; advanced arthritic changes in some rib facets; Schmorl's node depressions in two thoracic vertebrae; cribra orbitalia in left orbit but not in right; thinned left tympanic plate with very large dehiscence (possible cholesteatoma); right femur head mushroom shaped on a very short neck, though acetabulum appears normal; manubrium fused to first sternebra, but first sternebra separate from second; crowded lower anterior teeth; enamel pearls on upper molars; bony union of middle and distal phalanges in a fifth foot digit.

Burial 41 (Sex unknown, 2-4 years)

Remains: incomplete skull and parts of ten postcranial bones including rib fragments, partial atlas, two metatarsal diaphyses, a proximal hand phalange diaphysis, and a vertebral body.

Context: disturbed group of bones in Unit 21aa, Layer B; source of disturbance unknown.

Paleopathology: bilateral cribra orbitalia; porous posterior cranial vault.

Burial 42 (Female, 60+ years)

Remains: almost complete, variably preserved skeleton; most right foot bones and some left missing.

Context: articulated in Unit 21b, in a Layer A2 pit dug into Layer B; very tightly flexed on left and front, heading south, body facing west, head on left, partly face down, facing northwest; rocks on top of skeleton.

Paleopathology: labret wear facets on lower lateral incisors; general osteoporosis; slight arthritic lipping on occipital condyle; arthritic changes in all available limb joint surfaces including severe involvements in right elbow, both wrists, both knees, both ankles, and left foot; severe arthritic changes in most available vertebral joint surfaces, notably in the cervical and lumbar regions; abscess lesions at seven upper tooth sites; ante mortem loss of two upper teeth and one lower tooth, the latter a central incisor possibly lost from labret use.

Burial 43 (Female, 12-16 years)

Remains: skull (catalogue number PE:1), partial mandible (EU14:8), humeri (PE:11 and EU22:3), and left radius (EU5L:1).

Context: assembled from disturbed remains collected prior to and during site excavation.

Paleopathology: enamel pearl on an upper molar.

Burial 44 (Female, 50-59 years)

Remains: skull with upper teeth (catalogue number PE:3).

Context: collected prior to site excavation.

Paleopathology: enlarged right external auditory meatus with thinned tympanic plate (probable cholesteatoma); ante mortem loss of two upper teeth; six abscessed tooth sites.

Burial 45 (Male, 30-39 years)

Remains: skull (catalogue number PE:4), partial mandible (GS2/3:4 and LS:9), right femur (PE:8), and right tibia (PE:7).

Context: assembled from disturbed remains collected prior to and during site excavation.

Paleopathology: healed depressed fracture in frontal bone; slight arthritic lipping on occipital condyles; congenitally missing upper third molars.

Burial 46 (Female, 40-49 years)

Remains: skull and mandible (catalogue number PE:5), and right and left tibiae (LS:19 and GS4:1).

Context: assembled from disturbed remains collected prior to and during site excavation.

Paleopathology: labret wear facets on three lower anterior teeth; slight or moderate arthritic changes on occipital condyles; arthritic left knee (lateral tibia condyle); fine porousness in posterior skull vault about lambda; abscess lesions at two upper tooth sites; crowded lower anterior teeth; enamel pearls on upper molars; vascular grooves in tibia shafts.

Burial 47 (Female, 18-22 years)

Remains: skull (catalogue number GS2:1), mandible (PE:3), claviculae (EU5L:7 and EU5L:8), right scapula (PE:61), left humerus (PE:10), ulnae (EU5L:5 and PE:38), radii (EU5L:6 and PE:19), right tibia (PE:6), and right fibula (PE:36).

Context: assembled from disturbed remains collected prior to and during site excavation.

Paleopathology: enamel pearl on an upper molar.

Burial 48 (Male, 60+ years)

Remains: a skull, partial mandible, fragmentary claviculae and scapulae, a small humerus fragment, four left metacarpals, ten hand phalanges, and vertebrae from first cervical through ninth thoracic.

Context: partial skeleton from clustered bones (catalogue code GS3) exposed by backhoe in disturbed site overburden.

Paleopathology: arthritic changes in occipital condyle and temporomandibular joints; degenerative changes in most vertebral bodies; ante mortem loss of six upper teeth; abscess lesions at two upper tooth sites and one lower site.

Burial 49 (Male, 40-49 years)

Remains: partial skull and almost complete mandible.

Context: clustered elements (catalogue code GS4) exposed by backhoe in disturbed site overburden.

Paleopathology: abscess lesion at one upper tooth site; crowded lower teeth.

Burial 50 (Sex unknown, 3-5 years)

Remains: fragmentary skull, mandible, left clavicle, scapulae, left humerus diaphysis, 12 ribs, four cervical, and five thoracic vertebrae.

Context: clustered remains (catalogue number EU2:S2) in disturbed site overburden of Unit 2.

Paleopathology: cribra orbitalia in left orbit (right not studiable).

Burial 51 (Sex unknown, 9-12 months)

Remains: fragmentary skull with loose upper and lower teeth.

Context: isolated find (catalogue number EU4:S1) in Unit 4, Layer B.

Paleopathology: bilateral cribra orbitalia.

Burial 52 (Male, 60+ years)

Remains: partial skeleton including skull, incomplete left scapula, a distal left ulna fragment, two left tibia fragments, ten ribs, five left carpals and second metacarpal, left second metatarsal, atlas and sixth cervical vertebra, fifth through twelfth thoracic vertebrae, and first through third lumbars.

Context: clustered remains (catalogue code EU7L) in disturbed site overburden of Unit 7.

Paleopathology: general osteoporosis; compression fractures in four lower vertebrae; moderate arthritic changes on occipital condyles; severe arthritic changes in left shoulder; slight to moderate arthritic changes in left wrist bones; advanced or severe arthritic changes in vertebral apophyseal joints and rib facets; Schmorl's node scars in seventh and eleventh thoracic and first and second lumbar vertebral bodies; prominent vertebral osteophytes; porous occipital; ante mortem loss of 13 upper teeth.

Burial 53 (Sex unknown, 12-16 years)

Remains: mandible with five intact molars.

Context: isolated find (catalogue number EU8:3) in Unit 8, Layer B.

Paleopathology: no apparent changes.

Burial 54 (Sex unknown, fetus)

Remains: fragmentary humerus diaphyses, radius diaphysis, and fragmentary fibula diaphysis.

Context: clustered remains (catalogue number EU13:24) in Unit 13, Layer B.

Paleopathology: no apparent changes.

Burial 55 (Sex unknown, 4-6 years)

Remains: partial mandible (catalogue number B36:50), left clavicle (EU21C:3), and right humerus diaphysis (LS:25).

Context: assembled from disturbed remains in Units 19 and 21C.

Paleopathology: no apparent changes.

Burial 56 (Male, 40-49 years)

Remains: partial skeleton including an incomplete skull (less maxillae and teeth), incomplete lower jaw, fragmentary left clavicle, scapula and humerus, a small distal right radius fragment, and a right rib.

Context: recovered by Lakalzap Band during excavation for a water line in 1984, ca. 35-40 m northeast of the estimated 1983 site boundary.

Paleopathology: large ossified subperiosteal haematoma on skull vault; arthritic changes in right temporomandibular joint.

Burial 57 (Sex unknown, 8-10 years)

Remains: partial postcranial skeleton; includes a left humerus diaphysis and incomplete right and left femora, tibiae, and fibulae diaphyses.

Context: recovered by Lakalzap Band during excavation for a water line in 1984, ca. 35-40 m northeast of the estimated 1983 site boundary.

Paleopathology: no apparent changes.

Cultural Artifacts in the Greenville Site

Appendix B is based on descriptions of the Greenville artifacts completed by Patricia D. Sutherland in 1983 under contract to the Canadian Museum of Civilization. Her work entailed measurements of the specimens, formal or functional descriptive assignments, and individual illustrations on 3" x 5" filing cards. A computerized data base was also prepared. All dimensions here are reported in millimetres, in the order of length, width, and thickness; numbers in parentheses identify an incomplete dimension due to damage. In total, 243 items recovered from the site were given artifact designations. Twelve in disturbed contexts were clearly of historic European affiliation and will not be considered further. Photographs of some the artifacts are reproduced on Figures 46 through 52.

Stone Artifacts

Chipped stone

Twenty-nine objects were broadly categorized as chipped stone artifacts (e.g., Fig. 46). Their functions, assigned in some cases, were generally uncertain. In a few instances, it was difficult to determine whether an item had, indeed, been worked owing to the nature of the material. In 13 cases, the material was identified as schist or possibly schist, in five cases as slate or possibly slate, in three cases as slate or schist, in five as possibly andesite, in two as siltstone or possibly siltstone, and in one case the material was labelled unknown. Several items which showed definite signs of working, in the form of bifacial flaking, appeared unfinished.

There were 15 items of triangular or roughly triangular form. In most instances, it was difficult to tell which may have been the business end of the object; i.e., whether the expanded end may have been used as a scraper or the pointed end as an arrow or spear point, as an arming point, or as a knife. One additional item, roughly leaf-shaped in outline, may have represented a stemmed point. There were five roughly rounded objects, bifacially flaked at one end, suggesting scraping tools.

Scrapers. -- Eight relatively flat chipped pebbles, almost all possibly of andesite, were identified as scrapers. They ranged in length from 35.2 mm to 61.2 mm, in width from 28.4 mm to 56.2 mm, and in thickness from 5.4 mm to 10.9 mm. In each case, at least one end of the pebble had been bifacially or unifacially flaked.

Ground Stone

Ground slate tools

Five objects were placed in this category. Only one was sufficiently complete and formed to indicate a specific functional assignment. This was identified as an ulu-type knife, (125.9) x 63.9 x 4.5 mm (Fig. 47). It had been ground on only one face where random striae were visible, and had a roughened, flaked cutting edge. Two edges of the piece had been worked to flat, smooth surfaces. There were two other thin flat objects in the group. One was rectangular in outline, (79.6) x 47.6 x 3.3 mm. The dorsal face and lateral surfaces had been ground flat. There was some battering along both ends and adjacent parts of the dorsal face. The object might have been a tablet, mirror, or whetstone. The second piece was fragmentary and irregular due to damage. It measured (72.8) x (33.4) x (7.0) mm. Only one face was unbroken. It had been ground flat and smooth. Possibly, the piece represented part of a tablet, mirror, or knife. A fourth slate piece, (35.6) x 9.7 x 6.4 mm, was a pointed fragment with six ground or abraded facetted surfaces. It may have been an arming point or "pencil." No possible function was assigned to the fifth slate object. It was an elongated fragment, roughly half-moon shape in cross section, with one end tapered and rounded. Only the dorsal face, ground and polished, showed evidence of working. The object measured (44.5) x (11.5) x (3.7) mm.

Adzes

Two splitting adzes and one probable adze blade portion were represented (Fig. 48). None of the three items were recovered *in situ.* The adze blade portion, made of nephrite, was found one afternoon on the surface of Unit 21 and could have been intrusive. It had not been noticed earlier that day. One of the splitting adzes, a whole specimen possibly of porphyry sandstone, was found in a disturbed pile of rocks northwest of Unit 17 that had been placed there by a backhoe/front-end loader used to remove overburden from the site. The second adze, a virtually complete specimen made of sandstone or siltstone, was found on the site surface near screens set up to filter hand-excavated backdirt. Midden deposit adhered to the adze.

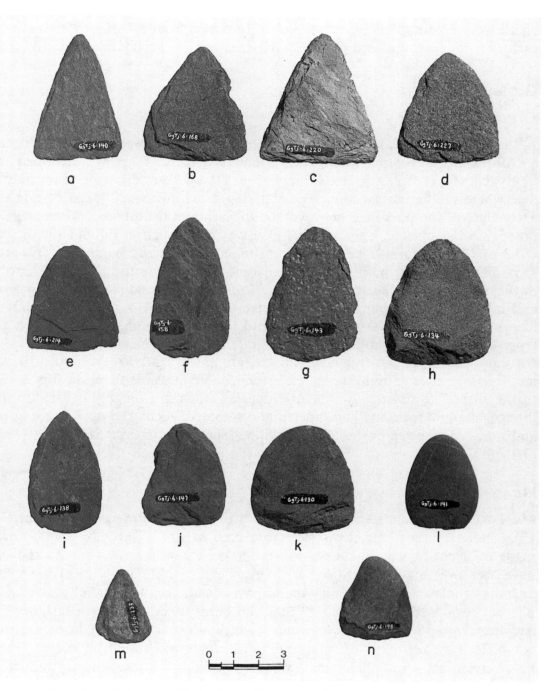

FIGURE 46. Chipped stone artifacts from the Greenville site: spear or arrow point (a);
knife or point (b, i); arming point or knife (c); arming point (d); preform, point
or scraper (e); preform for point (f); point, knife or scraping tool (g); scraper
or preform for arming point (h); scraper (j, n); possible scraper (l, m).

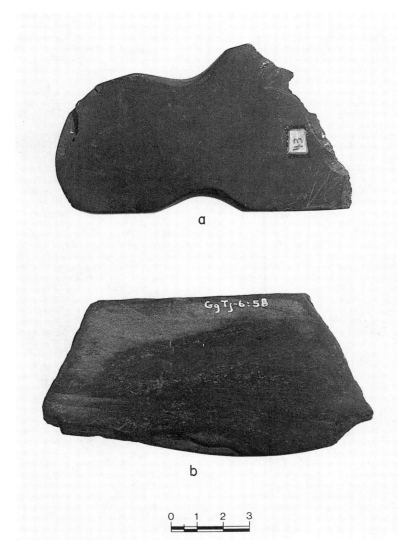

*FIGURE 47. Ground slate mirror or palette (a) and ulu-type
knife (b) from the Greenville site.*

Handles

There were four broken handles in the collection, three possibly made of
marble, and the fourth of porphyry sandstone. The last piece was distinctive, a
pecked and ground handle fragment of a stirrup maul with a nipple top. It was
not recovered *in situ,* but collected in 1981 from the surface of the disturbed site
overburden.

FIGURE 48. Splitting adzes from the Greenville site.

Mirror or palette

This was a ground slate piece, (110) x 65.4 x 9.1 mm (Fig. 47).   Both the dorsal and ventral faces had been ground relatively flat and there was a slight polish to the piece. About half-way along the object, the two faces were constric-

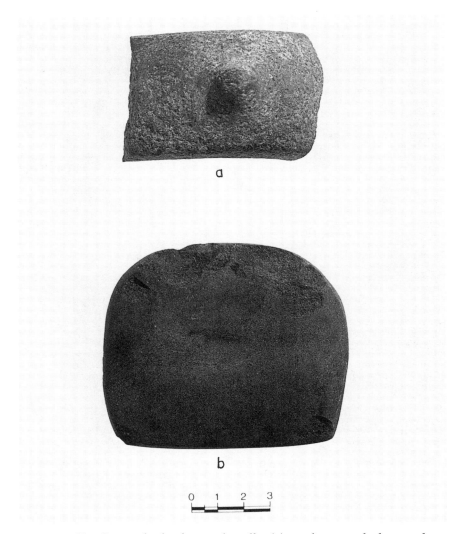

FIGURE 49. Ground nipple-top handle (a) and ground slate palette,
mirror preform, or whetstone (b) from the Greenville site.

ted, presumably for finger grips.   One end was vaguely rounded while the other
end was broken.   Similar specimens found on the north coast of British Columbia
have been called mirrors (when wetted), palettes for grinding pigment, or fine-
grained abraders.

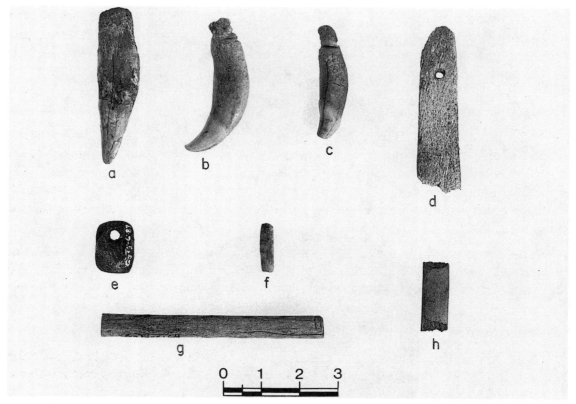

FIGURE 50. Decorative and other artifacts from the Greenville site: bear canine pendant or charm (a); harbour seal tooth pendants (b, c); bone pendant (d) and bead (f); stone bead or pendant (e); possible brow band fragment (h); possible drinking tube (g).

Bead or pendant

This small rectangular object, made of soapstone, measured 14.3 x 10.2 x 4.4 mm (Fig. 50). All surfaces were ground and polished, and one end featured a perforation that had been drilled from both sides.

Soapstone labrets

Three medial labrets were represented in the collection, only one of which was complete (Fig. 21, Chapter III). The complete specimen was a button or disc type on which the inner flange was slightly larger in diameter than the outer flange. Overall, this labret measured 28.7 x 21.5 x 8.7 mm. One of the two incomplete specimens, also a button or disc type, measured (39.1) x 28.8 x 14.6 mm. One side of the inner flange was broken off; the other extended well beyond the diameter of the outer flange. The second incomplete specimen was a fragment of a large button or disc type labret, sufficiently intact to indicate that the inner and outer flanges were almost equal in diameter. The fragment measured 61.6 x (31.0) x 13.5 mm.

Miscellaneous ground stone

Two flat objects were placed in this category. The larger of the two, possibly formed from andesite, measured 93.2 x (79.7) x (9.8) mm. One end was broken or chipped and there was chipping at the opposite corners on the dorsal face. The dorsal face had been ground and polished over much of its surface, and the lateral surfaces ground flat. The object may have been a palette, a preform for a mirror, or a whetstone.

The second object, formed of schist, measured (53.2) x (47.8) x 14.3 mm. Two edges were broken and the other two rounded and bevelled. One face was flat, the other irregular. The piece may have been an abrader.

Miscellaneous Stone and Mineral

One small piece, possibly calcite, appeared to have been worked, probably pecked, though no possible function could be ascribed to it. It was rectangular in outline, (27.2) x 11.4 x 5.4 mm.

A worked pebble, 52.0 x 24.0 x 16.2 mm, had the natural shape of a small adze/scraper. Most of its contours appeared natural except one end which had been pecked flat. It may have been a preform or small hammerstone. There was one round pebble in the collection, possibly quartzite, on which no modification was evident, though it might have represented a "worry" stone or charm. A very small piece of amber featured a ground end and probably drilled aperture, the piece broken at that point. It may have represented a bead. There were two samples of red ochre and three pieces of mica in the collection.

Bone Artifacts

Barbed points

Seven items were assigned this classification (e.g., Fig. 51). There were two complete specimens, both identified as probable leisters. One, made of bird bone, measured 37.2 x 6.5 x 2.0 mm. It was concavo-convex in cross section, pointed at both ends, and had three barbs including the distal tip. The second piece, possibly from land mammal bone, measured 24.5 x 3.1 x 2.2 mm. One end was pointed and the other cut and slightly notched, possibly for hafting. It featured two barbs.

A third item in the assemblage, virtually complete, was also identified as a leister. Measuring (40.1) x 5.5 x 4.2 mm, it was made from land mammal bone, one end pointed and the opposite end flat and tapered. The piece featured a single barb and was tear drop in cross section. A fourth probable leister was indicated by a damaged piece, (35.0) x 5.2 x 2.9 mm. There appeared to be a single barb notched into the distal end, but the specimen was incomplete in this area.

The three remaining barbed points were fragments, (55.0) x 13.4 x 4.7 mm, (74.5) x 19.7 x 5.9 mm, and (27.0) x 7.1 x 3.8 mm. Each piece appeared to be made from land mammal bone. The largest fragment, with three barbs, was regarded as a harpoon. Only one barb was visible on each of the other two fragments.

Bipoints

There were three bipoints in the collection, all made from land mammal bone and complete. One piece, roughly rectangular in cross section, measured 51.1 x 8.0 x 4.1 mm and may have served as a harpoon valve. A second piece, 68.1 x 10.2 x 3.8 mm, was identified as a splinter barb. The third piece was 68.1 x 13.6 x 3.2 mm.

Faceted points

Three fragments were assigned to this group. Only the longest, (49.6) x 13.0 x 2.7 mm, actually included a point. The other two, (25.0) x 10.5 x 3.2 mm and (14.0) x (12.2) x (3.3) mm, were segments, the longer of which might also have been interpreted as a chisel. All three objects were made from land mammal bone.

Awls

Seven objects were assessed as awls. One complete specimen, made of split land mammal bone, featured an elongated tapered point and an opposite spatulate end. The piece measured 89.3 x 12.1 x 4.0 mm. A second complete specimen, 87.0 x 8.1 x 7.1 mm, was made of bird bone. The morphology of the proximal end suggested a crane. The remaining five items, all of land mammal bone, were incomplete in one or another dimension: (120.8) x 8.3 x 4.9 mm; (90.0) x 13.8 x

5.4 mm; 69.1 x (12.6) x 5.8 mm; (58.8) x 1.0 x 5.2 mm; (44.9) x (9.4) x (4.9) mm.

Awls or punches

Seven items were identified as awls or punches. Three were made from land mammal bone, two possibly from land mammal, and two either from bird or mammal bone. One piece, 155.4 x 8.9 x 6.9 mm, may have been hafted. None of the remaining items were complete: (137.0) x (16.1) x (7.1) mm; (118.1) x 25.5 x 20.0 mm; (82.0) x (7.0) x (2.9) mm; (53.4) x (9.8) x (3.6) mm; (41.5) x 6.5 x 3.1 mm; (37.6) x 8.0 x 6.0 mm.

Awls or points

Two items, both incomplete, were in this group: (61.6) x 6.4 x 2.9 mm; (45.8) x (6.1) x (2.6) mm. The shorter of the two was made of bird bone; the other was not designated.

Awl, punch, or point

The single piece given this classification was possibly made from land mammal bone. It measured (48.1) x (8.8) x (3.2) mm.

Awl, punch, or wedge

This piece, made from land mammal bone and charred, measured (48.2) x 10.9 x 6.8 mm.

Spatulate tool

One bone piece was placed in this category. Made of land mammal bone, it was complete, though in poor condition, measuring 69.0 x 13.4 x 4.5 mm.

Ulna tools

Two items were identified as ulna tools. One, made from the bone of an albatross, measured 59.8 x 34.2 x 12.3 mm. The other, possibly of an immature land mammal, measured (101.9) x 37.1 x 14.0 mm.

Needle

One item, made from the ulna of a large bird, was placed in this category. It was incomplete in length, measuring (97.5) x 4.0 x 6.2 mm.

FIGURE 51. Bone artifacts from the Greenville site (I): probable leisters (a, b); awls (c, k); awl or punch (d); point (e, j); barb, possibly harpoon valve (f); splinter barbs (g, i); point or barb (h); possible point (l); wedge or chisel (m).

Bead

This piece, made of bird bone, was 13.0 x 3.6 x 2.8 mm. The dorsal face was rounded and polished, though the polishing may have been natural. The ventral face was naturally flat with some striae present. The ends had been cut but not flattened.

Whistle

This incomplete item, also of bird bone, was (28.7) x 9.7 x 9.6 mm. The distal end had been cut and ground to a finish and there was some polish visible. The opposite end was broken. The dorsal face featured a small, broken, oval aperture cut through the bone by incising.

Possible drinking tube

This tubular bird bone element (Fig. 50) measured 58.1 x 5.9 x 5.2 mm. The two ends had been cut and smoothed. On the surface next to one end, there were two wide incisions.

Possible pendants

There were two bone items in this group. One, made of land mammal bone, measured (45.6) x 11.4 x 2.7 mm. Rectangular in cross section, the dorsal, ventral, and lateral surfaces had been ground flat. The distal end was tapered along one lateral surface and thinned dorso-ventrally. Near this end there was a round perforation that had been incised dorsally and ventrally. Near the broken opposite end, the ventral face had peculiar perpendicular markings which resembled black paint.

The second item measured (37.6) x 8.4 x 2.7 mm and was not identified by faunal source. The ventral face was concave with exposed cancellous bone. The dorsal face was convex, exhibiting a natural polish. One end of the piece was broad, and the other end constricted and enlarged to form a knob.

Possible brow band fragments

There were two pieces in this group. The larger of the two, (60.9) x 11.5 x 2.8 mm, was identified from a mammalian source, possibly a skull fragment. The piece was expanded at one end, which was broken, and tapered at the other. The ventral face was concave and unmodified, while the dorsal face was slightly rounded with some transverse abrasion striae visible. The lateral surfaces were flat with some evident polish.

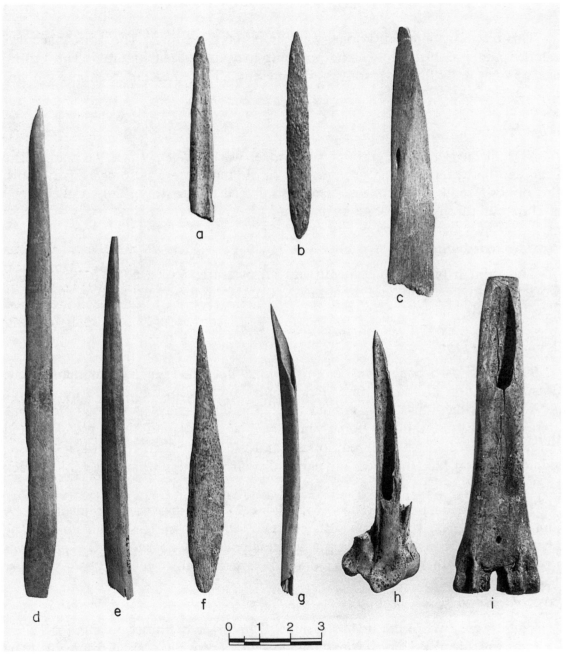

FIGURE 52. Bone artifacts from the Greenville site (II): point (a);
splinter barb (b); awls (c, e, h); awl or punch,
possibly hafted (d); awl with spatulate
end (f); needle (g); chisel (i).

The second piece, broken at both ends, was (19.3) x 17.2 x 1.7 mm. The dorsal face was slightly convex and polished, with transverse abrasion striae present. The ventral face was slightly concave, ground, and polished. Both lateral surfaces were slightly rounded, ground, and polished.

Wedges or chisels

Three bone objects were identified as chisels, one as a possible chisel tool, and seven as wedges or chisels. The largest of the chisels, 105.5 x 14.7 x 11.9 mm, was formed from a metacarpal of a Sitka deer (Fig. 52). The proximal end was largely unmodified though it featured some wear polish on the condyles which had been cut to cancellous bone, creating a flat surface. The distal end had been extensively modified, squared, and tapered ventrally and dorsally.

The remaining chisels and possible chisel tool were fragments of land mammal bone: (58) x 11.1 x 3.9 mm; (50.2) x 8.7 x 4.65 mm; (23.2) x 10.5 x 2.3 mm. Six of the pieces assessed as wedges or chisels were made of land mammal bone, while the seventh was not given a faunal identification. The seven items, each incomplete in one or another dimension, ranged in length from 19.8 to 68.6 mm, in width from 8.8 to 17.4 mm, and in thickness from 2.6 to 4.8 mm.

Miscellaneous bone points

There were 29 bone objects broadly classified as "miscellaneous bone points." For each piece, one end was clearly pointed or tapered. Other features suggested an array of possible functions but were insufficiently diagnostic to firmly place the items in one or another specific category. The possible function assignments and related number of items (in parentheses) were as follows: point (7); facetted point (1); splinter barb (2); barb (2); barb or needle (1); needle (1); awl (1); awl or point (1); awl or arming point for composite harpoon (1); arming point for harpoon (2); central arming element in composite harpoon (2); barb or harpoon part (1); harpoon with inset for a blade (1); wedge (1); arrow (1); arrow or other weapon tip (1). The majority of these pieces were of land mammal bone, while two pieces were either land mammal or bird bone.

Worked bone fragments

Sixty-four objects were broadly grouped as "worked bone fragments." All exhibited some kind of working (sawing, abrasion, etc.). Twenty-three were suggested to be points of some kind, and seven were assigned more specific possible functions: two as parts of awls or points; one as an ulna tool; one as part of a composite harpoon; one as a possible midsection of a barb; one as a barb, valve, or point; one as a pendant or preform for an arrow point.

Tooth Artifacts

Beaver incisor tool

This was an incomplete specimen, (24.1) x 7.8 x 8.2 mm. An enamel portion of the extreme distal end had been ground and polished, and abrasion striae were visible. Also, the tooth had been made thinner by cutting the length of the ventral face, possibly for hafting.

Possible incisor tool

This incomplete piece, measuring (22.5) x 4.3 x 3.1 mm, was identified as a rodent. The ventral face of the distal end was smooth, although there were no abrasion striae visible.

Pendants

Two worked teeth, both harbour seal canines, were identified as pendants. One piece, a right lower canine, measured 30.9 x 7.4 x 6.2 mm. Only the proximal end was modified; this root portion had been notched from two directions to form a constriction for attachment of a suspension line.

The second piece, a right upper canine, measured 36.6 x 10.4 x 7.5 mm. It, too, was only modified at its proximal end, notched in several places, presumably to form a knob for suspension by a thong or cord.

Possible pendant or charm

A right upper bear canine, this piece was 42.7 x 11.4 x 8.0 mm. The root and enamel portions were intact. The proximal (root) end had been thinned by grinding, perhaps for hafting or suspension.

Possible bead

This tooth, possibly from a sea mammal, was extremely fragile. The end of the root portion had been ground flat, while the end of the enamel portion was either ground or naturally worn. A natural aperture formed by the exposed pulp chamber could have been used for threading a suspension line.

Antler Artifacts

There was one possible antler artifact in the Greenville site collection. The item was the base of an antler from a Sitka deer. One end had been sawn to remove a tine, presumably for further working. A number of cut marks were visible elsewhere on the piece which measured (37.8) x 25.7 x 15.9 mm.

Human Remains from Other British Columbia Coast Archaeological Sites

TABLE 13. *Reference information on other British Columbia coast archaeological sites with human remains*

Region/ Site name	Borden designation	Number of individuals	Source of information
— Prehistoric —			
Prince Rupert Harbour:			
Baldwin	GbTo 36	22	Cybulski, n.d.a
Boardwalk	GbTo 31	120	"
Co-Op	GbTo 10	3	Calvert, 1968
Dodge Island	GbTo 18	20	Cybulski, n.d.a
Garden Island	GbTo 23	29	"
Grassy Bay	GbTn 1	1	"
Lachane	GbTo 33	73	"
Lucy Island	GbTp 1	3	Cybulski, 1986, n.d.a
Parizeau Point	GbTo 30	12	Cybulski, n.d.a
Ridley Island	GbTn 19	5	"
Queen Charlotte Islands:			
Blue Jackets Creek	FlUa 4	28	J. Murray, 1981; Cybulski, 1990
Central Coast:			
Namu	ElSx 1	42	Curtin, 1984
Strait of Georgia:			
Beach Grove	DgRs 1	25	Beattie, 1981
		1	Curtin, n.d.
		1	J.S. Cybulski[1]
Bliss Landing	EaSe 2	2	Beattie, 1981
Crescent Beach	DgRr 1	20	Beattie, 1981[2]
		13	Trace, 1981
		25	Conaty & Curtin, 1984
Deep Bay	DiSe 7	7	Beattie, 1981
Duke Point	DgRx 5	10	Cybulski, 1991a

(TABLE 13 continued)

Region/ Site name	Borden designation	Number of individuals	Source of information
(Strait of Georgia continued)			
False Narrows	DgRw 4	82	Gordon, 1974
		2	Burley, 1989
Glenrose Cannery	DgRr 6	22	Beattie, 1981
Helen Point	DfRu 8	9	"
Hill	DfRu 4	32	Hall & Haggarty, 1981
Little Qualicum River	DiSc 1	1	Bernick, 1983
Locarno Beach	DhRt 6	6	Beattie, 1981
Long Harbour	DfRu 44	16	Johnstone, 1989
Maple Bay	DeRu 12	4	Cybulski, 1988b
Marpole	DhRs 1	32	Beattie, 1981
		5	J.S. Cybulski[1]
Montague Harbour	DfRu 13	12	Mitchell, 1971
Whalen Farm	DfRs 3	13	Heglar, 1958
		1	Seymour, 1976
White Rock	DgRq 18	1	Lazenby, 1986
--- Historic ---			
Queen Charlotte Islands:			
Gust Island Rockshelter	FhUb 1	24	Cybulski, 1973
Central Coast:			
Owikeno Lake	EkSp 13	62	Cybulski, n.d.b
Hesquiat Harbour:			
(unnamed)	DiSo 5	4	Cybulski, 1978a
"	DiSo 9	57	"
"	DiSo 10	4	"
"	DiSo 11	4	"
"	DiSo 12	4	"
"	DiSo 13	7	"
"	DiSo 15	4	"
"	DiSo 16	11	"
"	DiSo 18	3	"
"	DiSo 19	8	"
"	DiSo 20	2	"

[1] Personal observations in 1975 and 1978.
[2] Number of individuals clarified in 1991 (Cybulski, 1991b).

TABLE 14. *Numerical distribution of deceased humans from other British Columbia coast archaeological sites by age group and sex* [1]

Region/ Site name	Infant	Child	Juvenile	Adolescent	Adult		
					Male	Female	Unknown

--- *Prehistoric* ---

Prince Rupert Harbour:

Region/ Site name	Infant	Child	Juvenile	Adolescent	Male	Female	Unknown
Baldwin	1	1	1	0	16	3	0
Boardwalk	9	2	4	6	63	33	3
Co-Op	0	0	0	0	2	0	1
Dodge Island	6	0	1	0	8	5	0
Garden Island	1	1	3	0	13	10	1
Grassy Bay	0	1	0	0	0	0	0
Lachane	1	3	5	6	37	21	0
Lucy Island	0	1	0	0	1	1	0
Parizeau Point	4	1	1	0	2	4	0
Ridley Island	1	0	0	0	3	1	0
Total Prince Rupert	23	10	15	12	145	78	5

Queen Charlotte Islands:

Blue Jackets Creek	0	2	2	0	13	5	6

Central Coast:

Namu	2	4	3	3	12	15	3

Strait of Georgia:

Beach Grove	1	1	3	1	9	10	2
Bliss Landing	0	0	0	0	2	0	0
Crescent Beach[2]	3	1	0	1	20	24	5
Deep Bay	1	1	0	0	3	2	0
Duke Point	2	2	1	1	2	2	0
False Narrows	6	5	12	5	25	19	12
Glenrose Cannery	4	1	4	4	0	4	5
Helen Point	0	0	1	1	4	1	2
Hill	7	0	0	5	7	3	10
Little Qualicum River	1	0	0	0	0	0	0
Locarno Beach	0	0	0	0	2	4	0
Long Harbour	9	0	1	0	2	4	0
Maple Bay	1	0	0	0	1	1	1
Marpole	3	1	3	0	14	12	4
Montague Harbour	0	0	1	1	6	3	1
Whalen Farm	0	2	2	2	4	3	1
White Rock	0	0	0	0	0	1	0

(TABLE 14 continued)

Region/ Site name	Infant	Child	Juvenile	Adolescent	Adult Male	Adult Female	Adult Unknown
(Strait of Georgia continued)							
----------------------------	-----	-----	-----	-----	-----	-----	-----
Total Georgia Strait	38	14	28	21	101	93	43
--- *Historic* ---							
Queen Charlotte Islands:							
Gust Island Rockshelter	4	0	2	0	7	8	3
Central Coast:							
Owikeno Lake	15	5	4	5	16	16	1
Hesquiat Harbour:							
DiSo 5	0	0	0	0	3	1	0
DiSo 9	10	10	4	3	15	13	2
DiSo 10	0	0	0	0	2	2	0
DiSo 11	2	0	1	0	1	0	0
DiSo 12	2	0	0	0	1	1	0
DiSo 13	2	2	0	1	0	1	1
DiSo 15	1	1	1	0	0	0	1
DiSo 16	3	2	0	0	2	2	2
DiSo 18	0	0	0	0	3	0	0
DiSo 19	2	1	1	0	1	2	1
DiSo 20	0	0	1	0	0	1	0
----------------------------	-----	-----	-----	-----	-----	-----	-----
Total Hesquiat Harbour	22	16	8	4	28	23	7
----------------------------	-----	-----	-----	-----	-----	-----	-----
Total Historic sites	41	21	14	9	51	47	11

[1] Infant category is 0-2 years; child is 2-6 years; juvenile is 6-12 years; adolescent is 12-16 years; adult is 16 years and older.

[2] Four individuals listed by Trace (1981) were not identified by age at death and sex. The other sex identifications shown here do not agree exactly with those reported by the various authors. They are based on my personal observations in 1991 (Cybulski, 1991b).

Notes on Radiocarbon Dates from Other British Columbia Coast Archaeological Sites

The sources of information for all radiocarbon estimates from archaeological sites other than Greenville which entered into the construction of Figure 11 in Chapter III are provided in Table 15. Following are some qualifications regarding their selection for inclusion in this study.

Prince Rupert Harbour

With the exception of a radiocarbon date from the Co-Op site test-excavated by Charles E. Borden and James Baldwin in 1954 (Calvert, 1968), all of the Prince Rupert Harbour estimates are from sites excavated between 1966 and 1987 under the aegis of the Canadian Museum of Civilization (MacDonald and Inglis, 1981; Simonsen, 1988a). At the time of this writing, a total 128 radiocarbon estimates had been obtained for 11 sites, 120 of which have been included here.[19] Although some have been published, the majority have not been evaluated in the context of analytical site reports by the archaeologists.

One hundred sixteen of the estimates I've included were from the ten sites with human burials (Appendix C). Forty were collagen dates obtained as part of my analysis of the burials, and I evaluated them and the rest (mainly charcoal but also a few shell dates) relative to their stratigraphic contexts as detailed in the field records for each of the sites (Cybulski, n.d.a). Following this analysis, I excluded from the total of 128 one of five estimates reported by George MacDonald (1969: 248) for Dodge Island, two unpublished dates for that site, one of 35 estimates for the Boardwalk site, one unpublished estimate for Garden Island, one unpublished estimate for Lachane, and two Ridley Island dates reported by Joyce May (1979) as being in disturbed contexts. In all but one of the cases, the sample estimates were clearly out of stratigraphic sequence, an observation also made for the three Dodge Island cases by Patricia Sutherland (1978) in her assessment of the stratig-

---

[19] The number of sites could be interpreted as ten as the Co-Op site may have been part of Lachane (MacDonald and Inglis, 1981:43). However, I have retained the separate designations since there is uncertainty on this issue (Simonsen, 1988a:2) and GbTo 10 has been separately reported archaeologically (Calvert, 1968).

raphy of that site. The final excluded case was the most recent date from the Boardwalk site, obtained from a sample of charcoal suspiciously in the context of a late 19th century European occupation (see, also, *Radiocarbon* 15:201 (1973)).

On the side of caution, it should be pointed out that I included 13 estimates in the construction of Figure 11 that I did not evaluate or which I thought might be questionable. They involved five estimates for Kitandach, a site from which human burials were not excavated and, therefore, one whose field records I did not study, an estimate for the Baldwin site that was not directly related to its formal excavation units, and four Lachane site estimates that were accumulated from a waterlogged part of the site not stratigraphically related to the areas that contained human burials. There were no obvious reasons to exclude the estimates. They appear to have been accepted as cultural indicators by the archaeologists (MacDonald and Inglis, 1981), as was one date each from Dodge Island, Garden Island, and Lachane which appeared in my assessment to be anomalously early (though not out of sequence) relative to dates at similar levels in the same or in other parts of the sites.

Statistical treatments and calibrations like those for the Greenville carbon 14 estimates (Chapter II) have not been completed for the Prince Rupert Harbour values. This work is in progress.

Blue Jackets Creek and Namu

Twelve radiocarbon estimates had been obtained for the Blue Jackets Creek site to the time of this writing. Four have been published by Patricia D.S. Severs (*nee* Sutherland) (1974), two attributed to her 1973 excavation of the site and two she attributed to earlier exploratory work by Knut Fladmark. Patricia Sutherland subsequently obtained eight estimates, four from human bone, which have not been published but detailed records are on file at the Canadian Museum of Civilization. All but one of the estimates were in the 3500 to 5500 years B.P. range and there is little reason to doubt the validity of any of them, particularly when interpreted statistically.

All of the Namu estimates included here were evaluated by their authors as archaeologically acceptable. Seven came from human bone samples reported by A.J. Curtin (1984).

Strait of Georgia

Over 136 radiocarbon estimates were assembled from various sources for the Strait of Georgia region. There were, in fact, several more to chose from, but I did not include estimates from sites on the State of Washington side of the border with the exception of Whalen Farm on Point Roberts, which has been assigned to the Canadian site ("Borden") designation scheme (Seymour, 1976). The exclusion of estimates from these sites, which have been comparatively considered by Canadian specialists in the region (Mitchell, 1971; Burley, 1980), does not seriously alter the structure of Figure 11. Nor did I include estimates from the Fraser Canyon sites reported by Donald Mitchell (1971) in his archaeological overview of the Strait of Georgia region. This group has more recently been treated as a separate entity (Mitchell, 1990).

Ultimately, 129 estimates from 40 sites were selected for inclusion in the figure, many of which appear in the carbon 14 tables of Donald Mitchell (1971:62-63) and David Burley (1980:32). A few of those estimates were excluded because of comments on potential or actual unacceptability made by those authors or by the original authors as reported in Roscoe Wilmeth's (1978) compilation of Canadian radiocarbon dates.

R.G. Matson (1976) rejected one of 11 dates he reported for the Glenrose Cannery site, Kathryn Bernick (1983) rejected one of six she reported for Little Qualicum River, and David Johnstone (1989) rejected one of three obtained for Long Harbour, all because they were stratigraphically inconsistent. These rejected dates have not been included in Figure 11.

In addition to the seven estimates reported by Rebecca Murray (1982) for the DgRx 5 site at Duke Point, I included one that I obtained from the bone collagen of one of ten individuals in a multiple mass burial. This date, 3490 ± 125 years B.P. (S-2350), was previously published but not evaluated in print. Rebecca Murray (ibid., p. 130) reported a radiocarbon date of 3080 ± 70 years B.P. (WSU-2229) from a sample of shell collected 30 cm above the burial in the same excavation unit, so the burial date appears acceptable (see, also, Chapter III).

Both Rebecca Murray (ibid.) and Kathryn Bernick (1983), who also used shell for some of her radiocarbon dates at Little Qualicum River, qualified and corrected these dates because of the so-called reservoir effect on marine organisms. They both used a correction factor of -801 ± 23 radiocarbon years proposed for the Puget Sound area. However, their original shell-based values (included in the construction of Figure 11) presented no problems relative to the wood charcoal dates they obtained. Moreover, R.E. Taylor (1987) has since shown that the marine reservoir effect is not constant and that it can be quite variable locally in positive as well as negative terms. My assessment of the few shell-based dates that were obtained for the Prince Rupert Harbour sites also indicated that they presented no problems for interpretation. All of this would suggest that shell-based radiocarbon dates are probably best left and archaeologically evaluated as originally reported by the laboratory that supplied them.

TABLE 15. *Sources of information for radiocarbon date estimates from other British Columbia coast archaeological sites*

Region/ Site name	Borden designation	Number of estimates	Source of information
Prince Rupert Harbour:			
Baldwin	GbTo 36	12	Cybulski, n.d.a
Boardwalk	GbTo 31	34	Cybulski, n.d.a[1]
Co-Op	GbTo 10	1	Calvert, 1968
Dodge Island	GbTo 18	4	MacDonald, 1969[1]
		8	Cybulski, n.d.a[1]
Garden Island	GbTo 23	7	MacDonald, 1969
		5	Cybulski, n.d.a[1]
Grassy Bay	GbTn 1	4	Wilmeth, 1978
Kitandach	GbTo 34	5	CMC records[2]
Lachane	GbTo 33	4	Inglis, 1976
		2	Simonsen, 1988a
		26	Cybulski, n.d.a[1]
Lucy Island	GbTp 1	2	Wilmeth, 1978
Parizeau Point	GbTo 30	2	Cybulski, n.d.a
Ridley Island	GbTn 19	2	May, 1979[1]
		2	Cybulski, n.d.a
Queen Charlotte Islands:			
Blue Jackets Creek	FlUa 4	4	Severs, 1974[1]
		8	CMC records[2]
Central Coast:			
Namu	ElSx 1	14	Luebbers, 1978
		7	Curtin, 1984
Strait of Georgia:			
Beach Grove	DgRs 1	4	Mitchell, 1971
		2	Wilmeth, 1978
Belcarra Park	DhRr 6	3	Burley, 1980
Birds Eye Cove	DeRv 15	4	Wilmeth, 1978
Bowker Creek	DcRt 13	2	Mitchell, 1971
Cadboro Bay	DcRt 15	1	Wilmeth, 1978
Campbell River	EaSh 1	1	Mitchell, 1971
Coldicutt Creek	DgRq 19	1	M. Skinner, 1991[3]
Courtenay River	DkSf 1	1	Mitchell, 1971
Crescent Beach	DgRr 1	4	Trace, 1981
Deep Bay	DiSe 7	2	Burley, 1980
Dionisio Point	DgRv 3	3	Mitchell, 1971
Duke Point 5	DgRx 5	7	R. Murray, 1982
		1	Cybulski, 1990
Duke Point 11	DgRx 11	1	R. Murray, 1982

(TABLE 15 continued)

Region/ Site name	Borden designation	Number of estimates	Source of information
(Strait of Georgia continued)			
Duke Point 36	DgRx 36	1	R. Murray, 1982
False Narrows	DgRw 4	1	Mitchell, 1971
Georgeson Bay	DfRu 24	2	Haggarty & Sendey, 1976
Glenrose Cannery	DgRr 6	10	Matson, 1976[1]
		2	Burley, 1980
		1	CMC records[2]
Helen Point	DfRu 8	4	Burley, 1980
J. Puddleduck	DkSf 26	2	Mitchell, 1988
Little Qualicum River	DiSc 1	5	Bernick, 1983[1]
Locarno Beach	DhRt 6	2	Mitchell, 1971
Long Harbour	DfRu 44	2	Johnstone, 1989[1]
Maple Bank	DcRu 12	1	Burley, 1980
Maple Bay	DeRu 12	1	Simonsen, 1988b
Marpole	DhRs 1	3	Mitchell, 1971
		1	Wilmeth, 1978
		1	Burley, 1980
Millard Creek	DkSf 2c	2	Capes, 1977
	DkSf 2d	1	Capes, 1977
Mission Hill	DkSg 2b	1	Wilmeth, 1978
Montague Harbour	DfRu 13	4	Mitchell, 1971
Musqueam North	DhRt 3	1	Wilmeth, 1978
Musqueam Northeast	DhRt 4	2	Borden, 1976
Pedder Bay/Ash Point	DcRv 1	1	Mitchell, 1971[1]
Pender Canal 1	DeRt 1	12	Carlson, 1986
Pender Canal 2	DeRt 2	1	Mitchell, 1971
		15	Carlson, 1986
Point Grey	DhRt 5	1	Wilmeth, 1978
Sandwich Midden	DkSg 2	1	Wilmeth, 1978
St. Mungo Cannery	DgRr 2	2	Calvert, 1970
		4	Wilmeth, 1978
Stselax Village	DhRt 2	1	Mitchell, 1971
Tsolum River Midden	DkSg 2a	1	Wilmeth, 1978
Whalen Farm	DfRs 3	2	Mitchell, 1971
White Rock	DgRq 18	1	M. Skinner, 1991[3]

[1]See text in Appendix D for qualifications.
[2]Records on file in Canadian Museum of Civilization.
[3]Personal communication.

Identification of Wood Samples from the Greenville Burial Site

by GREGORY S. YOUNG

Three deteriorated wood samples excavated from the Greenville burial site, GgTj 6, were identified in the Analytical Research Services section of the Canadian Conservation Institute, Ottawa. Despite severe deterioration of the wood, the identifications were narrowed to three possibilities: *Chamaecyparis* sp., *Taxus* sp., and *Thuja* sp.

Method

Portions of the three dry samples of wood, floral samples #8, #19 and #21, were soaked in water for several weeks to soften them sufficiently for sectioning by hand. Radial and tangential sections were examined by light microscopy.

Results

The wood samples were extremely deteriorated, and the cell structure that remained was often collapsed beyond recognition. This was particularly true for cross sections. Fortunately, all three samples were softwoods, and, therefore, the distorted cross sectional view, so critical in identifying hardwoods, did not completely prevent an identification. Documentation, however, of axial parenchyma and of the transition from early- to latewood was not possible. The remnant structure of the ray bundles, in radial view, provided the most information.

Floral sample #8

For this sample, radial sections revealed uniseriate ray bundles consisting of procumbent cells which often contained gummy deposits. The cells had thin, smooth vertical (end) walls with indentures and horizontal walls with secondary thickening. In a few cross fields, pits occurred in two rows, but in most cross fields, they occupied one row. The pitting was definitely not pinoid, but it was not possible to determine whether it was piceoid, cupressoid or taxodioid in the sections examined. Piceoid was less likely than the other two, because the pits in the samples were larger than typical for this type. Remnants of large bordered pits were visible in the radial walls of the wood tracheids.

Floral sample #19

Radial sections revealed similar anatomy to that in sample #8.

Floral sample #21

Radial sections revealed a similar anatomy to that in sample #8, but, in addition, one cross field pit was visibly cupressoid in shape. No vertical (end) wall structure was visible for the procumbent ray cells because of comparatively greater deterioration in this sample.

Discussion

The anatomical detail remaining in the test samples included the structures in the ray bundles needed to eliminate most of the softwoods from possibility. Gummy deposits visible in most rays were probably responsible for the somewhat better preservation of these structures compared to other anatomical features. The following discussion is organized according to the families within Coniferae that include genera indigenous to Canada.

Pinaceae can be divided anatomically into two subdivisions. Pinoideae consists of the genus *Pinus*. The test samples lacked normal fusiform ray bundles, dentate ray tracheids and fenestriform cross field pits typical of this genus. Abietoideae, the other subdivision, includes the North American genera *Abies, Tsuga, Picea, Pseudotsuga,* and *Larix.* These were not possible for the samples because all had nodular vertical walls in ray parenchyma.

Taxaceae includes *Taxus.* This genus is a possibility, because it contains the smooth, thin vertical walls in the ray cells which were seen in samples #8 and #19. The presence or absence of spiral thickening, which sets this genus apart from most others, could not be documented in the test samples because of the severe deterioration.

Cupressaceae includes *Chamaecyparis, Juniperus, Libocedrus,* and *Thuja.* Of these genera, *Juniperus* and *Libocedrus decurrens* were not possible because they also contain nodular vertical walls in ray parenchyma. The remaining two, containing similar structure, have the requisite vertical wall morphology in the ray cells.

The identifications therefore included three possibilities: *Taxus* (e.g., Pacific Yew), *Chamaecyparis* (e.g., Alaska Cedar) and *Thuja* (e.g., Western Red Cedar and Northern White Cedar). Without being able to document additional anatomy, particularly that visible in cross section, the identifications could not be narrowed further.

Common and Scientific Names of Animals Represented in the Greenville Site Faunal Assemblage

Common Name	Scientific Name
	--- Vertebrates ---
Mammals:	
snowshoe hare	*Lepus americanus*
groundhog	*Marmota monax*
beaver	*Castor canadensis*
deer mouse	*Peromyscus* sp.
meadow vole	*Microtus pennsylvanicus*
long-tailed vole	*Microtus longicaudus*
vole	*Microtus* sp.
vole & lemming subfamily	Microtinae
mouse & vole family	Cricetidae
porcupine	*Erethizon dorsatum*
small rodent	Rodentia
porpoise family	Delphinidae
whale	Cetacea
dog	*Canis familiaris*
coyote/dog	*Canis latrans/familiaris*
dog/wolf/coyote	*Canis* sp.
dog & fox family	Canidae
black bear	*Ursus americanus*
black bear/grizzly bear	*Ursus americanus/arctos*
marten	*Martes americana*
ermine	*Mustela erminea*
striped skunk	*Mephitis mephitis*
sea otter	*Enhydra lutris*
otter family	Mustelidae
domestic cat	*Felis catus*
carnivore	Carnivora
northern sea lion	*Eumetopias jubata*
sea lion family	Otariidae
harbour seal	*Phoca vitulina*
seal family	Phocidae
horse	*Equus caballus*
pig	*Sus scrofa*
mule deer	*Odocoileus hemionus*

Common Name	Scientific Name
(Mammals continued)	
moose	*Alces alces*
caribou/moose	*Rangifer tarandus/Alces alces*
caribou/mule deer	*Rangifer tarandus/Odocoileus hemionus*
moose & deer family	Cervidae
mountain goat	*Oreamnos americanus*
domestic sheep	*Ovis aries*
artiodactyl	Artiodactyla
Birds:	
albatross	*Diomedea* sp.
cormorant	*Phalacrocorax* sp.
green-winged teal	*Anas crecca*
greater scaup	*Aythya marila*
surf scoter	*Melanitta perspicillata*
common/Barrow's goldeneye	*Bucephala clangula/islandica*
large duck	Anatinae
bald eagle	*Haliaeetus leucocephalus*
turkey	*Meleagris gallopavo*
crane	*Grus* sp.
black-bellied plover/surfbird	*Pluvialus squatarola/Aphriza virgata*
cf. whimbrel	*Numenius phaeopus*
mew gull	*Larus canus*
herring/Thayer's gull	*Larus argentatus/thayeri*
glaucous-winged gull	*Larus glaucescens*
glaucous-winged/glaucous gull	*Larus glaucescens/hyperboreus*
gull	*Larus* sp.
black-legged kittiwake	*Rissa tridactyla*
gull family	Laridae
common/thick-billed murre	*Uria aalge/lomvia*
great horned owl	*Bubo virginianus*
raven	*Corvus corax*
cf. varied thrush	*Ixoreus naevius*
thrush subfamily	Turdinae
Amphibians:	
western toad	*Bufo boreas*
Fish:	
spiny dogfish	*Squalus acanthias*
salmon	*Oncorhynchus* sp.
salmon & trout subfamily	Salmoninae
salmon & whitefish family	Salmonidae
eulachon & smelt family	Osmeridae

Common Name	Scientific Name

(Fish continued)

walleye pollock	*Theragra chalcogramma*
walleye pollock/Pacific cod	*Theragra chalcogramma/Gadus macrocephalus*
pollock & cod family	Gadidae
redfish family	Scorpaenidae
arrowtooth flounder	*Atheresthes stomias*
arrowtooth flounder/petrale sole	*Atheresthes stomias/Eopsetta jordani*
flathead/sand sole	*Hippoglossoides elassodon/Psettichthys melanostictus*
Pacific halibut	*Hippoglossoides stenolepis*
starry flounder	*Platichthys stellatus*
flatfish	Pleuronectiformes

--- *Invertebrates* ---

Gastropoda:

top shell family	Trochidae
	Solariella/Margarites

Pelecypoda:

butter clam	*Saxidomus giganteus*

Cirripedia:

barnacle	Cirripedia

Malacostraca:

true crab family	Cancridae

Limb Bone and Skull Measurements and Indices for Human Remains from Greenville

TABLE 16. *Statistical summary of limb bone measurements and derived indices for Greenville males and females* [1]

Measurement/index	Side	Sample size	Mean	Standard deviation	Maximum value	Minimum value
		--- *Males* ---				
Clavicle:						
Maximum length	R	3	165.00	5.00	170.0	160.0
	L	1	168.00	--	--	--
Middle perimeter	R	2	35.50	4.95	39.0	32.0
	L	1	39.50	--	--	--
Thickness index	R	2	21.80	2.55	23.6	20.0
	L	1	23.50	--	--	--
Humerus:						
Maximum length	R	3	322.67	10.60	334.0	313.0
	L	3	328.67	15.57	345.0	314.0
Perimeter at deltoid	R	7	68.71	5.29	75.0	62.0
	L	8	69.75	6.07	79.0	62.0
Middle perimeter	R	3	63.33	3.21	67.0	61.0
	L	3	64.83	5.39	71.0	61.0
Perimeter under deltoid	R	9	60.22	3.59	65.0	54.0
	L	9	59.67	4.62	67.5	54.0
Maximum middle diameter	R	3	22.33	1.53	24.0	21.0
	L	3	22.33	1.53	24.0	21.0
Minimum middle diameter	R	3	17.00	1.00	18.0	16.0
	L	3	18.50	2.18	21.0	17.0
Maximum head diameter	R	5	47.50	1.50	50.0	46.0
	L	2	46.00	1.41	47.0	45.0
Minimum head diameter	R	4	44.38	1.25	45.0	42.5
	L	2	44.00	0.71	44.5	43.5
Robustness index	R	3	19.67	1.16	20.9	18.6
	L	3	19.73	0.96	20.6	18.7
Deltoid index	R	7	113.46	4.53	120.0	104.8
	L	7	115.93	6.68	125.8	106.7
Diaphyseal index	R	3	76.17	1.15	77.3	75.0
	L	3	82.67	4.25	87.5	79.5

(TABLE 16 continued)

Measurement/index	Side	Sample size	Mean	Standard deviation	Maximum value	Minimum value
Ulna:						
Maximum length	R	4	271.75	9.50	282.0	261.0
	L	4	266.75	10.75	280.0	255.0
Minimum circumference	R	5	34.70	2.91	39.0	31.5
	L	4	35.00	2.94	38.0	31.0
Robustness index	R	3	12.30	0.78	12.8	11.4
	L	3	12.60	1.35	13.7	11.1
Radius:						
Maximum length	R	3	248.33	10.69	260.0	239.0
	L	5	244.80	10.03	257.0	230.0
Minimum circumference	R	5	37.40	3.65	41.0	33.0
	L	6	40.42	0.80	42.0	40.0
Head diameter	R	6	23.25	0.88	24.0	22.0
	L	8	23.00	1.07	25.0	22.0
Robustness index	R	3	15.17	0.87	15.9	14.2
	L	5	16.40	0.65	17.4	15.6
Femur:						
Maximum length	R	9	427.00	12.56	447.0	412.0
	L	8	430.63	14.02	450.0	413.0
Oblique length	R	6	424.33	10.71	439.0	415.0
	L	5	430.80	13.54	450.0	420.0
Midshaft anteroposterior diameter	R	8	27.44	0.98	28.5	26.0
	L	6	28.00	1.26	30.0	27.0
Midshaft mediolateral diameter	R	8	25.94	1.47	28.0	24.0
	L	6	26.67	1.54	28.5	24.0
Subtrochanteric antero-posterior diameter	R	9	22.33	1.84	25.0	18.5
	L	9	23.94	2.43	29.0	20.0
Subtrochanteric medio-lateral diameter	R	9	33.50	1.68	36.0	31.0
	L	9	34.33	2.25	39.0	31.0
Middle perimeter	R	8	81.56	3.39	85.0	75.0
	L	6	84.92	2.15	89.0	83.0
Head diameter	R	9	46.83	0.97	49.0	45.5
	L	7	47.00	1.73	50.0	45.0
Robustness index	R	5	12.74	0.36	13.1	12.2
	L	4	12.65	0.65	13.3	12.0
Pilasteric index	R	8	106.00	5.66	112.5	96.3
	L	7	103.69	6.68	112.5	94.6
Platymeric index	R	9	66.80	6.20	73.4	53.6
	L	9	69.71	4.82	74.4	58.8

(TABLE 16 continued)

Measurement/index	Side	Sample size	Mean	Standard deviation	Maximum value	Minimum value
Tibia:						
Maximum length	R	10	347.70	14.23	367.0	327.0
	L	8	351.75	12.09	367.0	337.0
Anteroposterior diameter	R	11	34.50	2.26	38.5	30.0
at nutrient foramen	L	8	34.81	1.62	37.0	31.5
Mediolateral diameter at	R	11	21.55	1.80	26.0	20.0
nutrient foramen	L	8	21.31	1.71	24.0	19.0
Minimum circumference	R	10	71.30	2.26	75.0	68.0
	L	9	71.61	2.76	75.0	67.0
Robustness index	R	10	20.53	0.77	22.2	19.5
	L	7	20.27	0.87	22.0	19.6
Cnemial index	R	11	62.63	5.86	74.3	54.1
	L	8	61.38	5.68	68.6	51.4
Fibula:						
Maximum length	R	4	335.00	18.92	351.0	312.0
	L	5	333.40	16.65	352.0	318.0
--- *Females* ---						
Clavicle:						
Maximum length	R	3	141.83	4.86	146.0	136.5
	L	5	138.00	3.81	142.0	134.0
Middle perimeter	R	3	33.00	2.65	36.0	31.0
	L	5	30.00	2.92	35.0	28.0
Thickness index	R	3	23.27	1.25	24.7	22.4
	L	5	21.72	1.72	24.8	20.9
Humerus:						
Maximum length	R	7	294.86	11.11	317.0	284.0
	L	8	285.13	10.78	308.0	274.0
Perimeter at deltoid	R	9	63.22	3.63	70.0	59.0
	L	10	59.45	3.18	65.0	56.0
Middle perimeter	R	7	58.57	4.50	66.0	53.0
	L	8	55.00	3.25	60.0	50.0
Perimeter under deltoid	R	9	54.67	3.05	61.0	51.0
	L	10	52.20	2.14	56.0	49.0
Maximum middle diameter	R	7	21.00	1.41	23.0	19.0
	L	8	19.56	1.18	21.0	17.0
Minimum middle diameter	R	7	15.29	1.52	17.5	14.0
	L	8	14.75	1.20	17.0	13.5
Maximum head diameter	R	7	42.07	2.09	44.5	39.0
	L	7	41.00	2.40	46.0	39.0

(*TABLE* 16 *continued*)

Measurement/index	Side	Sample size	Mean	Standard deviation	Maximum value	Minimum value
(Humerus continued)						
Minimum head diameter	R	6	40.00	1.58	42.5	38.0
	L	6	39.50	2.32	44.0	37.5
Robustness index	R	7	19.84	1.41	22.4	18.4
	L	8	19.29	0.82	20.0	18.1
Deltoid index	R	9	115.66	2.51	119.6	111.1
	L	10	113.89	3.96	120.4	108.4
Diaphyseal index	R	7	72.69	3.21	77.3	69.0
	L	8	75.54	6.17	85.0	67.5
Ulna:						
Maximum length	R	6	236.25	9.14	247.0	220.0
	L	6	230.33	10.60	246.0	216.0
Minimum circumference	R	5	31.50	1.12	33.0	30.0
	L	7	31.07	1.79	34.5	29.0
Robustness index	R	5	13.36	0.54	14.1	12.7
	L	5	13.52	0.86	14.4	12.2
Radius:						
Maximum length	R	9	217.22	10.25	239.0	198.0
	L	8	213.94	12.29	229.0	194.0
Minimum circumference	R	9	35.11	2.00	38.5	33.0
	L	8	34.38	2.72	39.0	32.0
Head diameter	R	10	20.80	1.11	22.0	19.0
	L	7	20.79	1.52	23.0	19.0
Robustness index	R	8	16.03	1.06	17.3	14.4
	L	7	16.20	0.82	17.5	15.3
Femur:						
Maximum length	R	5	410.20	18.25	441.0	395.0
	L	6	399.50	22.95	442.0	375.0
Oblique length	R	3	415.00	21.28	438.0	396.0
	L	4	388.00	11.17	397.0	374.0
Midshaft anteroposterior diameter	R	5	25.10	0.55	26.0	24.5
	L	6	24.00	0.89	25.0	23.0
Midshaft mediolateral diameter	R	5	25.80	1.48	28.0	24.0
	L	6	25.67	0.82	27.0	25.0
Subtrochanteric antero-posterior diameter	R	8	22.00	0.53	23.0	21.0
	L	9	22.17	1.30	25.0	20.5
Subtrochanteric medio-lateral diameter	R	8	30.44	1.55	33.0	28.0
	L	9	30.89	1.75	34.0	28.0
Middle perimeter	R	5	77.90	1.95	80.0	76.0
	L	6	76.50	2.83	79.5	73.0

(TABLE 16 continued)

Measurement/index	Side	Sample size	Mean	Standard deviation	Maximum value	Minimum value
(Femur continued)						
Head diameter	R	7	43.50	2.02	46.0	40.5
	L	7	41.21	1.85	44.5	39.0
Robustness index	R	3	12.37	0.38	12.8	12.1
	L	4	12.60	0.24	12.8	12.3
Pilasteric index	R	5	97.54	5.82	104.2	89.3
	L	6	93.55	3.05	96.2	88.9
Platymeric index	R	8	72.43	3.49	78.6	66.7
	L	9	71.97	6.18	86.2	64.7
Tibia:						
Maximum length	R	5	318.80	22.44	352.0	295.0
	L	6	315.67	9.44	329.0	302.0
Anteroposterior diameter	R	8	29.31	1.28	31.0	27.0
at nutrient foramen	L	10	30.30	1.67	34.0	29.0
Mediolateral diameter at	R	8	20.38	1.30	22.0	18.0
nutrient foramen	L	10	20.90	1.37	24.0	19.0
Minimum circumference	R	7	63.64	2.69	67.5	60.0
	L	8	64.06	2.11	67.5	61.0
Robustness index	R	4	20.45	0.52	21.0	19.8
	L	6	20.03	0.70	20.9	18.9
Cnemial index	R	8	69.51	2.83	74.6	66.7
	L	10	69.10	4.63	75.9	58.5
Fibula:						
Maximum length	R	4	309.75	9.14	317.0	298.0
	L	3	308.83	11.73	319.0	296.0

[1] All data pertain to fully developed limb bones and all measurements are reported in mm.

TABLE 17. *Statistical summary of limb proportions and stature for Greenville males and females*

Character	Sample size	Mean	Standard deviation	Maximum value	Minimum value
--- Males ---					
Claviculohumeral index	3	49.83	0.55	50.4	49.3
Radiohumeral index	4	77.05	1.39	78.2	75.4
Tibiofemoral index	8	81.79	1.67	85.0	79.2
Humerofemoral index	4	73.90	1.24	75.0	72.2
Intermembral index	3	71.70	1.67	73.2	69.9
Stature (in cm)	14	163.54	3.16	168.6	159.6
--- Females ---					
Claviculohumeral index	5	48.04	1.99	50.3	45.0
Radiohumeral index	9	74.62	2.31	78.5	71.5
Tibiofemoral index	7	80.63	1.75	84.4	79.0
Humerofemoral index	8	72.39	1.28	74.5	70.8
Intermembral index	5	69.86	1.04	70.7	68.2
Stature (in cm)	11	152.95	4.44	163.5	147.1

TABLE 18. *Statistical summary of cranial measurements and derived indices for Greenville males and females*

Measurement/index	Sample size	Mean	Standard deviation	Maximum value	Minimum value
--- Males ---					
Cranial length	8	182.13	5.46	189.0	171.0
Cranial breadth	8	146.50	5.88	156.0	137.0
Minimum frontal breadth	7	97.71	1.98	100.0	94.0
Bizygomatic diameter	4	146.50	4.51	152.0	141.0
Basion-bregma height	8	134.63	5.73	144.0	126.0
Basion-nasion length	6	104.00	5.18	110.0	96.0
Basion-prosthion length	4	99.00	9.38	108.0	87.0
Upper facial height	5	72.80	7.16	83.0	66.0
Total facial height	4	117.25	4.57	123.0	112.0
Orbital height	8	36.13	1.96	40.0	34.0
Orbital breadth	8	44.50	1.41	47.0	42.0
Nasal height	6	51.83	2.99	55.0	48.0
Nasal breadth	5	26.40	2.19	29.0	23.0
Alveolar length	6	54.50	3.33	60.0	51.0

(TABLE 18 continued)

Measurement/index	Sample size	Mean	Standard deviation	Maximum value	Minimum value
Alveolar breadth	6	66.83	3.43	72.0	63.0
Mandibular length	8	108.13	7.45	116.0	93.0
Bigonial breadth	6	109.00	6.13	117.0	100.0
Bicondylar width	3	129.33	8.96	135.0	119.0
Symphyseal height	8	35.88	2.59	40.0	33.0
Ramus height	10	65.30	5.81	76.0	55.0
Minimum ramus breadth	11	39.18	2.52	43.0	35.0
Cranial index	8	80.48	3.39	86.2	76.5
Cranial module	7	153.90	4.06	157.0	145.3
Length-height index	7	74.01	3.50	80.0	68.5
Breadth-height index	7	91.54	5.08	98.6	84.6
Frontoparietal index	6	66.65	2.47	69.2	62.2
Mean basion-height index	7	81.81	3.85	88.3	75.7
Gnathic index	4	96.45	5.89	103.9	90.6
Upper facial index	3	48.37	3.52	52.4	45.9
Facial index	4	81.23	3.09	83.7	76.7
Orbital index	7	80.99	2.44	85.1	77.3
Nasal index	5	50.14	2.59	52.9	46.9
Maxillo-alveolar index	6	122.67	1.50	124.5	120.0
Transverse craniofacial index	3	101.03	3.15	102.9	97.4
Ramus index	10	60.20	5.51	67.3	50.0

--- Females ---

Measurement/index	Sample size	Mean	Standard deviation	Maximum value	Minimum value
Cranial length	11	178.18	6.11	188.0	168.0
Cranial breadth	12	140.50	5.04	149.0	133.0
Minimum frontal breadth	11	93.18	2.36	97.0	89.0
Bizygomatic diameter	7	136.71	4.79	143.0	130.0
Basion-bregma height	10	130.50	4.84	138.0	124.0
Basion-nasion length	11	99.91	4.09	108.0	93.0
Basion-prosthion length	8	102.75	5.26	111.0	96.0
Upper facial height	8	69.75	1.75	72.0	66.0
Total facial height	6	113.50	4.09	119.0	107.0
Orbital height	10	35.50	1.27	38.0	34.0
Orbital breadth	10	42.10	1.29	44.0	40.0
Nasal height	9	50.33	1.58	53.0	49.0
Nasal breadth	8	26.63	2.00	30.0	24.0
Alveolar length	7	55.29	1.89	59.0	53.0
Alveolar breadth	4	62.50	2.38	66.0	61.0
Mandibular length	7	105.00	5.92	111.0	96.0
Bigonial breadth	7	98.14	4.02	102.0	92.0
Bicondylar width	5	121.80	5.31	126.0	116.0

(*TABLE* 18 continued)

Measurement/index	Sample size	Mean	Standard deviation	Maximum value	Minimum value
Symphyseal height	6	32.67	1.86	35.0	31.0
Ramus height	11	58.64	3.41	65.0	54.0
Minimum ramus breadth	12	38.58	4.36	46.0	32.0
Cranial index	11	78.94	3.26	84.5	73.3
Cranial module	10	149.57	3.20	154.7	144.7
Length-height index	10	73.70	4.29	82.1	67.6
Breadth-height index	10	92.75	5.06	101.5	85.2
Frontoparietal index	11	66.38	2.66	70.4	61.1
Mean basion-height index	10	82.11	4.39	89.0	75.4
Gnathic index	8	102.89	2.37	106.0	100.0
Upper facial index	6	52.85	3.56	59.2	48.9
Facial index	5	83.22	1.71	85.4	81.0
Orbital index	10	83.44	5.08	90.0	71.7
Nasal index	7	52.33	4.21	61.2	49.0
Maxillo-alveolar index	4	114.73	5.60	122.2	108.9
Transverse craniofacial index	7	97.34	3.63	103.0	91.7
Ramus index	10	64.87	5.47	73.0	55.2

Frequencies of Non-metric Skeletal Variants for Human Remains from Greenville

TABLE 19. *Frequencies of non-metric postcranial variants in Greenville adults by sex and combined totals*

Variant	Males Freq.	%	Females Freq.	%	Total[1] Freq.	%
Atlas (C1) bridging:						
Posterior, complete	2/22	9.09	1/18	5.56	5/50	10.00
Posterior, partial	2/22	9.09	1/18	5.56	3/50	6.00
Lateral, complete	4/22	18.18	1/16	6.25	5/48	10.42
Lateral, partial	1/22	4.55	0/16	0.00	2/48	4.17
Atlas (C1) posterior arch:						
Foramen	1/21	4.76	3/16	18.75	5/47	10.64
Notch	5/21	23.81	3/16	18.75	12/47	25.53
Atlas (C1) condyle:						
Constricted or hourglass	8/22	36.36	6/16	37.50	18/48	37.50
Double or divided	1/22	4.55	2/16	12.50	3/48	6.25
Transverse cervical foramen:						
C1 (atlas), opened	1/21	4.76	0/16	0.00	1/47	2.13
C2 (axis), opened	2/18	11.11	0/17	0.00	3/45	6.67
C3, divided	0/13	0.00	0/18	0.00	0/37	0.00
C3, partly divided	0/13	0.00	0/18	0.00	0/37	0.00
C4, divided	0/16	0.00	0/17	0.00	0/39	0.00
C4, partly divided	0/16	0.00	0/17	0.00	0/39	0.00
C5, divided	4/17	23.53	1/16	6.25	5/42	11.90
C5, partly divided	2/17	11.76	1/16	6.25	4/42	9.52
C6, divided	9/15	60.00	4/16	25.00	18/42	42.86
C6, partly divided	2/15	13.33	2/16	12.50	4/42	9.52
C7, divided	0/9	0.00	2/12	16.67	3/28	10.71
C7, partly divided	1/9	11.11	2/12	16.67	4/28	14.29
Sternum:						
Sternal aperture	1/4	25.00	1/5	20.00	2/9	22.22

(TABLE 19 continued)

Variant	Males Freq.	%	Females Freq.	%	Total[1] Freq.	%
Clavicle:						
Costoclavicular tubercle	1/18	5.56	0/18	0.00	2/42	4.76
Scapula:						
Separate acromion tip	0/10	0.00	1/13	7.69	2/27	7.41
Suprascapular notch	11/12	91.67	10/10	100.00	22/24	91.67
Humerus:						
Septal aperture	1/21	4.76	3/18	16.67	4/46	8.70
Supratrochlear spur	1/23	4.35	0/19	0.00	1/50	2.00
Innominate:						
Acetabular mark	3/17	17.65	3/16	18.75	7/35	20.00
Accessory sacral facet	4/15	26.67	5/15	33.33	11/32	34.38
Femur:						
Third trochanter (true)	5/22	22.73	2/17	11.76	8/41	19.51
Third trochanter (ridge)	11/22	50.00	6/17	35.29	18/41	43.90
Fossa of Allen	13/20	65.00	0/13	0.00	14/36	38.89
- facet-like	6/20	30.00	0/13	0.00	7/36	19.44
- ulcer-like	6/20	30.00	0/13	0.00	6/36	16.67
- porous	1/20	5.00	0/13	0.00	1/36	2.78
Patella:						
Vastus notch	6/14	42.86	9/18	50.00	15/37	40.54
Calcaneus anterior and middle facets:						
Continuous unit	4/22	18.18	8/19	42.11	12/48	25.00
Constricted or hourglass	7/22	31.82	6/19	31.58	16/48	33.33
Two discrete facets	11/22	50.00	5/19	26.32	20/48	41.67
Emarginate anterior facet	4/21	19.05	1/19	5.26	6/46	13.04

[1] Totals include mature bones of indeterminate sex from disturbed contexts.

TABLE 20. *Frequencies of non-metric cranial variants in Greenville adults by sex and combined totals*

Variant	Males		Females		Total[1]	
	Freq.	%	Freq.	%	Freq.	%
Accessory sutures:						
Metopism	0/15	0.00	0/12	0.00	0/27	0.00
Os Inca	1/14	7.14	0/12	0.00	1/26	3.85
Accessory bones:						
Bregmatic bone	0/10	0.00	0/6	0.00	0/16	0.00
Coronal suture bones	0/15	0.00	0/14	0.00	0/29	0.00
Epipteric bone	0/10	0.00	0/9	0.00	0/19	0.00
Sagittal suture bones	0/9	0.00	1/7	14.29	1/16	6.25
Lambdic bone	0/12	0.00	0/10	0.00	0/22	0.00
Lambdoidal suture bones	5/21	23.81	11/21	52.38	16/42	38.10
- inclusions	2/21	9.52	0/21	0.00	2/42	4.76
Asterionic bone	6/24	25.00	1/23	4.35	7/47	14.89
Occipitomastoid bone	0/13	0.00	3/16	18.75	3/29	10.34
Parietal notch bone	2/21	9.52	3/25	12.00	5/46	10.87
Other vault variants:						
Supraorbital grooves	4/18	22.22	9/22	40.91	13/40	32.50
Supraorbital foramen	15/26	57.69	12/22	54.55	27/48	56.25
- notch	11/26	42.31	8/22	36.36	19/48	39.58
- multiple expressions	0/26	0.00	2/22	9.09	2/48	4.17
Sagittal sinus turns left	4/16	25.00	1/12	8.33	5/29	17.24
Parietal foramen absent	7/28	25.00	8/24	33.33	15/52	28.85
- multiple foramina	1/28	3.57	1/24	4.17	2/52	3.85
Facial skeleton:						
Two infraorbital foramina	1/16	6.25	0/19	0.00	1/35	2.86
Posterior zygomatic fissure	0/13	0.00	1/15	6.67	1/28	3.57
Palatine torus	3/12	25.00	2/11	18.18	5/23	21.74
Skull base:						
Pterygospinous bridge	0/23	0.00	0/23	0.00	0/46	0.00
- incomplete	7/23	30.43	7/23	30.43	14/46	30.43
Pterygobasal bridge	1/25	4.00	0/22	0.00	1/47	2.13
- incomplete	5/25	20.00	5/22	22.73	10/47	21.28
Spinobasal bridge	5/28	17.86	5/22	22.73	10/50	20.00
- incomplete	9/28	32.14	6/22	27.27	15/50	30.00
Foramen spinosum open	0/27	0.00	0/22	0.00	0/49	0.00
F. ovale/spinosum common	0/24	0.00	0/21	0.00	0/49	0.00

(*TABLE* 20 *continued*)

Variant	Males Freq.	%	Females Freq.	%	Total[1] Freq.	%
(Skull base continued)						
Divided hypoglossal canal	5/25	20.00	4/24	16.67	9/49	18.37
- partly divided	4/25	16.00	2/24	8.33	6/49	12.24
Condyloid canal absent	2/19	10.53	5/24	20.83	7/43	16.28
Divided occipital condyle	0/21	0.00	0/21	0.00	0/42	0.00
Precondylar variant	2/10	20.00	0/11	0.00	2/21	9.52
Ossified apical ligament	2/10	20.00	0/11	0.00	2/21	9.52
Paracondylar process	0/17	0.00	0/21	0.00	0/38	0.00
Clinoid process variant	0/16	0.00	0/22	0.00	0/38	0.00
Temporal bone:						
Thickened tympanic plate	8/36	22.22	5/25	20.00	13/61	21.31
Tympanic plate dehiscence	11/35	31.43	14/25	56.00	25/60	41.67
Auditory exostoses	0/37	0.00	0/25	0.00	0/62	0.00
Mandible:						
Mandibular torus	10/30	33.33	0/24	0.00	10/54	18.52
Mylohyoid arch	6/19	31.58	0/21	0.00	6/40	15.00
Multiple mental foramina	3/25	12.00	0/23	0.00	3/48	6.25

[1] Totals include mature bones of indeterminate sex from disturbed contexts.